Laugh or Cry

The British Soldier on the Western Front, 1914–18

Laugh or Cry

The British Soldier on the Western Front, 1914–18

Peter Hart & Gary Bain

Pen & Sword
MILITARY
AN IMPRINT OF PEN & SWORD BOOKS LTD.
YORKSHIRE · PHILADELPHIA

First published in Great Britain in 2022 by
Pen & Sword Military
An imprint of
Pen & Sword Books Ltd
Yorkshire – Philadelphia

ISBN 9781399068772

A CIP catalogue entry for this book is
available from the British Library.

Printed and bound by CPI Group (UK) Ltd, Croydon CR0 4YY

Pen & Sword Books Ltd includes the Imprints of Atlas, Archaeology, Aviation,
Discovery, Family History, Fiction, History, Maritime, Military, Military
Classics, Politics, Select, Airworld, Frontline Publishing, Leo Cooper, Remember
When, Seaforth Publishing, The Praetorian Press, Wharncliffe Local History,
Wharncliffe Transport, Wharncliffe True Crime and White Owl.

For a complete list of Pen & Sword titles please contact
PEN & SWORD BOOKS LTD
47 Church Street, Barnsley, South Yorkshire, S70 2AS, England
E-mail: enquiries@pen-and-sword.co.uk
Website: www.pen-and-sword.co.uk

Or
PEN AND SWORD BOOKS
1950 Lawrence Rd, Havertown, PA 19083, USA
E-mail: Uspen-and-sword@casematepublishers.com
Website: www,penandswordbooks.com

Contents

Preface

Those of us who were fortunate enough to meet veterans of The Great War were often struck by the sense of humour that pervaded their memories. Wartime anecdotes were usually accompanied by a quiet chuckle as they recounted funny tales, still remembered from nearly a century before.

They had found something to laugh about in literally everything around them; from the quirks of military life to the people they met and the places they served. In some cases even their darkest moments had been alleviated with a well-timed quip from a chum.

When the last of those thousands of old soldiers, who had fought in the war, finally faded away in 2009, it soon felt as if that humour had died out too.

Their laughter disappeared, to be replaced by a funereal sense that the First World War was no longer a suitable subject for funny stories, so I am delighted that Peter and Gary have written *Laugh or Cry*.

This wonderful collection of anecdotes highlights the ability of the British soldier to find those laughs in any, and every, circumstance, exactly as he had in every war before and since.

Whether in training, on parade, digging trenches, route marching, fighting the enemy or burying the dead, there was always a joke to be made, or a funny story to be told, to raise their spirits and take their mind off the work in hand.

The British soldier's sense of humour, along with his grousing, sentimentality, and those occasional moments of pathos, were just as important as his training, tactics and equipment. It kept his spirits up at times when others may have given in and plays a vital part in helping us to understand the Army of 1914–18.

This book is long overdue.

Taff Gillingham

Introduction

'The hottest place I was ever in, Zillebeke, there was a small lake there – and one wag had written up, "Boats let and hired; so much an hour!" That's what won the bloody war! Honestly – humour!'[1]
Gunner Harry Bretton, 87 Brigade, Royal Field Artillery

This is not a history of war on the Western Front. Far from it. This is a book that looks at the way humour helped the soldiers survive their terrible experiences. It will do this largely by using the words of the men themselves, as recorded in personal experience accounts in books, diaries, letters and oral history interviews. Reading accounts of the war can lead to a remarkably confused picture of the 'Tommy'. At the start of the war, he is pictured as a valiant fighter out to avenge 'poor Belgium', a heroic figure rarely to be found without a cheery quip and a chorus of 'Tipperary' on his lips. Then, after the war was over, there was a phase of dour books that sought to emphasize the mud, the lice, the spattered gore; with the Tommy now portrayed as an embittered brute, incapable of the finer feelings, blaspheming crudely, dependent on sex and alcohol to keep him going. As one might expect, the actual picture is far more nuanced. Both types exist, sometimes even within the same soldier under varying circumstances. Human beings are complicated, and there is no set pattern as to how they react to the outrageous stresses of war. Yet there are common traits that we can explore, and of these, one of the most interesting is the use of humour as an 'armour' against the slings and arrows of outrageous fortune.

Collected in these pages is much to throw light on the mind of the British soldier – up to his knees in mud, soaking wet, shot at with every weapon known to the Germans, bossed about by NCOs and officers, but in many cases still determined to see the funny side rather than surrender to utter misery. As a rule of thumb, does the British soldier moan? The answer is a resounding 'Yes!' He rarely stops complaining, grumbling, whinging, protesting, objecting, whining and griping, all the while muttering profane obscenities under his breath.

He grouses as all true soldiers do, if he did not grouse, then he could not be a true 'Tommy'. If you give him one thing, he wants another, it is not really that he wants or needs it, but it is the outcome of usually idleness, or [having] nothing to do; it merely means that he wants to get on a brisker business and get going, which two things are closely allied – proving I think that idleness, or a life without any real excitement, is his greatest enemy and can only be fought by grousing, which is a valve or safety exit.[2]

Lieutenant Lionel Sotheby, No. 1 Infantry Base Depot, Le Havre

Sotheby underestimates the British soldier: it was not just when they were idle or bored that they groused, it was a far more universal phenomenon, which, if ever harnessed, like a perpetual motion machine, could have powered the world. Much of the moaning was laced with humour of all sorts. They majored in sarcasm, they loved to see the pompous get their comeuppance, they practiced situationist comedy long before Monty Python. Almost everything that happened to them was grist to their sense of the absurd. As one reads these accounts, it is soon apparent that this is a measure of self-defence to distract from the trials and tribulations, the sheer horror that surrounded them. 'You have to laugh or you would cry' could have been their motto. But few put it more succinctly than this veteran:

'Not for one moment do I wish to imply that the war was anything but a horrible business, but a sense of humour was almost a necessity to prevent the combatants from going mad. There is no doubt that the men who took the war too seriously, and were able to see no humour in it, could not stand the strain. I say "combatants" advisedly, because a sense of humour was not confined to the British. Therefore, one or two notorious war books, dealing with the horrors of the war in which is depicted a state of affairs in which it would be impossible to remain sane, cannot be accepted as a true reflection.'[3]

Captain Hubert Rees, 2nd Welsh Regiment

Chapter 1

First Clash of Arms, 1914

God heard the embattled nations sing and shout: "Gott strafe England"
"God save the King" "God this" "God that" and "God the other thing".
"My God," said God, "I've got my work cut out."[1]

—John Squire

R eady for war? The British Expeditionary Force (BEF) was a small but well-trained regular force of, initially, only four infantry and one cavalry divisions that was thrown into a continental battle for which it was not prepared. In a war with nearly 200 French and German divisions smashing into each other on the Western Front, quality did not make up for quantity. The Tommies may have glumly acquiesced, or wildly enthused, at the prospect of Britain joining the war, but they could not help but ponder on what lay ahead of them. Most had a natural confidence in their own fighting abilities, but at the same time some were aware that this might not be easy.

It appears to me that things have now come to such a pitch that we cannot now abstain from joining in the war and still hold up our heads in honour. In fact, if we stay out, whoever wins, we shall presumably take it in the neck soon. The war will be a terrible business though, won't it?[2]
    Lieutenant Rowland Owen, 2nd Duke of Wellington's Regiment

As the British Army mobilized for war, the time-served reservists were recalled to the colours. Some took this development relatively calmly.

Fifteen pairs of critical eyes were directed on me simultaneously to see how I was 'taking it'. Would I break down and cry? Would I start blubbering because I was going out to be killed? Well, I did not start crying, neither did I 'blubber'. I was quite cheerful. I told them it would be over in 6 months and that I would consider myself lucky if I could get a shot at a Jerry before it was all over. Tom the blacksmith stated that it would not last 3 months. How could it last any longer with millions of

Prussians on one side and the French, English and Belgians on the other side? We'd go through them like a 'dose of salts'! Well, let us hope so![3]

Private Edward Roe, 1st East Lancashire Regiment

Others were more concerned, although in trying to escape the call-up few had the audacity to conflate their wife with farmyard animals.

Private Probert came from Anglesey and had joined the special reserve in peacetime for his health. In September, the entire battalion volunteered for service overseas, except Probert. He refused to go and could be neither coaxed nor bullied. Finally, he came before the colonel, whom he genuinely puzzled by his obstinacy. Probert explained: "I'm not afraid, Colonel, Sir. But I don't want to be shot at. I have a wife and pigs at home!"[4]

2nd Lieutenant Robert Graves, Wrexham Depot, Royal Welch Fusiliers

Some of the reservists struggled on their return to the army life. The boots were too heavy, the uniform too itchy, drill was too boring, there was too much shouting and, whisper it, perhaps they did indeed miss their wife and pig! But most knew from long and bitter experience that defiance was futile and so they knuckled under. There were exceptions, and Robert Graves, by nature a wonderful raconteur, loved to recall a splendidly scatological case of defiance that was brought to the Battalion Orderly Room in August 1914. He presented it as a mini-theatrical performance, complete with stage directions, dialogue and noises off.

Sergeant Major (off-stage): "Now, then, you Davies, cap off, as you were, cap off, as you were, cap off! That's better. Escort and prisoner, right turn! Quick march! Right wheel!" (On stage) "Left wheel! Mark time! Escort and prisoner, halt! Left turn!"
Colonel: "Read the charge, Sergeant Major."
Sergeant Major: "W.L. Davies at Wrexham on 20th August – improper conduct. Committing a nuisance on the barrack square! Witnesses: Sergeant Timmins, Corporal Jones."
Colonel: "Sergeant Timmins, your evidence!"
Timmins: "Sir, on the said date about two pm, I was acting Orderly Sergeant. Corporal Jones reported the nuisance to me. I inspected it. It was the prisoner's, Sir!"
Colonel: "Corporal Jones! Your evidence!"
Jones: "Sir, on the said date I was crossing the barrack square, when I saw the prisoner in a sitting posture. He was committing excreta, sir. I took his name and reported to the Orderly Sergeant, Sir!"

Colonel: "Well, Private Davies, what have you to say for yourself?"

Davies (in a nervous sing-song): "Sir, I came over queer all of a sudden, Sir. I had the diarrhoeas terrible bad. I had to do it, Sir!"

Colonel: "But my good man, the latrine was only a few yards away!"

Davies: "Sir, you can't stop nature!"

Sergeant Major: "Don't answer an officer like that!"

(Pause)

Sergeant Timmins (coughs): "Sir?"

Colonel: "Yes, Sergeant Timmins?"

Sergeant Timmins: "Sir, I had occasion to examine the nuisance, sir, and it was done with an effort, Sir!"[5]

2nd Lieutenant Robert Graves, Wrexham Depot, Royal Welch Fusiliers

As usual with the military, the men endured an awful lot of 'hurry up and wait', but at last they were ready to march off to war in mid–August 1914. They were often given a splendid send-off from the local civilians, followed by a great reception from the French upon their arrival on the continent. On occasion this got a little out of hand.

Ladies pursued them with basins full of wine and what they were pleased to call beer. Men were literally carried from the ranks, under the eyes of their officers, and borne in triumph into houses and inns. The men could scarcely be blamed for availing themselves of such hospitality, though to drink intoxicants on the march is suicidal. Men 'fell out', first by ones and twos, then by whole half-dozens and dozens. The colonel was aghast, and very furious – he couldn't understand it – he was riding![6]

2nd Lieutenant Arnold Gyde, 2nd South Staffordshire Regiment

As they marched into northern France and Belgium, they sang the usual marching songs, but included at least one fine new addition.

Poor Kaiser Bill is feeling ill,
The Crown Prince he's gone barmy,
And we don't care a fuck.
For old von Kluck,
And all his bleedin' great army.[7]

Whatever the mood of the men, some of the senior commanders were already under stress. Liaison officer Edward Spears had a unique view of the Chief of

General Staff, the august figure of Lieutenant General Sir Archibald Murray, in his Rheims hotel room as he tried to work out what the Germans were up to.

> Murray greeted me with the kindness he invariably displayed. He was worried, not so much by the situation, which he was trying to unravel on all fours on the floor, where enormous maps were laid out, as by the facts that the chambermaids kept coming into the room, and he had only his pants on![8]
> Lieutenant Edward Spears, General Headquarters, BEF

As the Battle of Mons raged on 23 August, 2nd Lieutenant Eric Dorman-Smith was in the thick of the action in command of a barricade facing a bridge over the canal. But the way he tells his story is most strange.

> I saw – directly in front of me – a German soldier sitting astride a low 3 foot wall at the bottom of the gardens of the houses directly across on the north side of the canal – about 200 yards away – rather less! He sat there looking, quite motionless, resting almost on the garden wall – he'd probably had a lot of marching. I said to the Fusilier next to me, "Private, shoot that man!" Then the voices from either side of me said, "Oh no, the officer must have first shot!" Someone said, "Take my rifle, Sir, it's a good one!" I realised it was up to me. So, I shot him! He fell down on our side of the wall and lay quite still. Almost at once another German got up onto the wall, sat on the wall, looking down at my victim! The voices said, "Go on, Sir! Have another shot!" I fired again and shot him! A third man did the same and I shot him! After that I handed back the rifle, saying, "Really it's somebody else's turn for this war now!"[9]
> 2nd Lieutenant Eric Dorman-Smith, 1st Northumberland Fusiliers

Men realized that this was a serious business, but even so, many could not help themselves from joking about it! It may have been a bluff, but it helped keep them sane.

> It also brought home to us that there really was a war on, a fact which up to then many of us had had some difficulty in visualising. After many years of complete peace, one's mental outlook required a considerable amount of readjusting which accounted for a brother officer asking me a few days later whether I felt savage. "Savage?" I asked. "What about?" "Savage with the Germans," he explained, with a serious and rather puzzled look.

"What I mean is – do you want to kill them?" "Not especially." "Nor do I, I expect we ought to eat raw meat or something!"[10]
    Captain Hubert Rees, 2nd Welsh Regiment

The 'Great Retreat' from Mons was interrupted by the Battle of Le Cateau. Although their situation was dire, as they prepared to give the Germans a 'bloody nose' to allow a continued ordered withdrawal, one British officer was furious that his men seemed to be incapable of taking even the most basic of military precautions.

> I was much horrified when I went to visit them to find that they had piled arms in an open space on a slope facing the direction of the enemy and had taken off their accoutrements and hung them up on the piles of rifles. Had artillery fire been opened there would have been a disaster. I was very angry! I rode round the troops who were supposed to be entrenched. In spite of what troops had learned in the Boer War, in spite of what they had been taught, all they had done was to make a few scratchings of the nature of a shelter pit, of no use whatever against any sort of fire. I came to the conclusion then, and never altered it during the war, that unless driven to it by his officers, the British soldier would sooner die than dig, but whether the reason for this was stupidity, lack of imagination or laziness I don't know, but probably it was a little of all three.[11]
>   Major General Sir Thomas D'Oyly Snow, Headquarters, 4th Division

As the columns of the BEF fell back, there were occasional panics, sometimes genuine, but as often caused by amusing misunderstandings.

> A message was passed down verbally with orders to pass it on, "Spies on the road ahead!" While wondering why, if that were so, the people in front hadn't done something about it, everyone assumed an attitude of extreme alertness and perhaps I surreptitiously grasped my revolver. Shortly afterwards a blessed sight appeared. Lying by the side of the road and obviously left there for us by the Army Service Corps were cases of bully beef and biscuits. For 'spies' read 'supplies' and there you have it![12]
>   Lieutenant Sidney Archibald, 6th Battery, 40 Brigade, Royal Field Artillery

They shared the roads with French refugees, but they could do little to help them, caught up as they were in their own life or death struggle for survival. However, Lieutenant Duncan Laurie had been much impressed by the young pretty wife of a French farmer, who was away serving with the French Army. Something made him want to help her.

> Wood and I were having dinner and as we had heard such dreadful stories of what the Germans were doing to the women, we decided we would try and go back and get the women from the farm at Ham. One old lady in the next house to the farm begged us to take her also, but it was quite impossible, and as she was old and plain, we did not think it mattered so much leaving her.[13]
>
> Lieutenant Duncan MacPherson Laurie, General Headquarters, BEF

The French victory at the Battle of the Marne in early September marked the end of the retreat and the beginning of the advance to the German defensive positions carved out on the hills above the River Aisne. Here, for the first time in the war, the soldiers of the BEF faced 'proper' trench warfare.

> The trench would be about 4 feet deep, that's all, with sandbags on the front. In between us and the German trenches there were some potatoes growing. One chap said, "I'm going to have some of those potatoes if they blow my blinking head off!" He got out of the trench; he got the potatoes, but a shell took his head clean off his shoulders. That happened, it sounds a bit fantastic but it's true![14]
>
> Lance Corporal Joe Armstrong, 1st Loyal North Lancashire Regiment

Scavenging for food to improve their rations was commonplace, and on occasion led to some unusual – and memorable – meetings in No Man's Land.

> When I was doing my rounds, I saw a hare sitting on the road in the moonlight, so I seized a rifle and rolled him over, and my platoon made the most of him! There was not much left when they'd done. One of my lads once went out of the trench (without permission) to a farm between the lines to steal chickens. While so engaged, he ran into a German who was doing the same. As neither had a rifle, they nodded and passed on.[15]
>
> Lieutenant Denis Barnett, 2nd Prince of Wales' Leinster Regiment

More and more British divisions were arriving, bolstered not only by the invaluable arrival of the Indian Corps, but also by the first of the Territorial Force battalions. The reinforced BEF joined in the 'Race to the Sea', with both sides trying to get round the opposing northern flanks until they reached the Flanders area of Belgium. Here the town of Ypres awaited them. The men of the BEF little knew how much suffering they would endure and the tens of thousands of lives that would be expended in defending that town. When the First Battle of Ypres began, it would be a titanic struggle as the British and French sought to hold back the massed German attacks.

> After taking bearings, I told the men to keep under cover and detailed one man, 'Ginger' Bain, as look out. After what seemed ages 'Ginger' excitedly asked, "How strong is the German Army?" I replied, "Seven million!" "Well," said Ginger, "Here is the whole bloody lot of them making for us!"[16]
>
> Sergeant James Bell, 2nd Gordon Highlanders

Sadly, in the fighting that followed, Ginger Bain was one of the first to be killed.

Many British units were overrun, and the Germans certainly took many prisoners. A prisoner's lot was not a happy one, but Sergeant Thomas Painting felt a certain amount of *Schadenfreude* during one incident.

> Our artillery opened fire and they were dead on the mark. It hadn't got a lot of noise, but it's got a nasty sweep, our shrapnel. The bullets burst and a German officer said, "Ah, Englander, the English artillery no good!" He'd hardly said that before he was killed – it was too good for him![17]
>
> Sergeant Thomas Painting, 1st King's Royal Rifle Corps

The fighting at Ypres dragged on into a freezing cold November. As they fell into the ways and means of long-term trench warfare, there was just one spot of relief with the onset in parts of the British line of the much-vaunted 'Christmas Truce'.

> The sergeant on duty suddenly ran in and said that the fog had lifted and that half a dozen Saxons were standing on their parapet without arms and shouting. I ran out into the trench and found that all the men were holding their rifles at the ready on the parapet, and that about half a dozen Saxons were standing on their parapet and shouting, "Don't shoot! We don't want to fight to-day! Don't shoot, we will bring you some beer, if you will come over!" Whereupon some of our men showed above the parapet and waved their hands. Then the Saxons climbed over the parapet and trundled a barrel of beer to us. Then lots of them appeared without arms and of course our men showed themselves. Then though we had been warned that the Germans would attack us, two of our men broke out of the trench and fetched the barrel. Then another broke out

and brought back a lot of cigars. All the Saxons then came out of their trenches and called out to us to come across.[18]

>   Captain Charles Stockwell, 2nd Royal Welch Fusiliers

The offer of beer was truly something that the freer spirits could not refuse. In some areas, the truce persisted for several days, and Private Herbert Williams recalled a drunken German who more than outstayed his welcome in a fraternal visit to the London Rifle Brigade trenches in Ploegsteert Wood.

>   On New Year's Eve, a runner came along, the officer knew I could speak German. "You're wanted to interpret!" I said, "What is it this time?" "Well, there is a drunk German in our trenches – and he won't go back!" I went up there, saw the platoon officer there, he said, "Oh, Williams, this chap here, he's drunk – it's all very well to meet them in No Man's Land, but he's actually in our trenches. He can see what a poor state they're in!" I thought to myself, "Well he's far too drunk to take any notice of anything like that!" This chap was standing up with a couple of bottles of beer, he wanted us to drink the health of the New Year and all the rest of it! The officer said, "Tell him he's got to go back!" I told him! He wouldn't take any notice; he didn't want to go back! This officer said, "If he stops here, he's got to be made prisoner, ask him if he wants to be made prisoner!" I did, "Gott, Nein!" He understood that, but he wouldn't go back! Eventually, the officer detailed another chap and me to take him back – so we escorted him – one on each side – this chap staggering about and singing at the top of his voice! We got up to the German wire and I thought, "Well I don't think I'll go right into their trenches – they might not be as lenient as we are!" We found a gap in the wire and headed him in the right direction and left him to it![19]

>   Private Herbert Williams, 1/5th London Regiment (London Rifle Brigade)

As the New Year began, the war was set in its ways.

Chapter 2

Back Home

Behind the BEF, right behind them, were the massed ranks of the Territorial Army and Kitchener's Army. They had been called to the colours and voluntarily recruited in their hundreds of thousands – and all of them had to be made into soldiers, fit to serve in the line against the might of the German Army.

> Men were pouring in. Men were ready to sign anything – and say anything. They gave false names, false addresses, false ages. They suppressed their previous military service, or exaggerated it, just as seemed to promise them best. Recruits had to sign as fast as they could. They did not trouble to read their papers. Whether our motives were to defend Britain, see the War, or get free food, we bundled ourselves into the Army in those hot, wild days of August 1914. What fun we meant to have! What fun![1]
> William Andrews

Intent as they were in filling the Army's ranks, recruitment sergeants frequently turned a blind eye to the age of young lads eager to enlist. Many were allowed to join although one or even two years below the minimum requirement. Army medicals varied greatly in how rigorous they were. But the doctors could also be cruel – or blunt – in their assessments of the physical attributes and distinguishing features of the callow recruits.

> He looked at me and he says, "Sallow complexion, prominent nose, mole on the right cheek." Before he'd done with me I felt a bit like Frankenstein! Then he says, "Initials?" I says, "F.A." He says, "You're going to have some trouble with that! 'F.A.' in the army doesn't stand for your initials!"[2]
> Private Arthur Dalby, 15th West Yorkshire Regiment

Once accepted by the Army, they were issued with a uniform and kit, although the pressure of numbers caused many delays in 1914. Indeed, many were given blue uniforms to tide them over before they got their much-cherished khaki. But there were other problems, as size was often an issue. Quartermasters were not necessarily sympathetic and had a somewhat 'one size fits all' approach. It didn't.

> I was a boy of seventeen years old. The uniform I was given was made for someone of about 28 stone. I didn't know whether I was inside or outside it. If the neck of the coat had been a little larger I'm afraid I would have slipped right through! When we were making a turn, I would be halfway round before my uniform would start to move – which always worried my drill instructor because I would never be in line with the other fellows.[3]
>
> Private Ernest Aldridge, 2nd Welsh Regiment

Many officers also had to be recruited. In the early days of the war, this was largely a class-based selection process, which in some cases was almost farcical.

> One day I was sent for by the colonel – I'd never seen him up to then. He said, "Your sergeant has recommended you! What would you like to be?" "Oooh!" I said, "A sergeant!" He said, "Would you? Do you swear?" "Oh no, Sir!" "Do you drink?" "No, Sir!" "Have you got a girlfriend?" I said, "No, Sir!" I hadn't even kissed a girl up to then – I was dead scared of girls I might tell you! "Well," he said, "I don't know! What the hell is the good of you being a sergeant? The only thing I can think of my boy is for you to be an officer![4]
>
> James Lovegrove, Royal Irish Fusiliers Depot

At the other end of the age spectrum from Lovegrove were the crusty old 'dugout' officers. These men had served in the Boer War or Sudan, and had usually left the Army, but were brought back to use their experience in training the battalions. They were often frustrated, being rarely allowed to be deployed on active service. Some were not the type of men to suffer in silence!

> Colonel MacLean was a rather aged and violently tempered old gentleman. We only saw him on battalion parades and manoeuvres – thank goodness. With his small, pointed moustache he reminded me of Mephistopheles. He was always mounted on his horse and from that vantage point would scream at us in a very shrill and terrifying manner, calling us all the foul names he could muster up. If he could find no valid excuse for this, he would soon make one up. Woe-betide anyone who had the misfortune to go before him on a charge – his sentence was always severe. Probably his irascibility was due to the fact that his advanced age

prohibited him from going to France, in spite of his numerous pleas. After the War, the old rascal took up Holy Orders and one day the newspaper placards bore the legend in huge type "Clergyman Assaults his Housekeeper".[5]

Private John Tucker, 2/13th London Regiment

Across the whole of the United Kingdom, the barracks and depots were crammed to the brim. Tented and hutted camps sprang up everywhere, but soon they too were full and thousands of men were placed in civilian billets. With a requirement to feed thousands, it is not surprising that the food was a simple fare. Some of the more sensitive recruits found mealtimes a real strain.

We held out our plates while a soldier in a grimy uniform ladled cabbage, meat and a greasy liquid on to them. We sat down on benches in front of tables that were littered with potato peel, bits of fat, and other refuse. We were packed so closely together that we could hardly move our elbows. The rowdy conversation, the foul language, and the smacking of lips and the loud noise of guzzling added to the horror of the meal. I was so repelled that I felt sick and could not eat. The man who sat opposite kept me under close observation. All at once he asked, "Don't yer want it, mate?" I said "No!" whereupon he exclaimed eagerly, "Giss it." A bestial, gloating look came into his face as he seized my plate and splashed the contents on to his own, so that the gravy over-flowed and ran along the table in a thin stream. He took the piece of meat between his thumb and his fork and, tearing off big shreds with his teeth, gobbled them greedily down.[6]

Gunner Frederick Voigt, Royal Garrison Artillery

The recruits' training was supervised by officers, but the real work was done by long-service NCOs. There is no doubt that they had their work cut out in trying to turn tens of thousands of civilians into what could pass for soldiers.

"Gawd bless my soul!" ejaculated Regimental Sergeant Major Cooper, an incarnation of the standardised British version of the great god Mars, as he surveyed his flock of lambs on the parade ground behind the barracks. "Don't know what the Army is coming to now-a-days. Look at that little lot of adjectival sewers. How's a mortal man ever going to turn *them* into soldiers. Well, I 'spose you've got to take it or leave it."[7]

Captain Randolph Chell, 10th Essex Regiment

Fresh-faced lads, straight from school, the office, church and their mother's knee were shocked by the vast range of abuse and swearing they experienced during training. Their instructors were godlike figures who bestrode the parade ground like titans.

> We noticed that most of the barking NCOs were tall, lean men, as stiff as pokers from the waist up, bellowing as though their throats would burst. Baker was blond with a ruddy complexion, a close-clipped moustache and an aggressive expression. First contact with him came as an electric shock. "Squad, 'tion! As were! 'Tion! As were! Good God! See what the Lord has sent me. What have I done to deserve this? You're a nice looking mass of bloody wrecks, aren't you? And they expect me to make soldiers of you. Alas, my poor regiment, that it should come to this. Thank God we've got a Navy. Looks as though you've all jumped over the wall from the bloody looney bin next door and you'll all be jumping back before I've done with you. You may be God Almighty in Civvy Street but you're fuck all here. I'll make you sweat blood. We tame lions here!"[8]
>
> Private Norman Cliff, Guards Training Depot, Caterham

The mornings began with the first parade of the day and some brisk physical exercise to separate the men from the boys.

> The company sergeant major brings the squad to attention, salutes, and reports all present. "Squad, number! Form fours! Right turn! By the left, quick march!" And away we go in a straggling mass, half asleep and very cold and hungry; and the business of another day has begun. We are led at once to a big 20-acre field, and double round it for 10 minutes by the officer's watch. This sounds easy, but 10 minutes is a long time to keep it up, and the old fat men are hideously distressed at the end of it. On the morning after pay-night the doubling is kept up for 20 minutes. The object of this is to sweat the drink out of the men. It is admirably calculated to serve its purpose. Then we are given 5 minutes "easy", and there is much gasping and blowing and spitting and wiping of red faces and *sotto voce* blasphemy. You see, the idea of this first parade is not so much drill-instruction as to freshen us up for the work of the day – and ease the stiffness out of the muscles. Then we are formed up in fours again and marched back to our own lines, very much awake indeed and very different from the sleepy scarecrows of an hour before.[9]
>
> Private John Staniforth, 6th Connaught Rangers

The drill sessions proper would start after breakfast. The idea was to get the men to move as a formed body of men, but also for them to be used to obeying orders without question. It was a brutal business.

> The full flood of his invective fell upon them. "I can work fucking miracles, I can!" He would cry. "I can make even a lousy, horrible crew of fucking fuckers like you into soldiers; and I will, too, by fuck!" If our marching was not to his liking, he would often quicken the pace to almost impossible speeds, "Left! Right! Left! Right! Left! Right! Left! Right! Left! Right! Left! Right! About turn! As you were!" Until we were pounding along with hammering hearts and bursting lungs, convinced that we must soon crack under the strain.[10]
> Private Frederick Noakes, Combermere Barracks, Windsor

Although most instructors were in reality just 'playing the role', the raw recruits were not to know this as the time-honoured abuse rained down on them.

> "Lion-tamers have got nothing on me!" "You may break your mother's heart, but you won't break mine! Squad! 'Shun!" One of his favourite devices for 'waking us up' was to give an order, countermand it, and give it again, a score of times, with lightning rapidity, "Form fours! As you were! Form fours! As you were!" Until we were dizzy with dashing to and fro, breathless and thoroughly tangled up; whereupon he would hurl imprecations upon our heads and slanders on our ancestry which, taken at their face value, were as blasphemously insulting as they were indecent![11]
> Private Frederick Noakes, Combermere Barracks, Windsor

Under this kind of stress, there was a real temptation to report sick with real – or imagined – ailments. Malingerers met with little sympathy.

> Well, we'd been having an awful lot of men shamming diarrhoea to get off parades; it's a favourite stunt, because it's so difficult to disprove. However, our doctor, Murphy O'Connor, made light of difficulties. Four heroes came up to him one morning when there was a long route march on for the battalion, all pleading fierce, though intermittent, diarrhoea. So, what does he do but sends over to the Army Service Corps depot for four plain white utensils of domestic earthenware. "Now," says he, "you sit on these pots till the regiment comes back, and then we'll have a look at your diarrhoea!" He marched them over to the guardroom, each with his little white pot under his arm; and

there in the cells these four great ruffians sat for 3-hours while a sentry
mounted guard over them with a fixed bayonet. When the battalion
returned, there wasn't as much as would cover a farthing in any
one of the pots! We've had no more malingerers on that tack since.[12]
   2nd Lieutenant John Staniforth, 7th Leinster Regiment

Route marches were a constant element of basic training. In those days, when
campaigning, the battalion marched almost everywhere – unless there was a
handy railway route. To get ready for these challenges, they had to build up their
endurance and basic fitness.

Weapons training was obviously crucial to any soldier. They would usually start
with rifle training. Here too they were in the hands of grizzled old instructors,
with their own sense of humour. Even officers under training were not immune.

The sergeant instructor is a type of his own. Our particular instruction-
patter started, "This morning I am going to show you the Mark III Lee
Enfield Rifle." We learnt it all by heart – we could hardly do anything
else. Our sergeant however had his method of keeping us on our toes.
Later in the day an innocent victim would be called out to give a
demonstration. "This morning I am going to show you," he would begin.
"Not this morning, sir," corrected the sergeant, "This afternoon!"[13]
   2nd Lieutenant Harold Mellersh, 3rd East Lancashire Regiment

The instructional patter was standard, as the men were taught the parts of the
rifle, had practical demonstrations in the method of aiming, then live firing on
the .22 range, before – at last – the real thing on the rifle ranges. They also had
to learn the art of bayonet training, which proved a gut-churning business for
the more sensitive recruits.

It was strenuous and interesting, if one could forget what the straw-stuffed
dummies we attacked were supposed to represent, though the sergeant's
blood-curdling directions to "Twist the bayonet in his guts!" and "Jump on
his face!" left little to the imagination. "Use every dirty trick you know!" he
would say. "Kick him in the privates; bash him with the butt; it's him or you!"[14]
   Private Frederick Noakes, Combermere Barracks, Windsor

More specialist training included the Vickers machine gun. Here too, instructors
used humour to get over their points.

The year was 1915 and the place the Machine Gun School of Southern
Command at Hayling Island. The commandant was lecturing on

machine gun tactics. He began, "My text is taken from the First Book of Samuel, the Seventeenth Chapter and the Forty-ninth Verse. 'And David put his hand into his bag, and took thence a stone, and slang it, and smote the Philistine in the forehead, that the stone sunk into his forehead; and he fell upon his face to the earth!' That, gentlemen, is the first recorded instance of superior fire power."[15]

> 2nd Lieutenant Eric Bird, Machine Gun Corps

The cavalry did not generally recruit anything like the number of men that poured into the infantry, but their recruits had to learn to ride in the 'roughrider' training schools. There was scant sympathy when they fell off the horse.

> There was a lane of jumps intended for horse and rider. Going over with the rider's arms folded – no stirrups! It was a lane, the horse couldn't jump out on either side. In all there were six or seven jumps. On one occasion, the horse and the rider in front of me stumbled. The chap who was riding it couldn't pull him up, because he hadn't the reins, he fell and hit his head on a tree trunk at the base of the jump – knocked him unconscious. Major Lloyd cantered up alongside the jump and he said, "If that man's dead, take him outside! We don't want dead men in here! If he's alive put him on his horse again!"[16]
>
> Trooper Fred Dixon, Surrey Yeomanry

Meanwhile the gunners had to master gun drill on the 13-pdrs, 18-pdrs or 4.5in howitzers. This was hard enough, but their new young officers also had to master the mathematics and practicalities of the science of gunnery. This took time.

Field training and tactical exercises were designed to check and refine their training for the new units. Here they would be inspected by the local brigade and divisional commanders. These could be tense and fraught affairs, as the history of the 15th Highland Light Infantry by Tom Chalmers proudly recalls when they were inspected by Brigadier General F. Hackett Thompson, commanding their brigade.

> This New Army Brigade didn't know the Regular Army tradition and were astounded by the general's first inspection. The tradition is succinctly expounded: "Fierceness on parade was the order of the day and ferocity increased with your rank!" Captains shouted a good deal and permitted themselves an oath or two, majors, mounted, swore a great deal. The colonel was generally angry with everybody and let them know it. But the Annual General Inspection reduced them all to comparative

silence, the intensity of the general's ferocity putting all minor efforts into the shade.[17]

However, even the sternest martinet sometimes met their match in an encounter with an ordinary soldier.

The general was taken aback when a hard-bitten private of the line, who had a fair growth of hair on a very blotched face, was tackled, "What's the matter with your face, man?" came the sharp and inevitable question. "It's the booze comin' oot, sur!" When the naive confession was interpreted to the brigadier the ice melted. He beamed and said, in almost benevolent tones, to the man, "That's the frankest answer I've ever had in my career!"[18]

Ready or not, they would soon be off to war.

Chapter 3

Off to War

I was on my six days leave which meant I was going overseas. My mother, without being told, knew I was off to France. The last day she followed me round the house until it was time for me to go. I got to the front door, and she was crying and holding me round my knees – I was forced to drag her to the front gate![1]

    Private Reginald Backhurst, 8th Royal West Kent Regiment

Battalions were desperately needed at the front. As soon as a unit had reached, or even approached, the required standard they were packed off to war. There was never enough time to achieve perfection; they just had to hope that their best would be good enough. As the Western Front beckoned, they would be inspected by the 'great and the good'. Here too, there could be a lot of unconscious humour.

Lord Kitchener was inspecting the Manchester City Pals in Albert Square, just before they went to France. We marched from Heaton Park to Albert Square, to meet Lord Kitchener! He was stood on the steps of the Town Hall and we marched past him. I'm carrying a signal flag – and I'm in the front of the company. As we got the word, "Eyes left!" I looked him full in the face! – he was like his picture – a big moustache! And he started laughing. I thought, "Well is he laughing at me?" Actually, he was laughing because we were all small men – none of us over 5 foot 3in. After that parade was over it was said, the generals came and spoke to us, they said that was [the] first time they'd ever seen Lord Kitchener laugh – when he saw us![2]

    Private Tom Haddock, 23rd (Bantams) Manchester Regiment

Another sign that they were soon to be bound for foreign parts was the commencement of an immunization programme against typhoid, often referred to as enteric fever.

The whole battalion paraded for inoculation against enteric. All company officers had been warned to parade their men in the morning,

explain to them what inoculation was, and what for, that there was
nothing to be afraid of, etc., and that, while it was not compulsory,
it was expected that every man would be done for his own future
good. The battalion duly paraded and formed up outside the camp
hospital. Lloyd, the adjutant, went in to be done first and to show a
good example. When he came out, looking extremely green in the face,
I was standing at the bottom of a few steps running up to the door of
the hospital. I said, "Are you all right, Lloyd? You look a bit dicky!" He
replied, "Yes, quite all right!" and fell down the steps in a faint! That
did it! There was a mighty rushing sound and we saw numbers of men
legging it back to barracks as hard as they could go.[3]

Lieutenant Evelyn Needham, 1st Northamptonshire Regiment

The injections were quite an intimidating process, often with blunt needles,
and led not only to a sore arm but could have other quite serious side effects.

The stuff was all sealed up in a bottle and looked rather like some
grouse soup we had for dinner the other night. The way the doctor
inoculates is to take a small squirt armed with a steel needle about an
inch long which he runs into the arm about the place where one is
vaccinated and scoots dead typhoid germs into the arm. The idea is
that the anti-typhoid germs in the body eat up the dead typhoid germs
and acquire the taste for them so that when live typhoid germs appear,
they are simply gulped down by the anti-typhoid germs before they
can say 'Jack Robinson!' It rather reminded me of acquiring a taste for
oysters. I wonder if dead typhoids are as beastly?[4]

Lieutenant Walter Coats, 1/9th Highland Light Infantry

They would not have been soldiers without a final 'blowout' before leaving.
In this, the officers of the 2/6th Lancashire Fusiliers seem to have excelled
themselves.

The final mess night in Colchester will live long in the memory of
all those who now survive. It was not surprising that excitement ran
high and that the revels were carried on well into the night. During
the course of the evening one unfortunate incident occurred! The
brigade gas officer happened to be in possession of some surplus tubes
of lachrymatory gas, and it was suggested to him that the gaiety of the
proceedings would be increased if this was suitably distributed where
people most did congregate. The idea was taken up with enthusiasm,
and the first tube was liberated in the anteroom amongst the bridge

players. They beat a hasty retreat, but four stalwarts returned complete with gas masks and completed the rubber. The second tube used was in the bar with more instantaneous results, as it was accompanied by thunderflashes produced by the brigade bombing officer. Then it was suggested that the padre, who was supposed to be reading in his room, should not be forgotten. The gas merchant ascended to his room, knocked, and on receiving a polite "Come in!" opened the door slightly and disposed of his third tube. He retreated with alacrity, but in good order. The result was surprising, as within a few minutes, members of a confirmation class which had been assembled in conclave with the padre – unknown and unsuspected – were clattering down the stairs mopping their eyes and uttering words which it is hoped the padre did not hear.[5]

2nd Lieutenant Charles Potter, 2/6th Lancashire Fusiliers

Our noble informant entirely fails to mention that he himself was that villainous brigade bombing officer!

Finally, the day came, as it had for so many hundreds of battalions before them, and it was time to march off to war. The farewells were sometimes tearstained, sometimes humorous, and not all farewell embraces were equally welcome.

Field Service Marching Order is heavy, the day is very hot, the crowd is distracting. At the bottom of Belvoir Street it is very thick, and right up Granby Street to the Midland Station people swarm round the troops shouting farewell to their sons, sweethearts and friends; shouting to anyone and everyone, for in this time of crisis everyone speaks to his neighbour. An old, dirty-looking, motherly woman accosts a young officer as he marches in front of his company into the station. "I shall be waiting for you when you come back, me duck!" she cries. He has never seen her before, and hopes he never will again, but the words stick in his memory.[6]

Captain John Milne, 1/4th Leicestershire Regiment

And so they sailed forth in troopships and transports from the great ports, proud scions of a maritime country – although in reality many had never even seen the sea before.

On board, a sergeant took me to the bow of the ship and above me was a bell and he said, "If you see anything unknown, ring that bell." The ship had set sail and I was looking down into the darkness and I could see a little light and I thought, "Oh, that must be somebody. I'll ring the bell." There was pandemonium throughout the ship, everybody running about, not knowing what to do. I could hear them all round me until an officer said to me, "What is it?" I said, "There's a submarine down there." I was stood down and afterwards I was told it was the pilot boat taking us out of the dock. So that's the kind of watchman I was![7]

Private Robert Burns, 7th Cameron Highlanders

Contrary to popular opinion, not all the British were natural sailors, much to the amusement of those who were!

Before long nearly everyone appeared to be seasick, and men were lying about in all sorts of postures or hanging desperately over the rail. I, however, although I had never been more than a mile off-shore before, on a pleasure steamer, was quite unaffected by the motion, and was able to get a good deal of amusement from the scene, in the usual unsympathetic manner of a 'good sailor'. I would see someone from my platoon come staggering up the companionway, and would say, cheerfully and maliciously, "How goes it, chum?" "Christ Almighty!" would come the answer, and there would be a frantic rush to the side.[8]

Private Frederick Noakes, Household Battalion

When they arrived, they were strangers in a foreign land. Everything was new and unfamiliar, which could lead to amusing misunderstandings.

'Our C.O. had never been in France before. Neither had the adjutant. So, when they saw a figure approaching them arrayed in gorgeous uniform, they jumped to the conclusion that it was some French general come to greet us. Accordingly, we marched past him at attention, with eyes left, and the band playing "Hielan Laddie". We found out afterwards that he was a private in the local gendarmerie!'[9]

Lieutenant Norman Down, 4th Gordon Highlanders

The cheering French crowds of 1914 had long drifted away. Now the troops were met by a stolid indifference, leavened only by the cheery abuse of small children, schooled in the intricacies of English by thousands of passing soldiers.

The inhabitants ignored us completely; they doubtless saw British troops arriving every day. Our only escort consisted of small urchins of both sexes. They ran beside our column imploring, "Gimme cigarette, bloody Tommee, gimme bleedin chocklick!" We thought they were clever little bastards to speak English so fluently and we tossed them a few cigarettes as a reward for their proficiency in army ruderies.[10]

    Rifleman Bernard Livermore, 9th London Regiment (Queen Victoria's Rifles)

The newly arrived drafts, or battalions, were swiftly moved into Infantry Base Depots, of which there were several clustered around the Channel ports. Here they were given some last-minute training, often to cover new developments in the terrible arsenal of war. One ominous development was gas warfare.

The instructor – a major – said there was one joke always made in connection with gas, and this was it: after a gas attack there are only two kinds of people left, viz., the quick and the dead, and the former were damned quick, i.e., in getting their respirators on. Very cheering![11]

    Lieutenant Joseph Maclean, Infantry Base Depot, Étaples

It seems that many of these instructors were not the most optimistic of men.

One elderly, dour, kilted Jock with bushy eyebrows used to start his lectures on gas warfare by looking fixedly at the subalterns for a few moments, then announcing, "Gentlemen, it is my duty to teach ye something about poison gas!" He would then pause, shake his head and continue, "but I'm thinking – what's the use – as most of ye will be mouldering under the sod in aboot a fortnight!"[12]

    2nd Lieutenant Basil Peacock, Infantry Base Depot, Étaples

They were often surprisingly imaginative.

For all the rough language in which the talks were given, they contained shrewd advice and sound common sense. Sometimes tins of pork and beans appeared among the rations. The beans were there all right, but the pork, if at all present, consisted of a minute cube of pork fat. This led an instructor to say, "If I can teach you men to take cover like that pork does in the beans no German will ever shoot you!"[13]

    Private George Warwick, 4th South African Infantry

One difficult task facing the inexperienced young subaltern was the role of orderly officer. It seems their duties encompassed the requirement to judge the quality of the beer served in the men's canteen, which proved a terrible hardship to one Lieutenant Lionel Sotheby.

The orderly officer is supposed to taste the beer and announce if it is good or not. I dislike beer intensely, and so told one of the privates in there to taste it, which he thereupon did, drinking practically two pints out of a jug before we could stop him, and then it was only because he was out of breath. That satisfied us the beer was alright. The sellers of the beer were [annoyed] because they said he should only have sipped it; the private, immensely furious, said that he could not taste beer until he had drunk three or four pints, and said he was trying to do them a good turn by saying the beer was good when he had not sufficiently tested. Having had enough of the squabble, I declared the beer good and decamped.[14]

Lieutenant Lionel Sotheby, No. 1 Infantry Base Depot, Le Havre

Usually, they were not at the depots long before moving towards the front.

The train journeys became the stuff of legend. The simple carriages were marked ominously with 'Hommes Quarante' or 'Chevaux Huit', meaning forty men or eight horses. These were often left in a filthy state by their previous occupants, whether human or equine.

Some of the trucks had obviously been used to transport the latter, for the floors were many inches deep in horse manure. So much so that one man complained to Captain George Campbell and pointed out the state of the truck that he had been detailed to occupy. George Campbell had a look and a sniff, and then turned to the 'Digger' with a grin and said, "Well, my lad, what do you expect me to do? Charter another train?"[15]

Lieutenant Walter Belford, 11th Australian Battalion

The train journeys were indescribably slow. British troop trains were very low down the priority list for the severely overstrained French railway system struggling with the endless demands of war. Progress was usually at a glacial pace, made worse by seemingly endless stops awaiting the passage of other trains.

Crowded together on straw-strewn floor harbouring a comprehensive collection of insect life, with no place to put equipment and rifles, surfeited with fresh air when the jolting of the train flung aside the doors or the more curious desired to enjoy the view, stifled when the doors were tightly shut, "Tommy Atkins" felt on these occasions, with some reason, that his comfort was hardly being considered. Starting and stopping with a series of sudden jerks, these trains rattled along downhill at an alarming speed, lurching, rolling, clattering to such an extent that one felt that only a miracle could prevent them from leaving the rails; but for the most part, they ambled along at a bare 5 miles an hour. The interminable halts, more often than not at some deserted siding, were exasperating to us, who were used to the definite schedules of our own railways.[16]

2nd Lieutenant Reginald Russell, 11th Queen's Own Royal West Kent Regiment (Lewisham Battalion)

Often, the men found that no proper arrangements had been made to feed or water them – in this the forty men were probably treated far worse than eight horses would have been.

Time passed and soon we were getting hungry. We got on with our eatables and then someone said, "What about making some tea?" We all liked the idea but how were we to make it? We had tea, sugar, milk and water but we wanted to boil the water. We all hunted round and someone found an empty biscuit tin, someone else found wood, and a few small pieces of coal were spotted in the corner of the truck. Some holes were made in the bottom and sides of the tin with an entrenching tool, the wood was split up and we were ready to light our fire. The fire was lit, and we got plenty of smoke. Soon we were all coughing with tears running down our faces. We tried blowing through the holes, swinging the tin from side to side, and even putting it on the edge of the door in an effort to make the fire burn up, but it was all no use. The fire would simply not burn up but only gave off clouds of smoke. We stood it for some time then one of the men said, "Fuck the fire!" and kicked it out on to the lines and so that was that.[17]

Private Harry Stinton, 1/7th London Regiment

And so they moved slowly, but inexorably, towards the front and their appointment with destiny.

Chapter 4

Conditions in the Trenches

Tatham smoked away at his pipe and at last, as we were plunging through mud and filth, he said, "This is what you might call the abomination of desolation, padre!"[1]
    Padre Maurice Murray, Royal Sussex Regiment

Life in the trenches was often nasty, brutish and frequently short. It required enormous resilience to survive in conditions that tested to the limit the physical and mental capabilities of the soldier. This was not unique to the Great War, but the static nature of the fighting heaped horror upon horror. How did they survive? Physically, it was a matter of a mixture of acquired instincts and skills, coupled with blind luck. Mentally, the men employed humour as a protective wall – or cushion – to dull the boredom, the fear and the agony, laughing at every aspect of the torments that surrounded them. Their humour ran the full gamut from A to Z. Pratfalls, sarcasm, toilet mishaps, over the top abuse, *Schadenfreude* and surrealism were all grist to their funny bones.

Things are queerly mixed. One picks up a man with his brains blown out (they will not keep their dear silly heads down!) and 5-minutes after we have forgotten the pitiful sight and are laughing over some jest. The particular jest here was a 'model' of HMS *Lion* that the men were floating about in the communication trench – this is 50 yards from the Boche! It was made from a piece of corky bark from a big pine. The gun turrets and funnels were also fashioned from the bark, and she had four guns – cartridge cases – for'ard and four aft.[2]
    Lance Corporal Douglas Bell, 1/5th London Regiment (London Rifle Brigade)

At the commencement of their tour of duty, the men would move along the communication trenches into their home for the next few days. The journey was often a physical trial. The trenches were narrow, crowded and strewn with perils underfoot and overhead.

It was an unwritten law that the leading men should pass back word of each obstacle as it was encountered, but it frequently happened that the warning was transmitted much more quickly than we moved – and would be forgotten by the time the obstacle in question was reached. A man half-way along the column would receive the word, "Step up!" or "Wire overhead!" and would keep a sharp lookout for a few moments, and then, when reaching the point referred to about 10-minutes later, would fall over the step, or be half-throttled by the wire.[3]

Private Frederick Noakes, 1st Coldstream Guards

Sometimes, the repeated warnings could irritate those behind, which in turn annoyed those attempting to help the ungrateful wretches lumbering in their tracks. A subtle retribution could be most gratifying.

Going up the trench, orders were passed down to keep low. The writer respected the command, so did those in front; but the fellow behind me in a spirit of bravado kept taunting me with the remarks, "What was I scared of?" Being of puny dimensions, it struck me he could ignore the order with impunity, so I ignored him! However, he kept on ragging and I was forced to ejaculate, "Shut up, you blethering idiot!" But to no avail and my dander was beginning to rise. Whenever there is a hole in the trench mat, the warning is usually passed from man to man, the word 'hole' being sufficient enlightenment to make one aware. It happened there was a hole and Buttress, who was in front of me, murmured, "Hole!" My chance had come! I remained silent and stepped over it, the next moment my tormentor fell in a heap. He extricated himself muttering imprecations on my head. The rest of the trip he was too busy watching his feet to annoy me.[4]

Private Donald Fraser, 31st Canadian Battalion (Alberta Battalion)

In certain sectors, the ground conditions were dreadful, almost beyond imagining.

Shell craters were superimposed on shell craters. Water filled them to varying depths. The pulverised, soaked earth made every step a supreme effort. No two steps were ever on the same level. We fell, rose and fell again, soaked to our very hides. "A man's a stupid big galoot to be here anyway!" growled Matthews. "But there is one bloody comfort. After you fall three bloody times, you don't bloody well care. You can't get any bloody wetter!" Splash! As he found an extra deep shell hole. Sulphurous language burst out as he broke water like a seal. He seized my extended rifle-muzzle and climbed out. Then he became silent. The situation was beyond even his lurid expressions.[5]

Private George Mitchell, 48th Australian Battalion

If it was their first time in a locality, then they were dependent on guides from the previous battalion holding that sector to lead them the right way. Or not.

> Guides are of two kinds: those who admit that they don't know the way and those who don't admit it! Ours was the latter class. He led us over all the wettest places, through the thickest brushwood, among the most formidable of our support line wire entanglements, over the widest and slipperiest trenches, and finally turned round and asked me which way I thought we ought to go now. If I had still had enough energy, I am sure that I would have killed him. It would have been for the best.[6]
>
> Lieutenant Norman Down, 4th Gordon Highlanders

When they finally reached the front-line trenches, a studied insouciance was a popular pose amongst the officers, especially those with a literary bent.

> The wood was in a very dilapidated state, and few of the trees stood more than 10 feet high. The stream consisted of rainwater trickling from one shell hole to another. "Ah," you ask, "but were the birds there, and did they sing?" We are afraid that we cannot answer that question from memory, but we have it on the authority of one of our most eminent 'Special Correspondents at the Front' that during one of the big battles the birds not only continued to sing, but chose the neighbourhood of the front line as a suitable place in which to do so; and in view of this incontestable (and doubtless first-hand) information, we are prepared to admit that it is possible that the birds did sing. Being truthful, however, we are compelled to admit that the only singing that impressed itself on our memory was that of the shells.[7]
>
> Major Herbert Wenyon, 8th Royal West Kent Regiment

This kind of mock-passive acceptance was not so prevalent amongst the Australians, who tended to express themselves more forcefully!

> There is the story of Lieutenant J. Archibald, always known as 'Archie', who had recently rejoined the battalion from England. In company with Company Sergeant Major George Lamerton, 'Archie' was endeavouring to reach the front line by the long, gluey communication trench. 'Archie' was rather stout and not in the best of condition, and the strenuous journey began to have its effect on him. After floundering through a specially bad bit of the trench, with mud and slop well over his boot tops, he was pretty well exhausted, and during a short spell he informed George Lamerton exactly what he thought of France and

the area round about Flers in particular. Lamerton feelingly endorsed his remarks. Then they proceeded on their journey. As they neared the front line the trench got rapidly worse, and 'Archie' put one foot into a place where a shell had burst not long before – and he disappeared in a smother of mud and water. With Lamerton's help he was dragged to his feet and propped against the wall of the trench, where he dripped mud from every part of his clothing and equipment. Gasping and spitting out several unpalatable portions of Picardy, he was a sight to move the Gods to tears, or laughter. Lamerton gravely scraped him down with a fragment of shell case, as he would have done a muddy horse. When 'Archie' found his voice, he burst out, "George, I'm fucked! I'm absolutely fucked! When I left, my girl fucking told me I had fucking to win a fucking medal, but if she fucking wants any bloody medals she'll fucking have to come out here and win them herself!"[8]
    Lieutenant Walter Belford, 11th Australian Battalion

It was traditional for a battalion moving into the line to accuse the previous occupants of the trenches of being unsanitary pigs of the highest order, whether they be French, of colonial origins, from another part of England, from another battalion of the same regiment, a different company or indeed anybody other than themselves.

    If they were in luck, soldiers of a new draft arriving to join the battalion would find an old hand who was ready, willing and able to show them the ropes. There was a lot to learn, and some degree of experience was vital to a prolonged survival in the trenches. Fresh-faced youths, excited at being in the war, all suppressed expectancy, needed to be calmed down and made to appreciate the realities of their situation. This was not a game.

I explain to him the lie of the land in front, point out the supposed machine-gun emplacements in the Jerry lines, our own posts in front of our wire, and a hundred other things a soldier should know about his particular part of the line. To all this I add my own pet theories and devices for cheating death. How to take a slanting look through the sandbagged loophole. One sees just as much and doesn't provide such a good target for a watchful sniper in the opposite lines. The spare cartridge stuck in the rifle sling. It is easier and quicker to insert than a new clip when one counts life by seconds. How to distinguish the different shells by their sound, and the necessity of judging accurately the interval between the bursts. The best way to approach a Jerry trench – erect and not bent double – then, if you are going to be unfortunate enough to be hit it will be on the legs and not in the stomach, and leg wounds aren't really

dangerous while stomach wounds are. And above all, I impress upon him the necessity of taking advantage of every bit of cover. Ignoring it may look brave and impressive, but if you have a desire to live out here it is much easier accomplished by making use of all the natural safeguards. In that way only can you get the last laugh, as a dead man can't even grin.[9]
Private Thomas Hope, 1/5th King's Liverpool Regiment

Sometimes the relieving troops were introduced to an unusual category of 'trench stores', something usually done to test their mettle early on.

I remember well a typically French macabre joke. Within the chalk wall at the entrance to my dugout was the top of a human skull which the French officer I relieved told me was so white and shiny because the French officers had got quite fond of it – they called it 'Francois' and used to stroke it as they went in and out of the dugout![10]
2nd Lieutenant Frederick Roe, 6th Gloucester Regiment

In the winter months, the trenches were often full of water and mud that overwhelmed all well-meaning attempts at drainage. Raining, raining, would it never stop raining? Mud and water crept up to their waists at times. Many waxed lyrical on the vexed subject of mud, which they considered an abomination sent by the gods of war to convert fine, upstanding soldiers like themselves into a kind of degraded mudfish!

I don't know what the world was like before it was mud, but I know what it was like when it was mud and, like Doug, I can now understand why Adam and Eve had no clothes, as I don't suppose they had any knives to scrape them with and they would be unwearable otherwise.[11]
Captain Walter Coats, 1/9th Highland Light Infantry

When they took over French trenches, they found the French had tried their best to hold back the water. But even such well-meaning efforts only created another nagging annoyance.

The ingenious Frenchmen had drained the communication trenches by a series of sumps dug in the trench bottoms. These were about 3 or 4 feet deep, lined with brickwork and bridged by duckboards. They served well enough for summer rains, but when the trench itself had a foot or more of muddy water in it, their positions could not be observed – and the duckboards floated away. However, we soon learned the positions of the sumps by falling into them. We all fell in – repeatedly. One would start out on a journey with the firm resolve to remember the sump at the fifth traverse; but at the last moment a shell or something else would distract attention. Officers suffered most because always they led the way. One night, I made the same double journey twice and duly fell into the same sump – waist deep – four times.[12]

2nd Lieutenant Eric Bird, 4th Gloucestershire Regiment

The water was cold, dank and hid a multitude of sins which were best not delved into. Men became irritable, although they could on occasion still see the funny side of things.

The water in the trench seemed to get higher each time we looked at it. We could no longer feel our feet. Part way up the legs and all the rest of the body were aches and pains. Some of the men going sick were taken out of the line, which made the duties of those left behind last a bit longer and harder. My chum and I were doing one hour's sentry; one hour's pumping or repairing trenches and then one hour's rest, right through the night. We had got our little fire going this night and were sitting one each side, with our feet dangling in the water. Every now and then, somebody came along and kicked into them. Then there were swear words from us, "Can't you mind where you're walking!" And from the men wading along the trench, "Take your so-and-so feet out of the so-and-so way!" We were dozing off to sleep when somebody else bumped into us. Of course, we let the usual swear words fly about, but the man out in the trench didn't return our compliments as usual. This being strange, we took a closer look at him and found it was the padre![13]

Private Harry Stinton, 1/7th London Regiment

Of course, countless amusing incidents occurred, but some much-repeated apocryphal stories circulated, one of which was still popular when one of the authors of this work, Gary Bain, was in the British Army sixty years later.

I am reminded of a Somme yarn during a damp spell. Officer passing – or wading – along the road sees a tin helmet move. Reaching out with his stick he tips it over and finds a head underneath. "Hello, who are you?" "No. 45678 Mechanical Transport, Driver Thomas Sticklebottom, Sir!" "Where's your lorry, then?" "Standing on it, Sir!"[14]

Captain Quartermaster Ernest Laman, 2nd South Wales Borderers

Dugouts came in many shapes and sizes. Some were just cubby holes hollowed out of the front wall of the trench, while others were cut-and-cover exercises with a reinforced roof. They were usually uncomfortable in the extreme.

The following lines were found in the diary of No. 2803 Private G.W. Cotterill of the 11th Battalion, and they describe the conditions exactly:

What is this slimy, dismal hole,
Where oft I'm lurking like a mole,
And cursing Germans heart and soul?
My Dug-out!
Where it is that beneath the floor,
The water's rising more and more,
And where my roof's a broken door?
My Dug-out!
Where is it that I try to sleep,
Betwixt alarms, then up I leap
And dash thro' water 4 feet deep?
My Dug-out!
Where is it that I catch a chill,
And lose my only quinine pill,
And probably remain until
I'm dug-out?[15]

Lieutenant Walter Belford, 11th Australian Battalion

The larger dugouts would have an atmosphere all of their own.

The low, oblong dugout is like the interior of a huge coffin buried 30 feet underground; the air is stuffy with damp and the frowsty smell of humanity, while the smoke from the brazier, to which our cigarettes and pipes add their quota, makes a haze through which the glimmering of half a dozen candle-ends struggles gallantly but ineffectually. There is a babble of voices and a clatter of equipment and rifles. Conversation is discursive and trivial, for the most part, but generally good-humoured and often humorous, though the language would hardly pass muster in a drawing-room. There might be arguments – wordy, repetitive, and leading nowhere – and a good deal of blasphemously expressed grousing, but it all amounts to very little. Three or four men are squatting on the ground in a group, playing 'nap' with a dirty pack of cards; one or two are trying to read, or catching lice in the seams of their tunics. Someone starts to sing, and others join in: the songs are usually popular ballads, or music hall hits, among which the favourites seem to be such sentimental ditties as 'Sweet Adeline' or 'It's only a Beautiful Picture' rendered with exaggerated feeling. Or it might be one of those lugubrious satirical 'classics' which poke fun at ourselves and the 'windiness' which we all feel but do not acknowledge.[16]

Private Frederick Noakes, 1st Coldstream Guards

Where possible they would occupy the cellar of an old building, or perhaps a captured German pillbox. Not until late in the war did the British provide their men with the deep concrete dugouts, blockhouses and pillboxes that were common on the German side from the middle of 1915. After all, the next 'Big Push' would surely end the war for good! The pillboxes had their own grim story and moved one officer to compose the following appalling doggerel, 'The Old Concrete Dugout', sung mournfully to the tune of a popular song of the day.

> There's an old concrete on the Bassevillebeck
> And it faces old Gheluvelt town!
> Though the rates and the taxes are not much per week,
> New tenants walk in with a frown!
> Altho' in the dugout of beds there are four,
> Of officers there are umpteen,
> It is out of the question to sleep on the floor,
> Past tenants have left it unclean!
> To settle the Boche that repose in the slime –
> They have lain there for many a week! –
> We sprinkle it freely with chloride of lime,
> That dugout on the Bassevillebeck!
> Of that old dugout the walls are so stout –
> Some 3 to 4 feet, less or more –
> A 9-inch direct hit would scarce knock it out,
> Yet a sniper sits watching the door!
> So keep your head low, as you pass to and fro!
> So much for "our song" which we proudly sing to each visitor in turn,
> and to the tune, of course, of "The Old-fashioned Town".[17]
> 2nd Lieutenant Frank Warren, 17th King's Royal Rifle Corps

This may seem bad, but the officers usually had better accommodation than the men – if it was available. The less principled officer would beg, borrow or steal to furnish his dugout, with seemingly a marked preference for simple theft – so much simpler all-round. Why explain?

The cellar, cleared of cobwebs, straw, bottles, and other litter, and embellished with a bed – great stunt; I stole it from the major's dug-out the first night, before he knew it was there – table, chairs, shelf, books, pictures, and so on, makes a most commodious habitation. You have to be a good shall we say, 'procurer' to look after yourself in these times, but we've fixed ourselves up quite adequately. Listen to our prospectus: "CAHERDRINNEY CASTLE. An exceptionally airy and well-ventilated bijou maisonette, with roomy basement accommodation; patronised by 'Jack Johnston' and other notorieties; gas laid on free of charge!" How's that for ducal living?[18]

Lieutenant John Staniforth, 7th Leinster Regiment

To try to keep out the freezing cold there would be a brazier, which was often more trouble than it was worth – and so difficult to pronounce without unfortunate misunderstandings all round!

The brazier is worth a mention. It is the usual trench type. That is, it used to be an oil drum. It has now, however, been extensively perforated with the pick end of an entrenching tool and is gorged daily with coke and wood and any other odd, burnable revetting material which our servants can borrow unobserved. These braziers are supposed to glow, but this is a height of ambition they only achieve when they belong to sergeant majors. In officers' dug-outs they merely smoke. But, in fairness to them, it must be said that they succeed in doing this remarkably well. One sticks it manfully until the candle is but a yellow flicker through the gloom and the fug quite unbearable and then one turfs the blessed thing out and protests to the servants.[19]

Captain Charles May, 22nd Manchester Regiment

Whatever the rank of their inhabitants, even the best-reinforced concrete dugouts were not 'safe'. The impact of the heavier shells could shake, rattle and roll the occupants like dice in a cup. Shaken and stirred might sum up their condition.

The illusion of security which, despite all previous experience, we were ever ready to nurture, was immediately shattered. The next shell burst with a roar above us. The dugout trembled as acrid fumes, billowing in through the door opening, blotted out the light and made us gasp for breath. The sergeant, awakened from a peaceful doze on the upper shelf, sat up quickly and bumped his head against the concrete ceiling. "Quick, quick," he shouted, "the dug-out's fallin' in!" We laughed uproariously, as though he had cracked the joke of all jokes. Tension relaxed.[20]

Private Norman Gladden, 7th Northumberland Fusiliers

When occupying captured German dugouts, many took a sarcastic pleasure in noting pre-war British exports being put to good use.

> The farmhouse had been flattened by shell-fire, but the enemy had reinforced the cellar roof and turned it into a strong redoubt. No. 15 Platoon commander, who made it his headquarters, noticed that on the steel rails which roofed the cellar were stencilled, 'Darlington, 1904' and felt safer![21]
>
> Captain Archibald Gilchrist, 10th King's Liverpool Regiment (1st Liverpool Scottish)

Some had more telling suspicions as to the origins of the British materials they found when they occupied a captured a German pillbox.

> When it was daylight, you know what we saw advertised in that pillbox? Portland Cement – our country had been exporting Portland cement to Sweden – and Sweden the devils had exported it to Germany! And those wonderful pillboxes were made of Portland cement! That's profiteering![22]
>
> Private Tom Phillips, 49th Machine Gun Company

Some things never change.

*   *   *

The problem with living on a contested battlefield was that corpses often surrounded the soldiers, especially following a battle. In our squeamish world it seems impossible to imagine sharing your living space with the recently – or not so recently – deceased; to coexist with these grim reminders of their mortality and the terrible dangers they faced. These inanimate 'things' had once been like themselves, walked, talked, ate and loved. The soldiers soon became impervious to it, seemingly hardened to any finer feelings. At first they were shocked, then a little numbed, until finally it all became a callous joke, with the corpse as a prop.

> There was a little stream running down through our trench at Hill 60. That was our drinking water. One foggy day somebody went scrounging round in No Man's Land, and they found a Scotsman and a German that had bayoneted each other and they were lying in the stream we were drinking out of. That was just a laugh![23]
>
> Quartermaster Sergeant George Harbottle, 1/6th Northumberland Fusiliers

Partially buried bodies were frequent. Either they had never been properly interred in the first place or they were uncovered by rain or shells.

> One of our most classic incidents occurred in this march up Pip Street. It was just the remark of one of those wonderful 'B' Company men from Stratford (by Bow). Somewhere just beyond the old German front line, he saw a somewhat decayed leg sticking up from the side of the trench, covered, to some extent, anyhow, by what had obviously been a green silk sock; the good quality of this article was still obvious. With a loud "Lor, Bill! What a toff!" this worthy from Stratford, passed on to his battle position. This was one of that class of priceless remarks peculiar to the British race in times of stress.[24]
>
> Captain Randolph Chell, 10th Essex Regiment

Whatever part of the body was left showing, you could be reasonably sure that it would soon attract ribald comment.

> The trenches were filled with dead Germans and natives (Gurkhas especially) and the occupants (also native) had quietly left the dead lying there or had buried them under 6 inches or less of earth, actually in the trench, where our men had to walk about the whole time. There was a dead Gurkha fairly embedded in the ground, but with one arm sticking out up in the air. As our men went by him, they shook him warmly by the hand with such remarks as, "Good luck to yer, mate!" "Cheerio old sport!" and other remarks of the same nature.[25]
>
> Captain Donald Weir, 2nd Leicestershire Regiment

Another problem with corpses, especially in summer, was the stench that oozed from them – the literal smell of death. Once inhaled, it was, for many, never forgotten, and some veterans claimed they could still smell it whenever their thoughts drifted back to the trenches.

> I was watching Steele, of the sanitary police, repairing the side of a trench, when a pair of boots came into view. He stopped and looked curiously when someone came along and pulled one of the boots. It came away and with it the leg bone. Here lay the remains of a dead Frenchman. In a trice there was a terrific odour which just about flattened us. Steele, however, quickly plastered up the place and we moved a few yards away to fresher surroundings. This unfortunate individual was only buried about a foot underground. I heard that there used to be a cross, but the

troops, being short of kindling, thought they could put it to better use and promptly removed it.[26]

Private Donald Fraser, 31st Battalion, Canadian Expeditionary Force

Another characteristic sometimes remarked upon was the willingness of the British soldier to volunteer to try to recover bodies left marooned in the hostile wastes of No Man's Land. While some admired their ostensibly altruistic motives, other harboured deep suspicions as to their real – and far less honourable – intentions.

No Man's Land was simply covered with dead. One dead officer lay just in the middle between the two front lines. He had on a wristwatch, field glasses, etc. He was surrounded with our dead and I had a shrewd suspicion that the Boche had a rifle trained on that spot and used to fire on it at intervals during the night. Several men wanted to go out and see who it was. What they really wanted was the wristwatch and glasses.'[27]

Captain Alexander Stewart, Cameronians (Scottish Rifles)

Newly captured pillboxes were often a charnel house. The German machine gunners rarely surrendered – and would in any case seldom be given the chance after killing and maiming so many of the attackers' comrades. A couple of Mills bombs would usually be tossed through the slit to finish the job once and for all. This could cause problems when it later came to occupying the pillbox themselves as part of the new front line.

We used to sit on top of those dead Jerries – and they were big fellows! Some had wind, "Damn this devil, it's alive!" sitting on his stomach! We had to pull these Jerries out, cart them by their legs. There were big shell holes just across the track. We dumped them all there. We couldn't lie down, couldn't sleep, the floor was too damp – about half an inch of water. I tried to lie down with my own tin hat holding my head off the ground, a Jerry tin hat holding my bottom and another Jerry tin hat holding my feet. I stuck it for a bit, but I was tumbling out of it, so I had to give up that idea.[28]

Private Tom Phillips, 49th Machine Gun Company

Some of the 'jokes' are quite chilling. Yet these weren't bad lads, they were just trying to keep their sanity in a mad world.

Two sergeants going out for a stroll came upon a German corpse with the steel helmet right down over the eyes. One of them lifted up the helmet in order to see the face properly. When the sergeant lifted the helmet, it pulled up the flesh with it, and the upper lip rose from over the ivory teeth with a ghastly grin. "Take that smile off your face!" said the sergeant, and let the helmet drop back over the eyes again. And they laughed.[29]

    Private Stephen Graham, 2nd Scots Guards

If they seemed oblivious to the evidence of the slaughterhouse that surrounded them, then a rock-hard pragmatism was their only possible underlying defence if they were not to be overwhelmed by the horrors.

I had some German canned horse and bully beef for dinner which I heated up in a 'billy cooker'. What, with drinking Fritz's coffee we found in some of their water bottles in No Man's Land about three to four weeks old, drinking boiled shell water and eating your meals with dead Germans' boots staring you in the face out of the parapet. Also, we are using the dead bodies of Fritz to step on in the trenches to get out of the mud – we don't take any more notice of a dead person now than we do of a rat.[30]

    Private Herbert Butt, 102nd Canadian Battalion (Northern British Columbia)

Yet even the most hard-bitten soldiers could feel revulsion or nausea at the state of utter decay that some older bodies had attained. It was impossible to conceive that the putrid mess in front of them had had once been a man, just like them.

On my preliminary investigation in the dim light, I could see only his field boots. I had come without my torch. Subsequently, on looking closer, I found that his flesh was moving with maggots. More precisely, I noticed that portions of his uniform were heaving up and down at points where they touched the seething mass below. The smell was pretty awful. None of the men would touch him, although troops as a rule are not noticeably fastidious. The job was unanimously voted to me, because it's supposed, quite wrongly, that doctors don't mind. I went down the stairway with a length of telephone wire and lashed it round the poor fellow's feet. We hauled him up and dragged him away for some distance. The corpse left behind it a trail of wriggling, sightless maggots, which recalled the trail in a paper-chase.[31]

    Lieutenant Lawrence Gameson, (RAMC attached) 73 Brigade, Royal Field Artillery

Not much could shock or disgust battle-hardened veterans, but some things could still crack the veneer that protected their inner being.

> We found a huge cat squatting on the chest of a dead German, eating his face. It made us sick to see it, and I sent two men to chase it away. As they approached it sprang snarling at them, but they beat it down with their rifles and drove it into the ruined houses. Then we covered the body with a sack, and went on. Later, we saw the sack we had thrown over the dead Jerry heaving up and down, and there was pretty pussy, still rending and tearing the body – so we shot it!'[32]
>
> Lieutenant Edwin Vaughan, 1/8th Warwickshire Regiment

The horrific combination of the innocent kitty and the rotting corpse was a step too far.

* * *

One of the wonders of life in the trenches was the regularity of the food rations with which the men were fed. Millions upon millions of tonnes of foodstuffs were required to feed the massed battalions of men, to give them three square meals a day, without fail, day in and day out, not just for a few weeks or months, but for year after year. It was a logistical nightmare, but the British Army managed it with barely a hiccup. However, there were no epicurean delights here: this was basic foodstuff, as was inevitable given the scale of the provisions required. In the line, meals were usually a mixture of tinned rations that the company quartermaster sergeants would send by nightly ration parties. Even this mundane task was not without risk.

> On our way back we came across a skull lying in the open with fragments of kit that identified it as German. Death grimaced menacingly from the skull, but Smart, a carefree youngster, waved to it with the remark, "Goodbye, old sport!" and we chuckled. We had not covered 10 yards more, before death struck with a sniper's help and Smart joined the unknown German in the fraternity of the fallen. A bullet through the head. He had mocked at death and Nemesis could not have been more swift.[33]
>
> Private Norman Cliff, 1st Grenadier Guards

Some enterprising Australians even found a means of profiting from such a mundane duty.

The boys would have to go down to Gordon's Dump, where the transports or other details would be met. Private Oscar Bauer, of 'A' Company, used to make use of the present writer's signature – all unknown to him, of course – to procure a case of whisky from the canteen. The money was subscribed by the troops interested, but an officer's signature had to be obtained before a case was allowed to be purchased. If the good "Scotch" in any way mitigated the horrors of the terrible experience the forgery was more than justified.[34]

Lieutenant Walter Belford, 11th Australian Battalion

Every night, the ration party would come up, carrying the food in sandbags. Amongst the tinned foods was bully (corned) beef, Maconochie's (a meat and vegetable stew), pork and beans (baked haricot beans with a small lump of fatty pork), cheese and tinned bacon. If they got jam, then it always seemed to be tins of plum and apple. Bread was a treat. It really was not a lot to look forward to.

There'd be a whisper over the top, "Rations boys!" There couldn't have been more than nine or ten in my section – a couple of loaves of bread, bully beef and Maconochie's. You could always tell when there was a load of casualties because instead of being four to a loaf there'd be two.[35]

Private Ivor Watkins, 15th Welsh Regiment

If they didn't get bread, then one staple of their daily diet was the standard army biscuit.

Always plenty of biscuits: about 3 inches square and a ½ inch thick. They were as hard as nails! You had to get a stone and break it down into small pieces. Then you'd soak it with water or tea. These ship's biscuits were worth having; everybody carried them. If you ran short you could always say, "Have you got a ship's biscuit?" And somebody would always have an extra one, there were always plenty. More than a standby, they were a staple food.[36]

Sergeant Jack Dorgan, 1/7th Northumberland Fusiliers

Many men rued the teeth they had broken on these rock-hard culinary delights. Not even false teeth were immune.

I had a full set of dentures. Of course, these biscuits – exactly like dog biscuits today – they snapped off all these teeth. I must have looked a

dreadful sight! I went to the medical officer, I said, "What do I do about this?" He said, "Well, you can soak them, can't you?"[37]
Private Edwin Bigwood, 7th Worcestershire Regiment

One ration never to be forgotten was bully beef, which arrived in huge quantities. The men grew heartily sick of it, but there was nothing else. Many swore they would never eat another can of 'bully' as long as they lived. Even opening the tins was a test.

We had a tin of bully beef. At the side of this thing was a key which you used to turn the top off. Mine didn't act and I got this jack knife to open this tin. Unfortunately, it slipped and my hand was jagged – see this – it's still there! A great jag and of course I bled like a pig. The boys bandaged me up.[38]
Private Donald Price, 20th Royal Fusiliers

Water added greatly to the burden of the ration party – it was bloody heavy!

We carried clean drinking water up to the line in old petrol tins. The taste of petrol and paraffin got into everything. Then there was the chloride of lime that they tipped onto the corpses and the Lysol, used as a disinfectant. In the background was that smell, that dreadful stink – all the time. I don't have to tell you; you can imagine it for yourself. A horrible, sweet smell. I suppose after a time you cease to notice it. You lost your sense of smell and your sense of taste. You'd make a dixie of tea.[39]
Private Noel Peters, 16th Middlesex Regiment (Public Schools Battalion)

Sometimes conditions were such that they couldn't get the water forward. There was usually plenty of water all around them, but there was a risk of it being polluted by gas.

A volunteer from among a group of mates would sample the water from a selected shell hole. For the next hour or so he would be watched with frank interest and speculation. If he survived the observation period without throwing any 'sixers', that water would be pronounced good, and promptly utilised. A great laugh went through the company on the next trip into the line. Members of "A" Section headed back to a shell hole, from which they had continuously drawn a most excellent supply but when they arrived on this occasion, the water had drained off. Lying peacefully on the bottom was a large and very dead "Fritz". "And the water seemed so good!" said one. "It was soup, you goat!" replied an unsympathetic onlooker.[40]

> Private George Mitchell, 48th Australian Battalion

Tea was a supposed panacea for all ills, but it had its work cut out in the trenches. In truth, though often denied by brainwashed ex-soldiers, British Army tea was a disgusting concoction, with far too much of each ingredient, then relentlessly brewed, or rather stewed, until it lost all possible self-respect as a drink. Many officers were simply aghast when offered a mug of this charmless drink.

> The tea, corrosively strong and sweet as a concentrated syrup, served in mugs with the enamel chipped off just where you put your lips. Contact with the naked tin can be avoided by drinking from the segment immediately above the handle. The state of the mugs can't be helped because they get such a bashing about, but there's no excuse for the ghastly brew.[41]
>
> Lieutenant Lawrence Gameson, 45th Field Ambulance, Royal Army Medical Corps

Yet the men loved it. Perhaps the combination of excess sugar and caffeine gave them a comforting 'high'. Brewing tea was not an easy matter in a flooded trench. Stories abound of lukewarm tea made with a candle, but most used a 'Tommy' cooker or a little non-regulation primus stove.

> The batmen soon used up the bottle of methylated spirit that they had brought into the trenches, so one of them suggested trying to start it with whisky, of which the officers had a limited supply – for medicinal purposes! It was simply amazing how much whisky that primus took to start it! One day while in the support line the batmen managed to get the stove going in order to make some afternoon tea. Admittedly it was a quiet sector. One of "D" Company's officers was passing the dugout occupied by the trench mortar boys, when suddenly there was an unholy rush and several of the troops became jammed in the door of the dugout in their eagerness to get inside. There was some cursing and swearing before the congestion was relieved, and then one of the trench mortar lads saw the officer gazing at them in mild surprise. "Quick, Sir! Duck in here!" he cried. The officer gazed around but could not see or hear anything dangerous. "What's up, anyway?" he asked. "A bloody rum jar [*Minenwerfer*] coming!" said the 'Digger'. "You listen!" Comprehension dawned on the officer, and he started to laugh. "Why, that's only our old primus!" The relieved troops sidled

out of the dugout looking very sheepish, but they were cheered up a bit when the lieutenant promised them some tea when the billy boiled.[42]

Lieutenant Walter Belford, 11th Australian Battalion

Some cheery souls tried to make a joke of the unending sameness of the food on offer.

I recall Granigan one evening tugging a dirty scrap of paper out of his breast pocket and beginning to read us an imaginary menu. 'Suckling pig, roast duck, turkey, and plum pudding! Come on, give me your order, gents!" The following day the ration party reached Centre Way just as that unhealthy avenue was being baptized with high explosive shells. A portion of the food was lost and Granigan arrived with his stew, but minus his tin hat. Rushing into our dugout, he placed the dixie on the floor, sat up on the lid, and fanned himself with his hand. "Oh, me little heart it's going pit-a-pat, pit-a-pat." "Where's that suckling-pig we ordered?" "Oh, I must tell you about that; I was coming along by the cemetery with the stew in one hand and the roast pig in the other – and would you believe it, a great big shell came, and took it clean out of my hand!" It was not brilliant humour, but that simple fun was as precious as the wisdom of Solomon.[43]

Sergeant Edgar Rule, 14th Australian Battalion

When they could get close enough to the front to set up their kitchens, the cooks would try their best. Yet the British soldier is rarely – or is it never – appreciative of the efforts of others on his behalf.

You'd take a lot of trouble to make a stew taste better. Maybe you'd scrounge some vegetables, real vegetables not the tinned kind, steal some onions and potatoes. Or sometimes you could get hold of some real steak. Now and then I'd scrounge a little curry powder off the Indians up the line at Festubert. Or there might be a few herbs that had survived the shelling in one of the little neglected gardens behind the miners' cottages. Anything to give it a taste! Some stout fellow would have a brazier going nicely and you'd put the dixie on to warm. And finally, you'd serve it out into their mess tins. And then, after all that, you'd hear one of the fellows say, "It all tastes the same!" Sometimes I'd get a notion to make a special dessert, to give them a treat. Tinned fruit spiced up with some rum and then add some apples and plums that I bartered for a couple of tins of bully beef, and then make some custard

to go with it. When I got it up to the line still intact the lads would say, "It all tastes the same!"[44]
    Private Noel Peters, 16th Middlesex Regiment (Public Schools Battalion)

One common story was of the man who got a parcel from home containing one of the fixed ingredients of their diet. Some of the trenches and dugouts were lined and reinforced with cases of unopened tins.

> One fellow got a parcel from his wife sent out from home. He opened up this parcel, we were all sitting opening our parcels and mail. Sid Baker, says, "Oh boys, look boys!" He held up a tin of plum and apple jam. A parcel from home and this tin of plum and apple was in it. We were building dugout walls with it! He laughed like to kill himself! His own wife had sent him a tin of jam![45]
>   Private Sibbald Stewart, 238th Company, Machine Gun Corps

Usually, parcels from home were much prized. Any choice titbits were dutifully shared with a soldier's best mates in the unit. Cakes, sweets and any other luxury items were all wolfed down as soon as possible.

> One evening, two of the fellows – 'Mary' so-called because of his clever impersonations of a cockney char in the battalion concert party, and 'Bermo' who hailed from Bermondsey – and I were trying to heat up a tinned meat-pie which I had just received from home, over a fire which had taken a lot of coaxing before it would burn, and in a mess tin which was almost too small for the purpose. Just as success was in sight and we had begun to anticipate an appetising supper, the air-raid warning was given, and we had to throw our nearly-boiling water on the fire. "Sich wyste, Mrs May," screamed 'Mary' in his falsetto stage-voice, "I never seed anything so disgriceful in all me born days!" But the pie was not entirely wasted – we ate most of it in the dark, lukewarm and half-congealed.[46]
>   Private Frederick Noakes, 1st Coldstream Guards

Scavenging for extra, or even more importantly, different, food was widespread. French and Belgian farmers often found their livestock – especially pigs and chickens – mysteriously missing. Where could they have got to?

> Heavy firing on our left towards Ypres and generally all round. More stew. A pig was foolish enough to come down the road. We shot him and shall very soon be eating pork chops.[47]
>   Company Sergeant Major Ernest Shepherd, 1st Dorset Regiment

Bored to distraction by the monotonous diet, the men were even tempted by the vista of the fresh vegetables growing in No Man's Land. Harvesting them, however, was a dangerous business, as scavengers faced the very real chance of being shot from both sides.

> One night, I was on the firestep and I heard a 'swish, swish, swish!' out in front. We had no listening patrols out. "Halt, who comes there?" a Scotch voice says. "Disnae shoot, disnae shoot!" and a Scottish soldier came rolling over the parapet, a sandbag in one hand and his haversack in the other – full of potatoes. He's been out scrounging potatoes from the potato field in front! He came out of a trench about half a mile along – he must have gone a long way in the dark – getting lost! As he rolled in his potatoes went all over the place! He was a great big Scot, his knees were all raw where he'd been kneeling in his kilt. His kilt was all muddy and he was scrambling on the floor getting up all these potatoes, he's swearing to himself and all of a sudden, he says, "Oh Bonny Scotland, what am I suffering for you the noo!" We roared with laughter.[48]
>
> Rifleman Francis Sumpter, 1st Rifle Brigade

It was not only risky; sometimes the hungry soldier had not entirely thought it through in the conditions that prevailed on the Western Front in the final two years of the war.

> We were in a part of the line where there had been a gas attack, but not recently. It had been a field of potatoes – and all these lovely new potatoes were growing. We thought, "Ohhh! What a feast! New potatoes!" We scrambled out over the top in the middle of the night and grabbed as many of these potatoes as we could. Ohhh! Didn't we feel ill afterwards. They'd been living in this filthy earth full of gas.
>
> Private Victor Kerridge, 1st Gordon Highlanders

* * *

Two special rations were much prized. Cigarettes and rum meant very little to non-smoking teetotallers, but they meant the whole world to the average man. Cigarettes were plentiful, but there still never seemed to be enough. Cigarettes became a kind of currency, passed between friends, shared to the last puff, or dog-end. Men craved cigarettes not only because they were addicted to nicotine, but because it gave them something to do with their hands, a distraction in times of great stress. One amusing story resonated across the decades. It summed up the ludicrous reasons for starting to smoke heavily and the awful difficulty in giving up – long after the original motivation had ceased to have any relevance.

> I always gave my cigarette ration to my batman, I used to have a hundred cigarettes coming out every month from Philip Morris, Turkish, and 100 also Turkish, from Bartlett in Piccadilly. I never smoked more than about fifty in a month until my batman came to me and he said, "You know, sir, that a major in one of the other batteries, he never wears a gas mask!" So I said, "Well he must be a bloody fool!" "He says that if he smokes cigarettes, they must be 'gaspers' continuously, he doesn't have to wear a mask." I did wear a gas mask always when things were bad, but I thought, "I'll try this business of smoking!" And instead of fifty a month I was smoking forty a day! It was many years before I could give it up![49]
>
>   Lieutenant Murray Rymer Jones, 74 Brigade, Royal Field Artillery

Just as important was the rum ration – especially in the winter months.

> The ration would come up in a rum jar: about 14 inches high, stone jar with a handle and a stopper. It had to be issued by an officer and an NCO. Being one of the only teetotal sergeants in the battalion, I was invariably the rum sergeant! We went along from sentry group to sentry group, dugout to dugout at the beginning of the night. Everybody would be up and waiting for it. Word soon spread, "The rum ration's on the job!" The officer would carry the rum jar and I would have a large spoon and the ration consisted of one spoonful. The rum we had was much stronger than the rum we have today! Although you may think a spoonful of rum is not much it was both beneficial and ample. The spoon was always licked by the fellow when he received his ration. That cleaned it ready for the next man![50]
>
>   Sergeant Jack Dorgan, 1/7th Northumberland Fusiliers

In a freezing cold flooded trench, rum was a lifesaver. Modern doctors may point out that alcohol promotes a dangerous loss in body heat, but the experience of the men in the trenches was markedly different. The men swore by it!

> Rum was our best doctor. To work and live in wet clothes, sleep in a hole in the ground and keep healthy would have been impossible without the rum issue. Taken neat on an empty stomach first thing in the morning, it went down like molten fire and, however wet or depressed we might be,

it sent our spirits soaring and created such an appetite that we could have eaten a dead man's boot.[51]

Corporal Harold Williams, 56th Australian Battalion

Which was perhaps just as well, given the unyielding nature of army biscuits! Older soldiers particularly appreciated the rum rations, savouring every drop and the warming 'glow' it brought to their long-forgotten extremities.

At dawn throughout this tour, I went round all posts armed with a rum jar. After the NCO in charge had reported his command present and his rifles clean, each man of the post filed up to me, and I issued him his 'tot' in a small metal cup. I never saw the rum more appreciated than it was during this tour. The "old toughs" who had been up all night in a water-logged sap-head would hold out their ration and say; "Best of luck, Sorr!" or "Best respects!" and drain the rum in one gulp. Kelly said to me one morning after he had drunk his tot, "Begorra, 'tis wonderful, Sorr! Trickling yet!" And they all in turn would lick their lips, stamp their feet, and so life would smile on them again. The ration rum was excellent, and as Kelly said, when frozen through after a long wet night, one could feel the rum trickling down into one's very toes![52]

Captain Francis Hitchcock, 2nd Leinster Regiment

The first introduction of raw spirits to men with little or no experience of alcohol sometimes had a bigger effect than was intended.

I was on guard at the battalion headquarters – a beastly cold, wet night – drizzling. There was a lance corporal and three of us on the guard. I was doing my turn out there and the corporal came out with a mug – some rum! "Have a drop of this it will warm you up!" I drank it, a nice ration there, he says, "You haven't drunk it all have you? That was for all four of us!" I wasn't used to spirits at all then! I was patrolling up and down this path and I found it very difficult to keep still, I was going backwards and forwards. I found after a bit, that if I ran up and down it I could keep on it better! So, I slung my rifle over my shoulder and there I was running up and down this path, backwards and forwards. Then I saw the adjutant coming along! I thought, "Good heavens! Drunk on guard in the face of the enemy – I shall be shot at dawn!" I propped myself up against a tree as he came and I said, "Halt! Who goesh there?" He said, "The adjshutant!" He was just as tight as I was![53]

Private Herbert Williams, 1/5th London Regiment (London Rifle Brigade)

There was much speculation on what the letters 'SRD' stamped on the rum jars meant. Some old sweats swore it meant 'Soon Runs Dry', but the general opinion was that it meant 'Seldom Reaches Destination', with the fickle finger of suspicion pointing at the officers and NCOs responsible for the rum issue.

> One spoonful, how it warmed the feet, how it took the place of a blanket, and what sleep it brought, and that contented feeling which made Private Atkins sit happily on the firing step softly crooning himself to sleep with this refrain:
> If the sergeants pinch the rum, never mind,
> If the sergeants pinch the rum, never mind,
> They're entitled to a tot, but they pinch the bloody lot,
> If the sergeants pinch the rum, never mind.[54]
> Captain John Milne, 1/4th Leicestershire Regiment

Considerable evidence can be proffered in support of the sentiments expressed in this popular song. Often, they *had* pinched the rum!

> Mr Whitehouse was orderly officer and, with a corporal, dispensed the rum-ration to the front-line posts. But he had apparently been sampling it himself on the way, for by the time the post next to ours had been reached the jar was empty and he himself was distinctly 'merry'. He ordered the corporal to take it back to company headquarters and swear that it had been only half-full to begin with, and in the meantime, he crawled into a bivvie and tried to entertain us with incoherent and often unrepeatable songs. Our amusement was tempered somewhat by the fear that his attempts at singing would be audible in the German lines and provoke retaliation![55]
> Private Frederick Noakes, Household Battalion

One private was lucky enough to catch his sergeant major in the very act of stealing their rum ration. His response was in the finest traditions of the British Army – he sought to profit from his good fortune by blackmailing the culprit.

> I had to go back and get something in the support line. I missed my way and went up a *cul de sac*. There was the sergeant major off in the corner there with a big bottle of rum! He was filling up his water bottle! He was startled to see me, he said, "Errr, will rum be good?" I got the lid of his billycan and poured out neat rum. Of course, I drank quite a good deal of rum! Then I went back up to the front line – and they came round with the rum ration. I could have won the war as easily as anything! Absolutely![56]
> Private Edwin Bigwood, 7th Worcestershire Regiment

The Australians reacted to suspected dishonesty from one of those in charge of the rum with a splendid stream of spittle-flecked abuse.

> Temporarily in charge was the quartermaster sergeant's clerk, known as 'Old Harry'. He was sandy-headed, watery-eyed, flabby of skin, and verging on middle age, and as cranky as a houseful of old maids. The troops suspected that when opportunity arose, he treated himself handsomely to rum and other things. Peter Hughes hated him but, driven by the crying need of a nip, he approached "Old Harry", and in the nicest tones at his command, said: "Harry, give me a nip of rum?" "Indeed, I will not," snarled Harry. "You won't, you rum-thieving old bastard!" said Peter. "I'll have rum to drink when they are trying to grow lilies on your grave!"[57]
>
> Corporal Harold Williams, 56th Australian Battalion

Given these suspicions, teetotallers were often put in charge of issuing rum to try to reduce 'natural wastage' through theft. The priorities of the men were well-illustrated when one man nearly had a most unfortunate accident while dutifully carrying the precious rum jar.

> I was going across some duckboards across a swamp – and stumbled, nearly fell in. A chap grabbed me, pulled back! I said, "Thanks, pal!" He said, "No it's not you – it was the rum jar I was saving!"[58]
>
> Private Percy Jackson, 2nd Middlesex Regiment

If there was ever a time the Germans were truly hated, it was when they scored a direct hit on the rum jar – the very fulcrum of many men's desires. One Cockney war story summed it up brilliantly.

> Just before the battle of Messines we of the 23rd Londons were holding the Bluff sector to the right of Hill 60. 'Stand down' was the order, and the sergeant was coming round with the rum. 'Nobbler', late of the Mile End Road, was watching him in joyful anticipation when a whizz-bang burst on the parapet, hurling men in all directions. No one was hurt but the precious rum jar was shattered. 'Nobbler', sitting up in the mud and moving his tin hat from his left eye the better to gaze upon the ruin, murmured bitterly: "Louvain, Rheims, the *Lusitania*, and now our perishin' rum issue. Jerry, you 'eathen, you gets worse and worse. But, my 'at, won't you cop it when 'Aig knows abaht this!"[59]
>
> Private Edward Oliver, 23rd London Regiment

The idea of the august figure of Field Marshal Sir Douglas Haig sharing his outrage is perhaps amusement enough.

* * *

The war was filthy business, and so were the men. Covered in mud and miscellaneous 'shite', and infested with lice, the trenches were a truly unpleasant environment. Try as they might, it was difficult to maintain any standard of cleanliness.

> When an occasional opportunity arose in the early dawn hours, I stripped, and my batman threw dirty water taken from shell holes in a canvas bucket all over me much to the amusement of nearby onlookers. Removing blankets lying on the wire bunks, and casting them aside on the ground, I began to wonder if I was developing delusions. The blankets were moving in all directions, and on closer examination, I realised that this was caused by the infestation of millions of lice. My machine gunners also became infested, and whenever possible, removed their shirts to pick off any visible lice. On one occasion, I heard one say to another, "There goes another Arsenal supporter!" as he threw it away. I gathered that the remark was made on account of its colour.[60]
> Lieutenant Horace Paviere, 167th Company, Machine Gun Corps

Lice were here, there and everywhere, infesting the clothes of the men, the NCOs and many of the officers.

> Squirming, biting lice congregated beneath the straps of my equipment. Instead of being satisfied to wander at large around our shirts, having a nip when the call for nourishment arose, these "chats" would assemble for their divisional sports, race meetings and free fights, wherever a belt or strap bore heavily. Then, at any extra pressure, they would make concerted or spasmodic rushes.[61]
> Private George Mitchell, 48th Australian Battalion

The men new to the front sent desperate appeals to their families for various brands of insect powder advertised as 'Good for body lice'. They soon found that such advertisements were entirely accurate as the powder was indeed good for lice – they thrived on it!

> The greatest shock a recruit gets when he arrives at his battalion in France is to see the men engaging in a 'cootie' hunt. With an air of

contempt and disgust he avoids the company of the older men, until a couple of days later, in a torment of itching, he also has to resort to a shirt hunt, or spend many a sleepless night of misery. During these hunts there are lots of pertinent remarks bandied back and forth among the explorers, such as, "Say, Bill, I'll swap you two little ones for a big one!" or, "I've got a black one here that looks like Kaiser Bill!"[62]

Private Guy Empey, 1st London Regiment

'Chatting' and the associated banter was a universal pastime amongst the men.

No matter what precautions were taken, everyone was lousy; insecticides were of little avail, and the utmost one could do, in our circumstances, was to wage an unending war against the pests by cracking them between thumb-nails or burning their eggs out of the seams of our clothes with a lighted cigarette-end or candle flame. They were slow-moving and easily caught, but they bred so fast that the most unremitting efforts could do no more than keep their numbers down. We made a joke of our lousiness, as we did of most things that were unavoidable. In common parlance, a louse was known as a 'chat' and the word was also used as a verb, 'to have a chat' meant not light conversation, but to hunt in the folds of one's shirt! Newcomers from England were solemnly assured that on the other side of No Man's Land all the lice bore 'Iron Cross' markings on their backs and did the goose-step in formation.[63]

Private Frederick Noakes, Household Battalion

2nd Lieutenant Robert Graves, always a reliable source of apocryphal stories, summed it up nicely:

Lice were a standing joke. Young Bumford handed me one, "We was just having an argument as to whether it's best to kill the old ones or the young ones, sir. Morgan here says that if you kill the old ones, the young ones die of grief; but Parry here, sir, he says that the young ones are easier to kill and you can catch the old ones when they go to the funeral!"[64]

2nd Lieutenant Robert Graves, 2nd Welsh Regiment

As for keeping their uniform clean in the trenches, that was simply impossible. This gem of a story from a medical officer sums it up perfectly:

One of our Scottish infantrymen was perched on a ledge in the wall of a sodden trench. The trench was almost knee-deep in liquid mud.

The ground outside and the approaches was a viscid, glutinous morass. Pitiless rain was pouring down. He was pulling a sock through the clenched fingers of his left hand. Mud oozed through his fingers and around the top of his sock as he pulled the sock, which, saturated with mud was as slimy as an eel. I asked him what he was doing. He answered simply, with no dangerous Scottish twinkle in his eyes, "I'm doing a bit of washing, Sir!"[65]

Lieutenant Lawrence Gameson, (RAMC attached) 73 Brigade, Royal Field Artillery

It will be of no surprise to find that the trench latrines were not a particularly pleasant, or indeed secure, environment. This was not a place for quiet contemplation, with perhaps a smoke or a read of the latest newspaper. They were a functional necessity, with everything reduced to the bare essentials.

A hole, everybody had to go in there, officers and all. No paper, we had to do the best we could. We couldn't be bothered about anything else, the quicker you did it and got your trousers up to be ready, the better. It would be an awful thing to be caught with your trousers down. It was a quick move![66]

Private Ivor Watkins, 15th Welsh Regiment

In winter, they were not places to linger with backsides exposed willy-nilly to the elements, but summer brought its own problems.

There would be short latrine trenches leading out at the back of the traverses – but they soon got foul. And in the summer the flies and the smell were very bad! You got used to the smell, curiously, you can get used to almost anything, but you can't get used to flies! At least I can't! The flies were an awful nuisance![67]

Lieutenant William Shipway, 1/4th Gloucestershire Regiment

Lieutenant Shipway was not alone in his hatred of the flies.

The latrine, two empty biscuit tins let conveniently into the sides of a small recess cut out of the trench, was that afternoon the assembly place of a myriad of buzzing flies, whose noise seemed sufficient to drown the premonitory scream of an approaching shell. I had little inclination to tarry in such an unsavoury and dangerous spot![68]

Private Norman Gladden, 7th Northumberland Fusiliers

There was nothing quite like the sense of utter vulnerability men experienced when under shellfire whilst ensconced on the toilet.

> Latrines in the front-line trench were a big hole – and you sat on a plank – resting loosely on oil drums – nothing firm! There would be half a dozen of us on it! And Jerry dropped a 'Whizz-Bang!' and it dropped just the other side of the trench – and the whole ruddy lot fell in the shit. Oooh you bugger! That was a nasty one from Jerry – that was dirty – that wasn't playing fair! You can imagine that – that was the funniest thing I've seen! Yes! I was one of them! My God we didn't half pong! You couldn't go down into dugouts![69]
> Corporal John Fidler, 1st Cameronians (Scottish Rifles)

Many men must have died in the latrines, but some recalled the happier consequences of German shells.

> One day a shell hit the officers' latrine, sending the screen flying. I was shocked to see a man still sitting there on the throne and I thought he must be dead. I ran as hard as I could and arrived to find Ellison up and adjusting his trousers. He said with a grin, "It was lucky that the shell came when it did as I was feeling a bit constipated!"[70]
> Lieutenant Julian Tyndale-Biscoe, 'C' Battery, Royal Horse Artillery

There were also more mundane accidents that were indelibly associated with the latrines.

> One of the small men drafted to us from the Bantam Regiment and whose boots were at the cobblers, borrowed those of a comrade. Visiting the muddy latrine and perching himself on the pole, his short legs preventing his feet from resting on the ground, he lost balance and fell backwards into the disgusting contents of the pit. He had to be helped out, leaving his companion's boots, which were several sizes too large for him, in the bottom of the morass. What occurred afterwards between him and his pal I never learned, but [I] expect the air was pretty thick and no doubt his ear also! Incidents such as this, although often rather crude, gave us much amusement and helped to relieve the otherwise dreadful monotony and discomfort of our lives.[71]
> Private John Tucker, 2/13th London Regiment (Kensington Battalion)

As ever, the Germans were blamed for everything: they were even accused of arranging their latrines up on the heights above the British lines so that the 'run-off' slurry dribbled down – slowly but inexorably – towards the British trenches. War is cruel, but surely not that cruel?

* * *

'Rats as big as cats' is a clichéd phrase familiar to all those who encountered Great War veterans. The popular vision of the trenches has long been one of trenches swarming with rats, an unstoppable tide of filthy rodents grown fat from gorging on the dead. In fact, rats were a localized nuisance, thriving mainly in areas where they were already well-established in civilian life – thus farms, storehouses and canals hold an irresistible attraction to the discerning rat. One exasperated officer summed up the nuisance they posed:

> Rats! Now at home, in small numbers and well under the control enforced by long-established civilization, rats present no particular terrors or inconvenience except, perhaps, to a sensitive female. But in the trenches, where food was abundant and engines of destruction, at least as far as rats were concerned, few, they waxed plentiful, and their audacity increased with their size and their numbers. Not content with running all over the duck-boards, and all but refusing to step aside and let you pass, they ran riot in your dugout, gnawed your clothes, devoured your food, scampered all over you as you slept, and in one notorious case caused grave inconvenience to a medical officer by removing bodily his set of false teeth. In the front line they climbed on the sleeping soldier and gnawed through his haversack to reach his iron ration. In the 'bivvy' they nibbled holes in a man's socks as he lay on the ground. In fact, so bold were they that you could fire two or three rounds at a rat and hit all round him before he would condescend to move at all, and then he would only twitch his whiskers and remove himself in a leisurely fashion to some less disturbed spot. The services of Mr. Browning's 'Pied Piper' would have been invaluable to us.[72]
>
> Captain Charles Wurtzburg, 2/6th King's Liverpool Regiment

In badly infested sectors they were indeed present in massed battalions, swarming over the trenches.

> Whether it was the chalk trenches, or the numerous dead bodies buried there that attracted them I don't know, for they were quite at home and even had the manners to stand aside while you passed them in the trenches, and they looked quite offended if you kicked at them. Some of

the boys swore that the rodents carried tin openers with them, for food was only safe when it was carried on the person.[73]

Corporal George Ashurst, 1st Lancashire Fusiliers

Some trenches were almost overrun as the rats waged a ceaseless battle for supremacy with the soldiers who had dared to enter their subterranean lairs.

Thousands of them, enormous brutes with an utter disregard for man. The walls of the trenches and dugouts were honeycombed with their runs and at night they swarmed over everything. The men had the greatest difficulty in keeping their food protected. It was useless to hang a loaf of bread by a string from the roof of a dugout. The rats grinned contemptuously, waited till one's back was turned, slid down the string, and the bread vanished. The only way to preserve perishable food was to cut it into small pieces and pack it in a mess-tin. Rat-hunting became a regular trench sport and though many men developed great quickness and efficiency with stick or bayonet there was no noticeable reduction in the number of rats.[74]

Lieutenant Archibald Gilchrist, 10th King's Liverpool Regiment (1st Liverpool Scottish)

The loss of rations was often significant, although many in authority were inclined to think that the soldiers themselves had eaten the iron rations, contrary to King's Regulations, and were using the rats as a convenient excuse.

The iron rations of our unit had disappeared gradually, and our quartermaster indented for 241 – our total number – at one go-off, a somewhat wholesale order. And then started a correspondence which ran, "Reference your indent of – for 241 iron rations. It is not understood how all your iron rations have disappeared. Please explain!" To which the quartermaster replied, "These rations have been lost mainly through the action of rats!" What he meant was that the rats had in many cases eaten through the linen bags in which the iron rations were carried, and that the tins had fallen out through the holes so caused while the men were on the march or in billets. However, in came, "Please explain how rats can eat through tin?" Here the quartermaster with a troubled mind, brought the correspondence to me, and we tried them with, "It is pointed out for your information that the rat prevalent in the district is not the small black rat, but the large, grey Hanoverian rat!" The correspondence ceased and we got the rations handed over! 'Q' had evidently not got a good textbook on natural history at hand.[75]

Major David Rorie, 1/2nd Highland Field Ambulance, Royal Army
Medical Corps

It is not surprising that some sensitive souls were unable to master their
atavistic horror of the rats that seemed all around them. Naturally, this sign of
weakness was taken advantage of by those less troubled.

> One wretched officer, who had a horror of rats, was very popular
> with his brother subalterns because, not daring to go to sleep at night
> in the trenches, he always volunteered to take everyone else's tour of
> duty and would return, worn and haggard, to company headquarters
> dugout after morning stand-to and try to snatch what sleep he could
> curled up on the table. Even then he would lie awake wondering if the
> rats would fall on him from the roof. They were erudite rats too. One
> of them was discovered disappearing backwards into a hole with an
> unopened copy of the *Weekly Times* in its mouth.[76]
> Lieutenant Archibald Gilchrist, 10th King's Liverpool Regiment
> (1st Liverpool Scottish)

Hunting tigers out in India had nothing compared to the thrills and spills of
rat hunting. One simple ruse accounted for many of the more easily fooled rats.

> Sometimes we indulged in a little amusement, and at the same time
> helped to lessen the activities of these four-footed thieves. Placing a
> piece of cheese about three inches from a rat hole we waited patiently,
> rifle at the ready and finger on trigger, for the lightning dash we knew
> the rat would make before long. Soon a little twitching, whiskered nose
> would protrude from the hole; the army cheese would be too tempting a
> morsel to miss. Out would shoot half the rat's body, and as quickly the
> finger would press the trigger, bang, and Mr Rodent's body would be
> flung over the back of the trench, almost in two halves.[77]
> Corporal George Ashurst, 1st Lancashire Fusiliers

Rats were not the only nuisance in the trenches. Mice were sometimes mentioned,
but one new 'menace' was that of the slippery frog.

> The battalion had long looked on rats as a necessary evil, but frogs were a
> new experience and nearly as unwelcome. By day, they remained hidden
> in the trench drains and in out-of-the-way corners but at night they
> swarmed into the fire-bays and communication-trenches and became
> a general nuisance to all who had to walk the duckboards in the dark.

To tread unexpectedly on a frog is disconcerting. It is as slippery as a banana-skin and makes an unpleasant popping sound if solidly stepped on which is distinctly unmanning. One hyper-sensitive subaltern when on trench-duty at night always insisted on his runner preceding him to clear the frogs from his path and when, one day, he found one in his newly-completed dugout he gave orders for the floorboards to be lifted and the frog removed before he would take possession. When his batman shortly afterwards produced the results of his labours, one hundred and fifty frogs in a sandbag, the subaltern was noticeably shaken, and his friends declare that he has never been the same man since.[78]

Captain Archibald Gilchrist, 10th King's Liverpool Regiment (1st Liverpool Scottish)

A relative rarity was the wild rabbit or hare. If they couldn't catch them to eat, then soldiers would use them as target practice as they gambolled about in No Man's Land.

The arrival of a hare, which had prudently decided to evacuate Bourlon Wood, and ran the length of our line and that of the 19th Hussars. All the men fired at it; the hare escaped to our left flank amid prolonged cheering.[79]

Captain Alan Lascelles, Bedfordshire Yeomanry

The hare was either very lucky indeed or the beneficiary of some very poor shooting!

The men also attracted various abandoned furry animal friends, which were quickly adopted as pets or unit mascots. One such was 'Snips' the Cat!

Hearing a plaintive mewing coming from a ruined house just behind the line, Lance Corporal Merritt climbed out of the trench to investigate. He addressed much lurid language to the Boche who, having spotted him, were taking pot-shots, but he eventually returned safely with a half-starved kitten. Hard-boiled Merritt's love for that kitten was astonishing. Woe betides any who dared disturb its sleep or begrudge its food! Its bed, when at rest, was an upturned steel helmet; during the journeys to and from the line and when the battalion was on the move, it travelled on the packs of the various members of the section, who all became greatly attached to it. 'Snips' with his physical development permanently retarded by poverty-stricken kitten-hood, never became a prize specimen of cathood, but his courage was not impaired, and he would often attack and kill rats of his own size. 'Snips' was reported

"Missing" on the Somme and had to be struck off the strength accordingly.[80]

> 2nd Lieutenant Reginald Russell, 11th Queen's Own Royal West Kent Regiment (Lewisham Battalion)

Trench pets do not seem to have had a terribly long life expectancy, and while the men were often upset at their demise, they still could not resist a joke or two in the aftermath.

> There is a little grave about 2ft by 3ft in the middle of a bust-up farm, and on the cross there is this, "Here lies Tim, a little brown dog, killed by a shell during the bombardment of this house by the Germans on April 23, 1915. R.I.P." That was the end of our mascot. He went out of the trench into the farm to see why the bricks kept jumping about. He did his bit all right. The Rifle Brigade had a kitten, but she was shot by a sniper while walking on the parapet with her tail straight up in the air. Please send a bullet-proof tortoise.[81]
>
> Lieutenant Denis Barnett, 2nd Prince of Wales' Leinster Regiment

Sometimes there could be too much of a 'good thing' and some heartless officers had no compunction in taking drastic action to reduce the growing dog population.

> Dogs have suddenly appeared in the trenches. Good dogs, apparently sprung from nowhere. I have given orders for any seen to be shot. It is a pity, and one feels very sad about it, but I am too suspicious of 'Fritz', I think him quite capable of inoculating the brutes with some beastly disease and then letting them loose on us. I may be wrong, but in war one cannot take chances – especially against Fritz. 'Bang!' One has just been shot as I write. It is whimpering out its life alongside my dugout. Poor beast! It seems a dirty trick – but there you are![82]
>
> Captain Charles May, 22nd Manchester Regiment

Another officer in May's battalion remembered that not all the dogs went quietly. One at least put up a heroic battle for life.

> There is an order that all dogs seen in the trenches are at once to be killed, as they may be bearers of messages or poison from the Boche lines and are extremely dangerous. We have killed several before but never experienced anything like this. We were informed of this dog being seen while we were having breakfast in the dug-out, and the sergeant major passing at the time went off to shoot it with his revolver.

We heard a shot and afterwards found it had hit the dog's head but missed his brain. He fired another shot, which also hit the dog's head, and the next thing came for our dugout. It had gone absolutely mad, and was foaming at the mouth, and blood was pouring from its eyes. It was a large, black dog, and naturally gave me a shock. I got out my revolver like lightning but found I could not shoot as the sergeant major was coming up behind, and I might have hit him. He also could not fire for fear of hitting me. Luckily, he got hold of the dog by the tail just as I was going to give it a hard kick under the jaw, and he carried it away, much to my relief. The sergeant major flung it to the ground and gave it a kick which turned it over. It then got up again, and he put another bullet through its head, and as it appeared quite dead, it was flung over the parapet, and orders were given for it to be buried at night. An hour later, going down the trench 100 yards from this spot with the sergeant major, we heard a rifle shot, and afterwards learnt that the dog had been seen to move, and a shot had been fired which hit it all right. Almost immediately after we saw it on the parapet above us – it had come the 100 yards quite by accident up to us again. It was bleeding and foaming as before and sprang down over some barbed wire coils onto the trench bottom, where three rounds rapid fire from the revolver finished it.[83]

Lieutenant William Gomersall, 22nd Manchester Regiment

In amidst the squalid horror and carnage of the trenches, many of the men cherished any small interactions with the elements of nature that were not rats.

A small bird sang on a stunted tree in Mansell Copse. At the break of dawn, we used to listen to it and wonder that amongst so much misery and death a bird could sing. One morning a corporal visiting the fire posts heard the bird singing and muttering, "What the hell have you got to sing about?" fired and killed it. A couple of the lads told him to fuck off out of it. We missed the bird.[84]

Private Albert Conn, 8th Devonshire Regiment

*   *   *

Overall, the combination of the flooded trench, the corpses, the lice and a limited diet was not really conducive to sustained good health. One of the most obvious ailments that developed was trench foot. Immersion in freezing cold water and mud made feet become first tender and then agonizingly painful. If not treated, then men could lose their toes or even need to have their foot amputated. George

Ashurst was an early victim, but even amidst his agonies in hospital he found plenty to laugh about.

> They put me in a room with three others with frozen feet. Our feet were uncovered in bed, sticking up at the foot of the bed. They were just bathing them, powdering it and drying – no massage. The doctor used to come round in the morning and just feel at your toes and feet. "How are you this morning?" "Not so bad, Sir!" All the time he had a needle – we didn't know that for quite a while – and he was shoving it in your toes. You didn't move – you didn't feel it! The doctor knew when you jumped your feet were getting right. He knew life was there again. Then – "Ooooh!" – terrible, horrible pain, just a touch of anything and you'd scream out. You used to go to the toilet on your hands and knees with your toes cocked up. A fellow would be coming back and when you got together, "Woof! Woof!" A bit of a dogfight – the nurses used to laugh at us.[85]
>
> Private George Ashurst, 2nd Lancashire Fusiliers

It was eventually discovered that whale oil rubbed into the feet every day had a preventative effect, although one cannot help but wonder at the mental processes of the person who first thought of it! Once the 'cure' had been discovered, the rate of trench foot in a unit was often regarded as an accurate indicator of the state of morale and discipline in a battalion. As such, officers became sticklers for enforcing the regulations.

> It became a crime for any man to go sick with trench-feet or frost-bite. Colonel Corfe, knowing full well the properties of whale oil and the preventative effect of the rubbing of the feet therewith, was most particular that instructions should be carried out to the letter. So much so, that for many months the first question he would fire at the men, as he made his daily round of the line, would be "Have you rubbed your feet to-day?" This expression became so familiar that it formed the theme of one of the many ditties. To the tune of 'Mademoiselle from Armentieres' the troops would pour their full hearts into:
>
> The Colonel on his rounds one day, Parlez-vous?
> The Colonel as he passed our way, Parlez-vous?
> The Colonel on his rounds one day,
> Said, "Have you rubbed your feet to-day?"
> Inky-pinky, parlez-vous?[86]
>
> 2nd Lieutenant Reginald Russell, 11th Queen's Own Royal West Kent Regiment (Lewisham Battalion)

The vicissitudes of trench life could manifest themselves in other relatively trivial complaints, that in the case of Donald Price had most amusing consequences, or at least amusing from any other perspective but his own.

> I developed a boil on my thigh. You've got to understand how we were dressed: I'd got my equipment on – fighting order, an overcoat, a goatskin, a leather jacket and my waders on. I'd got my boil down here. The doctor came along in the morning as usual and he says, "Anything doing?" I said, "Yes, Sir, I've got a boil." He said, "Let's have a look at it." Well now I've got to get my trousers down. Imagine it: an overcoat and all my equipment. Raining like hell. I struggled with all this; I opened my coat and got me pants down. He says, "Bend down!" I bent down and my arse touched the firestep. Well, the firestep was sodden and as I soon as I put a little bit of weight on it gave way and I went with it. With my bare arse and my boil in this muck. The doctor looks at me and he says, "Well, get up!" I got up: my trousers and me covered in crap – and my boil had burst![87]
> Corporal Donald Price, 20th Royal Fusiliers

Given the reliance at times on the rock-hard 'dog' biscuits, coupled with the dodgy state of dentistry in pre-war Britain, it should be no surprise that there was a multitude of incidences of severe toothache.

> I was having teeth trouble, so I thought, "I know what I'll do, I'll have a day out behind the lines!" I went along to sick parade next morning, "What's the trouble with you?" I said, "One of my teeth here, I've got toothache! I think it ought to come out!" "All right!" We walked 7-kilometres to the next village, behind the lines. We line up in the street outside, "Next, please! One at a time!" It's a schoolroom, when it's my turn to go in! There's a barber's chair there, there's a man holding something behind his back! Another man standing behind the chair! "Well, Sonny, what's your trouble?" "This tooth!" "That one there? All right!" "Arrrrgggggh!" That was it! Out in no time! "Next please!" We laugh at these things now! Same as you laugh at the films when you see somebody fall over and break their leg! We laugh! But they don't![88]
> Private Harry Wells, 'C' Battery, 175 Brigade, Royal Field Artillery

The men were usually terrified of dentists – and with very good reason. The British Army had not yet organized a proper dental service, and most medical personnel had no idea what they were doing.

I had a very bad attack of the toothache. I was going crackers! I said, "I'll have to do something!" I reported it to a Yankee medical officer attached to us. He said, "Do you want to go to Arras to the infirmary?" I said, "Yes!" I was terrified in case he'd say he'd pull it out! He drove me to Arras and the courtyard there was circular, with little holes right round – they were all like wards. We just got in and a bloody big guardsman came out of one of these places – screaming his head off! It put the fear of God in me! I said, "Turn round, let's go back!" When we got back, he said, "Do you want me to do it?" I said, "Yes!" He just put me against a tree and pulled it out! Bloody near killed me![89]

Gunner Leo McCormack, 'C' Battery, 175 Brigade, Royal Field Artillery

Another physical ailment sent to try their patience was 'Trench Fever'. The symptoms varied and were often difficult to distinguish from other complaints, but a sustained raised temperature was a common factor.

One day towards the end of the month, after a very wet trench tour of six days, I felt ill at lunch time. By the evening I had a high temperature. The doctor came and looked at me and said in a matter-of-fact voice. "You have got rheumatic fever!" Here was an inglorious end to my military career. Fifteen months training, two months of wallowing in mud, and I was to be sent home a wreck – probably with a crocked heart. But the doctor was wrong. I was sent in succession to a field ambulance, casualty clearing station and base hospital with, all the time, a temperature which zig-zagged from sub-normal to 103 degrees. I was successively accused of influenza, typhoid and muscular rheumatism. At No. 2 Red Cross Hospital in Rouen a young doctor heard my story, looked at my temperature chart and said: "You have got trench fever. We have just invented it!"[90]

2nd Lieutenant Eric Bird, 4th Gloucestershire Regiment

Bird was sent to a convalescent home in the French Riviera for a couple of weeks. The formal name for his complaint was 'Pyrexia of Unknown Origins', a superb medical diagnosis that explained not a lot: it meant he had a raised temperature for an unknown reason. It afflicted tens of thousands of men and was afterwards thought to be an infection spread by lice.

It may well have been at the root of Lieutenant Walter Coats' problems. When he fell ill, he made a great ironic play of one of his stock phrases in his letters home:

I am still flourishing though the doctor says that if I am not more flourishing tomorrow, he is going to send me to hospital. As I don't want to go, I am at present lying down trying to become more flourishing. I don't think there is very much the matter with me. I am off my feet and feeling like a washed-out dish cloth and periodically sick but these are all minor discomforts. The doctor says he thinks it is jaundice. It is nothing to worry about at any rate. I was so much better this morning the doctor gave me my choice as to whether I would go to hospital or stay and let him treat me. He said if I went to hospital, I would probably be sent home and end up in the 3rd Battalion, so I said I would stay here. There is really not much wrong with me and I should hate to go home without a decent reason.[91]

Lieutenant Walter Coats, 1/9th Highland Light Infantry

This perception that diseases were not an honourable way out of the trenches was shared by many.

To be stricken down in the battlefield is much nicer than to be stricken down in billets with some awful disease. To die a glorious death is the former and to die a glorious death when dying for one's country, but at the same time a horrid one to fall foul of is the latter. One may and well say:

Typhoid to right of us
Old flu to left of us
Cholera on top of us
Diphtheria in front of us
Dysentery quite close to us
Yellow fever sitting at the very tip top of us
With e'er a death around.

That's how the matter stands putting it in words and apart from enjoying the firing line I must say it is much more agreeable to me to be there, and meet death if need be in action than to fall foul of one of those horrors. I only wish the Germans would capture our infected and so infect some of the sausage worshippers.[92]

Lieutenant Lionel Sotheby, 2nd Black Watch

The medical officers had a difficult task. How exactly were they to swiftly determine whether a man was seriously wounded, really ill or merely malingering? One superb story illustrates the dilemma perfectly!

A 'Jock' came stumbling in carrying a casualty. The medical officer asked the casualty where he was wounded. "On the cheek, Sir!" was the reply. The M.O. signed to the 'Jock' to drop his burden, and that worthy, somewhat disgruntled to learn that the object of his heroic exertion was merely superficially wounded, let him slide off his back and land with a resounding thud on the tiled floor. This treatment elicited a loud groan from the sufferer. The M.O. continued his examination, "I see no wound on your cheek, my man," said he. A tearful voice replied, "I mean the cheek of my arse, Sir!"[93]

> Captain Charles Potter & Lieutenant Albert Fothergill, 2/6th Lancashire Fusiliers

The doctors were always on their guard, and as they gained in experience, they learnt the little 'ways' of the soldiers. Few of them were fooled for long. And of course they had their own not-so-subtle punitive measures.

> Nothing puts the wind-up Private T. Atkins, so much as mines. He positively hates them, whether ours or the enemy's. If he hears rumours of mining or strange sounds underneath his trench, he becomes fidgety and morose. He also takes umbrage if the Royal Engineers arrive and begin tunnelling anywhere in his neighbourhood. He knows mining means counter-mining, and in his opinion the place becomes unhealthy and he decides it is getting on his nerves and vaguely wonders if it is worthwhile showing the medical officer his hammer toe, which he has borne so manfully for years, in the hope that he may be ordered a slight respite behind the lines in some salubrious spot well removed from ammonal and TNT where his toe may have rest. The M.O. is all sympathy; he has a miraculous cure for hammer toes. He hands him a "Number Nine" and sees him swallow it.[94]

> Captain John Milne, 1/4th Leicestershire Regiment

A 'Number Nine' was a fairly powerful laxative. At least that would give the soldier something to think about and would certainly take his mind off his hammer toe.

Persistent malingerers would soon find themselves deeply unpopular amongst their comrades. One man skiving meant that others had to take up the slack in the routine workload and the often-dangerous daily tasks of trench life.

> We had some amusement over Skinner, the smallest man in the company. The line did not appeal very strongly to him, so he lost no opportunity in endeavouring to develop trouble. At Boescheppe he found that there was something the matter with his knee – the ligaments were on the bum was his plea. His weakness of heart was very apparent, so he obtained no sympathy from anyone. We collected several of the

biggest men we could find and had him hoisted on to a stretcher. They carried him very reverently to the medical officer's quarters, a retinue following him ready to relieve should his bulky form of 90-pounds prove too heavy for them. There was much laughter as the procession moved off. Ushered into the doctor's presence he refused to have anything to do with him, threatening him with the guard room for malingering. Skinner arrived back on foot. A few days later he was sent to the base and ultimately to "Blighty" to swell Canada's mighty army of misfits.[95]

Private Donald Fraser, 31st Canadian Battalion

Although not much spoken about, there were many cases of self-inflicted wounds designed to secure a minor injury that would get them out of the discomforts of the trenches and away from danger. However, not all of them had thought it through.

The brightest reported attempts are those of two smart lads. One took his boot off and shot himself in the foot after which with great difficulty he put his boot on again. The other thought that the tell-tale mark of the powder must be got over, so he balanced a tin of bully beef on his foot and fired through that. He was hardly prepared when the medical officer asked him how small pieces of meat and tin came to be in his wound.[96]

Rifleman John Moloney, 2nd New Zealand Rifle Brigade

Sometimes such attempts really backfired, to the ill-concealed amusement of their 'friends', at least in the versions told with glee by Robert Graves!

A bloke in the Munsters wanted a cushy, so he waves his hand above the parapet to catch Fritz's attention. Nothing doing. He waves his arms about for a couple of minutes. Nothing doing, not a shot. He puts his elbows on the firestep, hoists his body upside-down and waves his legs about till he gets blood to the head. Not a shot did old 'Fritz' fire. "Oh," says the Munster man, "I don't believe there's a damned squarehead there. Where's the German Army to?" He has a peek over the top – crack! He gets it in the head. *Fini!* Another story: "Bloke in the Camerons wanted a cushy, bad. Fed up and far from home, he was. He puts his hand over the top and gets his trigger finger taken off, and two more beside. That done the trick. He comes laughing through our lines by the old boutillery. "See, lads," he says, "I'm off to bonny Scotland. Is it na a beauty?" But on the way down the trench to the dressing-station, he forgets to stoop low where the old sniper's working. He gets it through the head, too. *Fini!* We laugh, fit to die![97]

2nd Lieutenant Robert Graves, 2nd Welsh Regiment

Chapter 5

Fighting in the Trenches

One bottle of morphine pills, one for semi-consciousness, which has
the effect, when being wounded, of making you not mind anything,
in fact laughing grotesquely at a German if he wants to finish you off
with a bayonet.[1]
    Lieutenant Lionel Sotheby, 2nd Black Watch

L ife in the trenches was one of routine, a stale tedium slashed by moments
of sudden nerve-shredding terror. This could be said of most wars, but
the contrast was particularly stark in the Great War. A tour of duty
would include three-day stints in the front, support and reserve lines before
going out to rest and sometimes right back into reserve. Contrary to popular
opinion, they were not always in the front line, but the British Army expended
a huge amount of staff effort in circulating round the companies, battalions,
brigades and divisions so that the men knew they would have a chance of
remission in the near future. But the days spent in the front line were still a
terrible trial, especially in winter or when the front was 'active', a word that
conceals a multiple of hellish realities. The soldier's day would start at around
dawn, with 'stand to'.

Activities of every description stopped entirely an hour before daylight.
There was no whistle blown, no signals given, but quietly every working
party finished what they were doing, every patrol was brought back
into the trench, all of the sentry groups were put on the alert. That was
called, 'stand to!' Over the whole of the front-line trenches there was a
silence. In that hour, you just stood there quietly, every man out, officers
and men all in the front-line, bayonets fixed, one in the breech and an
ample supply of ammunition for whatever might occur.[2]
    Sergeant Jack Dorgan, 1/7th Northumberland Fusiliers

Then, day or night, there would be the sentries, men assigned to monitor what
was going on across No Man's Land and to guard against being surprised by the
Germans. During the day they would listen out, taking the occasional peek from

behind the sandbags or using a simple periscope, which in itself was an inviting target for German snipers.

> We were issued with mirrors, about 5 by 3 inches, which we could clip onto our bayonets. They were less obvious than the usual type of box periscope. We could get some idea of what the shelling was doing to the Boche forward trenches, not that anyone could see much because there was some ground that was a little higher than our position. I saw very little. Almost as soon as I raised my mirror above the trench, glass spattered everywhere. Jerry had some talented snipers at Beaumont Hamel and this one shot out several of our new trench mirrors. An officer of another battalion was passing with his runner. "Let's see how good he is with a tin hat!" he said and hooked mine up with his walking stick. The sniper responded to this challenge immediately and my tin hat spun to the trench floor with a large dent in it. The officer took my bent tin hat and gave me his in exchange. I often wondered what tale of daring-do he told. And in what place of honour my hat ended its days?[3]
>
> Corporal Alf Damon, 16th Middlesex Regiment (Public Schools Battalion)

They were far freer to look over the top at night, although darkness did not provide protection from the speeding bullet of the fixed rifle or spraying machine gun. The NCOs were charged with ensuring that the sentries were following the rota and staying awake, although it seems some rather evaded this responsibility.

> You each do an hour in the night, say from nine o'clock onwards, until five or six next morning. The sergeant didn't want to keep awake and come along and fetch each one out on guard when the hour was up. I was the only one with a wristwatch so the first night I handed my watch over to the first one – and each was to pass the watch on after the hour. I was to be the last one. Well, when I came on, I could see it wasn't anywhere near the time, because it was still very dark! What they'd done is that they hadn't done their hour, they'd each one wound the watch on a bit to look like the hour! Did about quarter of an hour, wound the watch onto the full hour, woke the next person and said, "Here you are!" So, I came on very early and had 2 or 3 hours! It was funny – much laughter next day. I didn't lend the watch in future![4]
>
> Private Arthur Smith, 9th Royal Fusiliers

Once 'on duty', the men peered into the Stygian darkness. It was common for men to imagine they saw movement – was that a German patrol sneaking towards them, or just a tree stump?

One dark and quiet night I thought I could see movements in the depths of the crater. I heard rather suspicious rustling sounds – it might be a Boche creeping round the side of the crater to put my post out of action. Two pointed shapes, in the dark just like spikes on helmets, steadily advanced. I whipped a Mills bomb out of my pocket and was ready to pull the pin out. Then I discovered that the pointed spikes were the ears of a large rat in the immediate foreground![5]

Private Bernard Livermore, 2/20th London Regiment (Blackheath & Woolwich Battalion)

There were the usual 'tall stories' passed around of the interaction of officers and the sentries they were inspecting. One favourite was very much as follows:

Those trenches were very wet indeed. The rum that we had used to come up in earthenware flagons, just over a foot high. I was on sentry duty during the daytime, and the brigadier came round. I was standing just poised on the top of one of these rum jars to keep out of the water. When he came round, like a good soldier, I thought I ought to stand to attention and I jumped off the rum jar and was then up to my knees in muddy water. He said, "Oh, you needn't have done that!"[6]

Private Marmaduke Walkington, 1/16th London Regiment (Queen's Westminster Rifles)

The irascible Major Gerald Burgoyne was certainly dissatisfied with the performance of one of his sentries.

Another two casualties this morning. A fool on guard goes to sleep with his rifle at full cock. On being awakened to go on sentry he shoots himself through the foot, the bullet going on into another man's legs. What can one do with fools of this kind?[7]

Major Gerald Burgoyne, 2nd Royal Irish Rifles

Sentries had to be alert, as there were a variety of activities that could be carried out under cover of darkness in No Man's Land, and they had to be wary of shooting their own men. In front of them were rows of barbed wire, which had to be checked and refreshed as the weeks went by. Any wiring party would be vulnerable to the Germans opening fire if they detected their presence. This was particularly the case before the screw-in pickets reached the front. Up until then, stakes had to be hammered into the ground – not a naturally quiet procedure.

A wiring party in the Loos salient – twelve men just out from home. Jerry's Very lights were numerous, machine-guns were unpleasantly busy, and there were all the dangers and alarms incidental to a sticky part of the line. The wiring party, carrying stakes and wire, made its way warily, and every man breathed apprehensively. Suddenly one London lad tripped over a piece of old barbed wire and almost fell his length. "Lumme," he exclaimed, "that ain't 'arf dangerous!"[8]

    2nd Lieutenant Thomas Farmer, East Kent Regiment

As can be imagined, wiring was not a popular duty. One unscrupulous officer took advantage of this in dealing with an unexpected problem that had arisen amongst his men.

I was stopped by a rifleman who asked if he might speak for a minute. "Certainly! What can I do for you?" "If you please, Sir, I am a conscientious objector, and I feel that I cannot obey the orders given me!" "But, how did you manage to get here in the firing line? This is the first time I have heard of it!" "If you please, Sir, I have a mortal terror of killing anything, but when I read of the terrible things the Germans had been doing to the men and women of France and Belgium, I thought it was my duty to come and help them, but now that I have been in the trenches, I am more of a conscientious objector than ever, and my conscience will not let me shoot!" "Very well, hand over your rifle and bayonet; we will not ask you to shoot anyone. Instead of doing sentry we will give you another job, that of mending the wire in front of our trenches. As soon as it is dark you will 'go over the top' and mend the wire that has been broken." "Thank you, Sir!" said the man, who appeared to be greatly relieved. When darkness fell, he was given a pair of cutters and ordered to go into No Man's Land and mend any breaks he could discover in the wire. He had been gone but a few minutes when "Wheep!" went a bullet close by his head and "Phut! Phut! Phut!" Two or three more in the ground at his feet. He was back in the trench in no time calling out for the sergeant and on his coming shouted, "Give me my fucking rifle, I'll teach the fuckers to shoot at me!" His request was complied with and I suppose he lived happy ever after, at any rate I heard no more of him or his objections![9]

    Lieutenant Colonel Vernon Dickins, 9th London Regiment (Queen Victoria's Rifles)

But other perils lurked in the dark in No Man's Land, as Harold Hayward found on a wiring party. His plight would certainly amuse his comrades.

The first time we went over wiring, of course everything was, "Schhh, schhh, schhh! Going out over the top tonight, go quietly!" Not a word to one another. We were going to make a proper continuous line. I just happened to step to one side and I went up to my neck into a French latrine. I said, "Help, help!" They said, "Schhhh! Schhhh!" I thought, "I'm not going to die like this!" When my parents asked, "What caused his death?" [they'd be informed,] "That he fell into a latrine and was drowned!" They pushed their rifles down and I caught hold of two of them and they pulled me out – but no-one would come near me for the rest of the time in the line![10]

Private Harold Hayward, 12th Gloucestershire Regiment

* * *

The effect of small–arms fire was reduced with the men under cover in the trenches. But that did not mean that rifle and machine-gun fire did not swell up to an awesome amount on occasions, normally through some nervous sentry firing and thereby triggering a response which quickly escalated out of all recognition.

Perhaps an inquisitive Boche, somewhere a mile or two on the left, had thought he saw someone approaching his barbed wire; a few shots are exchanged – a shout or two, followed by more shots – panic – more shots – panic spreading – then suddenly the whole line of trenches on a front of a couple of miles succumbs to that well-known malady, 'wind up'. The firing becomes faster and faster; then suddenly swells into a roar. Everyone stands to the parapet and away on the left a tornado of crackling sound can be heard, getting louder and louder. In a few seconds it has swept on down the line, and now a deafening rattle of rifle fire is going on immediately in front. Bullets are flicking the tops of the sandbags on the parapet in hundreds, whilst white streaks are shooting up with a swish into the sky and burst into bright radiating blobs of light – the star shell at its best. Presently there comes a deep 'Boom!' from somewhere in the distance behind, and a large shell sails over our heads and explodes somewhere amongst the Boche; another and another, and then all becomes quiet again. The rifle fire diminishes and soon ceases. Total result of one of these firework displays: several thousand rounds of ammunition squibbed off, hundreds of star shells wasted, and no casualties.[11]

2nd Lieutenant Bruce Bairnsfather, 1st Warwickshire Regiment

All this sound and fury achieved very little. Relatively safe at the bottom of the trenches, the men often found it amusing, at least until the shelling started.

At 8pm the enemy opened up a fierce volume of rifle and machine gun fire and continued until 2am, much to our amusement. As one of the wits remarked, "The commander of the opposing troops must have large shares in an ammunition factory!"[12]

Company Sergeant Major Ernest Shepherd, 1st Dorset Regiment

Newcomers to the trenches were often given valuable advice under fire, as American volunteer Guy Empey discovered when serving with the London Regiment.

Occasionally a bullet would crack overhead, and a machine gun would kick up the mud on the bashed-in parapet. At each crack I would duck and shield my face with my arm. One of the older men noticed this and whispered, "Don't duck at the crack of a bullet, Yank; the danger has passed, you never hear the one that wings you. Always remember that if you are going to get it, you'll get it, so never worry!" This made a great impression on me at the time, and from then on, I adopted his motto, "If you're going to get it, you'll get it!" All my nervousness left me, and I was laughing and joking with the rest.[13]

Private Guy Empey, 1st London Regiment

This was a common fatalistic reaction to the constant danger. One thoughtful officer summed up as follows:

The only way to be here is to be philosophical. We have evolved a philosophy accordingly. What do you think of it? If you are a soldier, you are either (1) at home or (2) at the Front.
If (1), you needn't worry.
If (2), you are either (1) out of the danger zone or (2) in it.
If (1), you needn't worry.
If (2), you are either (1) not hit or (2) hit.
If (1), you needn't worry.
If (2), you are either (1) trivial or (2) dangerous.
If (1), you needn't worry.
If (2), you either (1) live or (2) die.
If you live, you needn't worry: and –
If you die, YOU CAN'T WORRY![14]

Captain John Staniforth, 7th Leinster Regiment

Even when it was relatively quiet, there would be a steady trickle of casualties to be evacuated. For most men, a 'Blighty' – a wound that meant they would be sent back for treatment to Britain – was much to be cherished.

On one occasion a stretcher case was noticed on the trolley with a huge, satisfied smile on his face and a large notice on his breast which bore the legend, "Blighty first stop!"[15]

Lieutenant Walter Belford, 11th Australian Battalion

Machine-gun fire was deadly for men caught in No Man's Land or exposed for too long above the parapet, but if the men stayed deep in their trenches, it did not feature as a great source of casualties. Indeed, some men chose instead to admire the relative artistry of the machine gunners.

One particular machine gunner had the knack of going, "Pom-diddley-om-pom! Pom-Pom!" He'd wait a few minutes, "Pom-diddley-om-pom! Pom-Pom!" Jerry would reply, "Pom-Diddley-Brrrrrttt!" It may seem silly and amusing now, but he could never follow that sequence.[16]

Private Ivor Watkins, 15th Welsh Regiment

Far more deadly, was the single aimed shot of the concealed sniper. The German trenches were usually on slightly higher ground and their sniping often proved lethal. There was no warning; just the sharp 'crack' of the rifle.

One of our lads, Charlie Reid, he was a great little fellow. He stood up one day outside a trench dugout, pulled out a German helmet and put it on his head. There was a pair of spectacles attached to it, so he put the spectacles across his face, stood up and said, "Ho, boys!" He folded his arms and stood up there and a German sniper sniped him right away – he was gone – through the head. You had to watch every movement we made, keep your eyes open to see there was nobody watching you.[17]

Private Sibbald Stewart, 238th Machine Gun Company

Vulnerable points in the line were marked down by snipers on both sides: perhaps where a bay had been blown in by a shell and not yet properly repaired, or any point where the Germans could get a good peek into the British lines. Men became aware of the danger spots and warnings notices were erected – not all serious.

Some jester had pinned up an ironical notice on the wall of the support line trench, just before it crossed the sunken road to Puisieux, "If you don't want to become a landowner in France, keep well down whilst crossing the sunken road!"[18]

Lieutenant Edward Liveing, 12th London Regiment (Rangers)

Even being forewarned and careful did not always prevent unpleasant consequences.

Sergeant Martin Delbridge met his death in a most unfortunate manner. He was cautioning some new hands about 'bobbing up and down' when observing over the parapet. He explained that quick movements were almost sure to attract the attention of the enemy. After showing the troops how not to observe he then said, "You ought to raise your head slowly, like this!" Suiting action to the word, he slowly raised his head above the parapet and was immediately shot through the brain.[19]

Lieutenant Walter Belford, 11th Australian Battalion

Many snipers did not shoot from the front line, but preferred to conceal themselves in a 'hide' in No Man's Land or just behind their front line. This was, after all, a specialist trade, with the practitioners not only excellent marksmen, but also experts at concealment. And they were patient; able to lie unmoving until their prey made a fatal mistake.

Charlie Shaw was a gypsy – and he was my mate – we used to work together as a pair. We used to be looking out and he was very good at observing. This morning we got up there early, we were both looking – he had a telescope and I had the big binoculars – we could see all what was going on. On the German side, two men came over the top carrying spades. We watched to see what they were going to do. As they came walking down the slope facing us, our side, they stopped halfway down, and they began to dig a hole. They dug and dug away till they'd dug a big hole. We wondered what the hole was for. They went away and came back again with what looked like great big tin blocks of which they fitted into this hole – it fitted right in tight! I said, "What do you think that is, Charlie?" He said, "I don't know about you, Jack, looks to me like a toilet!" I said, "A toilet, do you think they're going to build one out there facing us?" "Well, it looks like it! I'm going to keep my eye open!" Off they went, over the top, back again. Within about 20 minutes from over the top we could see another man come. He looked like an officer, by his uniform. He got down to where this hole was – and he began to pull his trousers down – he sat down on this hole! As he sat there he pulled out a paper and started to sit back and read! Charlie says, "Blimey, look at that! Are we going to allow that, Jack?" I says, "No, what are you going to do?" He said, "I'm going to have a pot at him!" He'd got the rifle you see – we'd got Hotchkiss telescopic sights on the rifle! He looked through the telescope, "Can you see him?" He said, "I've got a good view! Look through the telescope and see what you think?" I said yes, "Just on a mile!" "Right, I'll set the range!" He says, "Get ready! Are you watching? I'll open fire!" 'BANG!' Up jumped that officer, and he ran as fast as he could with his trousers hanging down! Old Charlie must have just missed him![20]

Private Jack Rogers, 7th Nottinghamshire and Derbyshire Regiment (Sherwood Foresters)

The ordinary soldier rarely fired his rifle – and if he did, he would often miss the kind of snapshot target that was most common in trench warfare outside of a full-scale attack. Robert Graves claimed to remember an outstanding example of enthusiastic incompetence:

A chap from the new draft. He had never fired his musketry course at Cardiff, and tonight he fired ball for the first time. It went to his head. He'd had a brother killed up at Ypres and sworn to avenge him. So, he blazed off all his own ammunition at nothing, and two bandoliers out of the ammunition-box besides. They call him the 'Human Maxim' now. His foresight's misty with heat. Corporal Parry should have stopped him, but he just leant up against the traverse and shrieked with laughter. I gave them both a good cursing.[21]

2nd Lieutenant Robert Graves, 2nd Welsh Regiment

Sniping was a brutal business and perceived by most front-line soldiers as cold-blooded killing; indeed, snipers were often not particularly popular men within their own trenches.

When going round the trenches, I asked a man whether he had had any shots at the Germans. He responded that there was an elderly gentleman with a bald head and a long beard who often showed himself over the parapet, "Well, why didn't you shoot him?" "Shoot him?" said the man; "Why, Lor' bless you, Sir, 'e's never done me no 'arm!" A case of 'live and let live,' which is certainly not to be encouraged. But cold-blooded murder is never popular with our men.[22]

Brigadier General Lord Edward Gleichen, Headquarters, 15 Brigade

If a man was under observation, then the sniper's decision to kill, or not to kill, could hang on a thread. Woe betide those who drew extra attention to themselves.

Many amusing things were seen, or said to be seen, through the observers' telescopes. The old white-haired Boche, digging near Monchy, who looked so benign that no one would shoot him, became quite a famous character, until one day his real nature was revealed,

for he shook his fist at one of our low-flying aeroplanes, and obviously uttered a string of curses, so one of the snipers shot him.[23]
   Lieutenant John Hills, 5th Leicestershire Regiment

The very best snipers created their own 'legend' and became hated figures in the opposing trenches as the number of casualties attributed to them increased. Sometime a sniper, or snipers, took such a toll that serious efforts were made to eradicate them once and for all.

   Some of their marksmen put up boards. When a sniper had shot one of our men, he would hoist his score for example, "Eighty-seven, not out!" or some other impressive figure. One of them claimed to have shot more than a hundred. We plastered his bit of line with every missile we could, and at night crept up and threw bombs where we thought he was lurking.[24]
   Lance Corporal William Andrews, 1/4th Black Watch

Good sniping locations in No Man's Land were of great value, and both sides scrambled to occupy them during the hours of darkness so that they could shoot from them all through the next day.

   There was an old shell-ruined house between the opposing trenches. This was of course a sniper's paradise; and every evening at dusk it became a race between the two parties which could occupy it first. At last, this became a nuisance, and we said to the Royal Engineers, "This is the limit; suppose you blow it up once for all!" The R.E.s however, said, "Suppose you dig a new front-line trench and bring the house within your lines; then you will have it to snipe from in perfect security." We thought that was a good idea, and next night we went out and laid down nice white sandbags to mark the proposed new line and guide the diggers, and sat down to wait for a dark night to complete operations. When it came, out went a couple of battalions with picks and shovels and went at it hell-for-leather, digging in the dark and following the line of sandbags, not without a fair number of casualties from rifle and machine gun fire and bombs which opened up on them. When dawn broke, they stood up in their new trench and surveyed the landscape – and found the house still in front! The Boche had got there first and shifted the line of sandbags![25]
   Lieutenant John Staniforth, 7th Leinster Regiment

*   *   *

Early in the war, the British had a complete absence of viable trench mortars and hand grenades. They were completely unprepared for trench warfare and found themselves seriously embarrassed by the German weaponry. In true British style, the most ludicrous makeshift measures were taken to stem the gap, including raiding museums to secure weapons from a bygone age.

> Things are actually beginning to get a bit hot. We have nothing to compete with the Boche in the way of trench mortars and have to use any old thing we can lay hands on. To make things more unpleasant, they hold most of the high ground in a 2 to 3 mile semi-circle in front and to our flanks. In fact, we are in a sort of saucer. The following came out in orders, "Trench howitzer introduced by VI Corps named 'Toby'. Used with great effect. Found in Paris and last used in 1700." 'Toby' seemed highly pleased at being put on the active list after 200 years on the reserve list![26]
>
> 2nd Lieutenant Julian Tyndale-Biscoe, 'C' Battery, Royal Horse Artillery

Later in the war, the highly functional 3in Stokes mortars and other heavier mortars were deployed to the front. They could slather shells across the Germans front line and were highly efficient weapons – a kind of pocket artillery for the infantryman. Naturally, the infantry abused the mortar crews, accusing them of drawing German counter-fire.

> The trench mortar crowd was not too popular, however, for though most of the boys were interested in the entertainment while it lasted and were delighted when one of the big bombs lobbed in the enemy trenches, yet they were not so pleased to see the trench mortar sections dismantle their weapons and make off for their lives as soon as they had fired a few shots and thus leave the poor infantry to collect all the return hate. It was not long before the Trench Mortar Battery was called 'The Cut-and-Run Brigade'.[27]
>
> Lieutenant Walter Belford, 11th Australian Battalion

It was also claimed that the trench mortar crews claimed far more hits than they ever achieved in reality.

> My trench mortar came into action. It sounds much more important to say "Came into action" than the more commonplace "Pooped off!" Up, up, it went through the trees, and down with a thud into the German trench opposite. It was a tremendously lucky shot. With a contemptible

little 'Pop!' it exploded. My observer came rushing down from his post, his face flushed with excitement, and shouted out that we had bagged a German officer, who had been exposing himself to look at the commotion which had suddenly arisen on his flank. Of course, I didn't believe him, as trench mortar enthusiasts are even more egregious liars than snipers.[28]

Lieutenant Norman Down, 4th Gordon Highlanders

The trouble was the Germans had the dreaded *Minenwerfer*, a fearsome weapon that could project large shells into the general area of the British trenches. When the trenches were close together, this was a terrible disadvantage. All the soldiers could do was try to dodge the incoming deadly missiles. It was not an accurate weapon, but this was partly what could trigger panic. It was excruciatingly difficult, especially at night, to judge exactly where the shells were going to land – and hence evade the blast.

As the action of most of these missiles was generally very local, it was often a source of great amusement to onlookers to see their mates making a quick dash out of the way of some particularly obnoxious ironmongery. On one occasion, Lieutenant Wally Hallahan was particularly amused at the antics of the company batmen, who were scared into unusually fast action by a bomb landing near their 'possie'. These lads made a dash for a nearby bay of a trench and almost collided with another bomb. This sent them hell-for-leather back to their original position, just in time to run into a third burst. How they escaped being casualties was a mystery, but Wally always reckoned that if 'Fritz' had not considerately stopped his little bit of hate in time that the batmen must have dropped from pure dizziness, as they had kept running round and round on practically the same spot. Wally nearly hurt himself with laughing, yet he was one of the most tender-hearted of men and would have been the first to have run to the boys' aid if any of them had been hit.[29]

Lieutenant Walter Belford, 11th Australian Battalion

Some chose to see it as a game, and of course the British accused the Germans of cheating.

When he starts to serenade us with the local *Minenwerfer*, there is a 'Poof!' and there up in the air, for all the world like a big beer bottle, is the latest little bit of hate. Up, up, up, it goes and then starts to come down. As it falls you can make out roughly where it should land, and you at once proceed "at the double" to the end of the 'Playground' furthest away. It is a fine game, with just the right element of luck – sometimes the wind blows the bomb to your end! And one which encourages initiative and rapid power of decision – two qualities much sought after in military circles! As usual the Hun has not played fair, and this morning he started two 'Minnies' going from different places and directed at opposite ends of the 'Playground'. That's the Hun all over, never able to see that a game's a game![30]

Lieutenant Norman Down, 4th Gordon Highlanders

The *Minenwerfers* were a constant menace, battering away at the front-line trenches. They may not have been accurate, but they packed a punch when they landed 'home'.

We found the trenches very much as we had left them except battered into an almost unrecognizable condition by the enemy's latest trench weapon, the heavy *Minenwerfer*. Unlike the 'Rum Jar' or 'Cannister' [*sic*], which was a home-made article consisting of any old tin filled with explosive, this new bomb was shaped like a shell, fitted with a copper driving band and fired from a rifled mortar. It weighed over 200lbs, was either 2 feet 2 inches or 3 feet 6 inches long and 9 inches in diameter, and produced on exploding a crater as big as a small mine. It could fortunately be seen in the air, and the position of the mortar was roughly known, so we posted a sentry whose duty was to listen for the report of discharge, sight the bomb, and cry at the top of his voice, "Sausage left!" or "Sausage right!"[31]

Lieutenant John Hills, 5th Leicestershire Regiment

There were sausages all around them at times!

As we were only about 30 yards from the enemy lines, bombing went on all day. The German bombs, shaped like a long sausage, could be seen coming through the air. Our sentries would shout, "Sausage right!" or "Sausage left!" as they came over. One night we were strengthened by reinforcements, including several Cockneys. The next morning, one of our sentries saw a bomb coming over and shouted, "Sausage right!" There followed an explosion which smothered two of our new comrades in mud and shreds of sandbag. One of the two got up, with sackcloth twisted all round his neck and pack. "'Ere, Bill, wot was that?" he asked one of our men. "Why, one of those sausages!" Bill replied. "Lumme," said the new man, as he freed himself from the sacking, "I don't mind the sausages, but," he added, as he wiped the mud from his eyes and face, "I don't like the mash!"[32]

Private H. Millard, East Surrey Regiment

As for hand grenades, the British soon generated a supply of improvised 'bombs', but they were by no means 'soldier-proof'; many were far more of a danger to their own side than to the Germans. In addition, there seemed to be no limit to the wild stupidity of even their officers, who were supposed to know better, but clearly didn't.

The Germans have been using large numbers of hand-grenades and trench mortars with disastrous results to our men. So we too have to practise these weapons in order to be able to hold our own. Perhaps they will improve someday, but the type of bomb now produced for our edification is made from an ordinary 'plum and apple jam' tin with an attached fuse which has to be lit by a match before throwing. This is obviously unsatisfactory in wet or windy weather, when it is difficult to get the match to light, but it is the only sort available at present, and the troops have to be taught to use it. Strange to relate, they have had no bombing instruction during their peace training, and no one, except a few engineers, knows anything whatever about the bomb and its habits. Sometimes these are harmless enough. One of the first produced was put by some irresponsible idiot on the heating stove in the officers' mess, and then forgotten. It was not spotted for some time, not, indeed, until it was nearly red hot, and the individual in question was ordered to remove it and drop it in a bucket of water. During this process, most of us made ourselves extremely scarce, feeling profoundly grateful that it had not exploded in the mess.[33]

Lieutenant James Hyndson, 1st Loyal North Lancashire Regiment

Even when a viable hand grenade in the form of the ubiquitous Mills bomb arrived at the front in 1915, there were still dangers to employing them in the close confines of a trench.

The hand grenade is great fun: the pictures of it in the official books explain it sufficiently. The great point is to avoid hitting the back of the trench with it as you throw it. If this happens you will be unable to relate your experience to your friends.[34]

2nd Lieutenant Adrian Hodgkin, 1/5th Cheshire Regiment

The trenches were usually too far apart to allow bombs to be thrown from trench to trench, but various primitive devices were developed which promised to project the bombs into the distance. They were basically nothing more than big catapults, but there seemed to be an awful lot that could go wrong.

> The corporal in charge of it came to me and told me that he couldn't quite understand the new release on it, and would I come and show them how it worked. It takes three to work, two of whom disappear round the nearest protecting wall of sandbags, before the third looses it off. When it was, in my opinion, ready to fire, I sent the men under cover and lit the fuse. Five seconds after the fuse is lit the bomb explodes. Then I released the firing lever. Nothing happened, except that the bomb stayed quite still with the fuse burning merrily away. I had another shot, but without success, and stood there wondering what I should do. When the fuse had less than a second to burn, I had a brain-wave, and decided to leave for the corner instead of waiting to be blown forcibly to an unknown destination. Just as I disappeared round the corner the bomb went off, blowing the catapult out over the top of the trench, and tearing a hole in the last disappearing pleat of my kilt. As I was rounding the corner at full speed the commanding officer was rounding it in more leisurely fashion from the opposite direction. I had the misfortune to knock him over![35]
>
> Lieutenant Norman Down, 4th Gordon Highlanders

Later in the war, rifle grenades appeared, another form of small-scale 'artillery' for the infantry to deploy at their immediate beck and call.

> In the apex of the salient Company Sergeant Major Barker, of 'D' Company, had found a rifle grenade machine – simply the barrel of a rifle mounted on a fixed stand, at a point within comfortable range of the enemy trench. Now, Barker had in the training days in England been bombing sergeant and was anxious to give a practical demonstration of the skill he had acquired in the handling of these treacherous and dangerous weapons. Moreover, the officer commanding 'D' Company was determined to show his company that 'live and let live' was not to be their motto, so his support in the venture was assured. Accordingly, that same night Barker, with a small host of supporters, was to be seen in the vicinity of the lethal weapon. All took such cover as they could while Barker loaded the machine with a 'Newton Pippin' and prepared to do his worst. "Look out!" "Bang!" With a thin whistling sound, the grenade wended its way towards the enemy. Tense silence. A second later an uninteresting report over the way. Hardly had that noise subsided than a sinister 'Pop!' was heard. "What was that? Keep low!" A rushing,

hissing noise approached, becoming rapidly louder. "Clang! Clang!" as 'pineapple' after 'pineapple' burst in and among the party, covering the prostrate soldiers with mud as they flattened themselves against the ground. A swift creeping, shuffling, and the party were hurrying away blindly trying to escape from 'those damned things'! For the remainder of the night the shoot was 'off'![36]

Captain Charles Wurtzburg, 2/6th King's Liverpool Regiment

As was so often the case with the Germans, retaliation was swift and out of all proportion to the original 'offence' to their *amour propre*.

* * *

To the men in the trenches, sometimes the only thing that really mattered was the artillery. It dominated their lives. Minute adjustments to a dial sight on a German gun several miles away could mean life or death. The uncertainty of it all caused tremendous stress and was the origin of the shell shock which we would now equate to post-traumatic stress disorder (PTSD). But it also promoted a kind of fatalism that somehow allowed most of them to survive the experience without going stark staring mad, which would have been a rational response to huge shells crashing down on their trenches.

The Cockneys had their own peculiar sense of humour. They were speaking the Cockney 'language' which we didn't altogether understand. Always very cheerful whatever the circumstances. Most amazing crowd of people. When the Germans sent over their 'Jack Johnsons', an enormous shell, it was so big and heavy you could see this great thing moving about in the sky. When it fell down to the ground it made the most enormous hole. Several of these Cockneys were sitting in the bottom of this trench and an officer came by and said, "What are you doing down there?" They said, "Well, if you know of a better hole, go to it!" This was one of the Bruce Bairnsfather sketches.[37]

Private Leonard Gordon Davies, 22nd Royal Fusiliers

Gradually many of the men got used to shellfire. They couldn't ever really enjoy it, but it became part of their daily life for the periods in the trenches.

They shell us day and night, because we have some field pieces just behind. They circle round with shrapnel, high explosive, etc., so far they have missed us. Oh! it's simply fine. I don't know if my head is going or what, but I laugh and sometimes roar at the shells when they fly quite close. It takes people differently; others curse and swear at the Germans.[38]

Lieutenant Lionel Sotheby, 2nd Black Watch

Shells could even provide an opportunity for a little disrespectful dark humour.

A fussy little major from another battalion blew up, all beans and bounce. "Where is company headquarters, my man?" he asked. A 5.9in [shell] landed in a thunderous flame-pierced blast of destruction. "It was just where that shell landed. I couldn't say where it is now!" He gave me a dirty look, opened his mouth to say something, but changed his mind. "If you go now, Sir, you will arrive just as the next shell lands!" He gave me another black look but took the hint and waited.[39]

Private George Mitchell, 48th Australian Battalion

If they survived, then they gained experience of the characteristics of the different types of German shells: the intimidating 'Jack Johnsons', the 'Whizz-Bangs' and, perhaps most feared of all, the ubiquitous batteries of 5.9in guns.

A shell fell with a roar a hundred yards or so beyond us. We took but little notice of it, for by now we were, in common with the rest of the battalion, beginning to get that shell-sense which told us whether the shell was 'ours' or whether it would fall at a safe distance. After the third one had fallen, however, we began to realise that the gunners over the way were aiming at that particular little spot in Belgium – and with 5.9s. With the arrival of several more within a few yards of us, we got down and made a still closer inspection of one particular little piece of trench, spending a very '*mauvais quart d'heure*' before the gunners decided that they had completed their work satisfactorily. For myself, I must own to a horrible feeling of funk, and yet I can distinctly remember a sense of pride in that we two modest members of the 'Poor Bloody Infantry' were important enough to be accorded the attention of a whole battery of 5.9s and that the expenditure of some fifty shells had accomplished nothing more than covering us with dirt, and half-choking us with fumes![40]

2nd Lieutenant Reginald Russell, 11th Queen's Own Royal West Kent Regiment (Lewisham Battalion)

The ability to recover from even the closest escape seems incredible to the eye unschooled by practical experience of men at war. The following quote is horrific, but the underlying message is nonetheless still clear:

Five of us were round a brazier in the front line, frying some bacon, when a shell exploded among us. Clarke was killed outright; Fisher so badly wounded that he died an hour or two later; Furniss was wounded too. Frank Evans and I were knocked out for several minutes but did not receive a scratch. It was a pretty grim introduction to trench life. Poor Fisher had the top of his head sliced off like an egg and I was bespattered with his brains. I wanted to be physically sick, so did Frank Evans, but we quickly realised that would never do, so we carried on. I cleaned myself up a little and managed to swallow some breakfast. It was one of our shells too, a Belgian battery firing short.[41]

Private Norman Ellison, 1/6th King's Liverpool Regiment

Despite the loss of friends and the horror of being spattered with brains, Ellison was able to face his breakfast. Men tried their best to remain positive-minded, but it was difficult when the evidence of their own mortality was everywhere.

Birchall says that he doesn't want to get killed a bit. He wants to die at the age of ninety-five and be buried by the vicar and the curate, and his funeral attended by all the old ladies of the parish! He strongly objects to large objects of an explosive nature being thrown at him, and then his remains being collected in a sandbag and buried by ribald soldiery and dug up again two days later by a 5.9![42]

Captain Lionel Crouch, 1st Buckinghamshire Battalion

Sadly, although Captain Edward Birchall managed to outlive the writer, Lionel Crouch, who was killed on 21 July 1916, Birchall died a few weeks later on 10 August 1916. He was just 32 years old.

Some men seemed to be unaffected by even the worst bombardment. It was accepted by most that such men were 'special'. They were certainly not normal. One young lieutenant remembered an encounter under trying circumstances with Lieutenant Hugh Colvin VC:

Colvin came into my concrete dugout and there were various odd shells round about while he was in there. A small shell hit the corner outside of the concrete which didn't do a great deal of damage. The place was lit by candles stuck in bottles and of course all the candles went out and there was a general air of fumes and so forth – that's all that really happened. But the place was pretty hot inside and the ceiling was covered with flies. When I lit the candles again, Hugh Colvin was sitting in a chair opposite and he just looked up at the ceiling and said, "You know, that didn't even shake the flies off the ceiling!" He was a

very calm character with no nerves, no imagination at all. A marvellous bloke, marvellous, very capable and a very brave type too.[43]
   2nd Lieutenant John Mallalieu, 9th Cheshire Regiment

In some ways, more remarkable is the simple insouciance of the unsung hero who was discovered – despite shells crashing down all around – sat on the fire step exuding an air of calm.

"You seem happy enough despite the bombardment?" "Oh, I'm happy enough, Sir!" replied the postman. (Though equal in rank with Lionel, he addressed everyone with an educated voice as 'Sir', whether officer or in the ranks.) "You can have a bombardment any time, Sir," he said, "but it is not every day that you get a cheese sandwich!"[44]
   Private Lionel Renton, 16th Middlesex Regiment (Public Schools Battalion)

Perhaps even stranger was the officer in the 13th Royal Fusiliers who had developed a most unusual – and dangerous – hobby!

It was not always pleasant to stroll with the second in command. He had become an amateur of shells and noted new varieties with all the enthusiasm of a naturalist. At recent excavations, ominous of further gifts, he would pause and prod hopefully with a stick, oblivious of the urgent tapping of his companion's foot. So, too, he would thrust his head over the parapet as a shattering detonation rent the air, and gaze mildly at whirring clods, barbed wire and garbage. "By Jove, that's a funny one!" He would remark, "I haven't seen one burst like that before!" And vainly attempt to persuade my own craven soul to share his hobby.[45]
   Captain Guy Chapman, 13th Royal Fusiliers

Amidst all the frequent calamitous losses, close escapes were also common, and it was these that the average soldier chose to concentrate on.

Only one gun seemed to be in use, but shells fell as regularly as the tick of a clock, and we soon realised that the deliberate, and methodical gun-fire was intended exclusively for our two dug-outs, and that we were caught like rats in a trap. First on one side, then on the other, those shells dropped around us and we wondered how long it would be before the German gunners succeeded in making a direct hit. At last, with a dull thud, a shell landed so near that we felt the dug-out crumple up, and in an instant all was darkness. There were four us of in that little shelter of earth; Jimmy Lawson, Jack Baird, Bob Muir, and myself. Lawson alone showed any fright, while after the first shock I laughed, and the three of them today would tell you that I began to whistle the regimental march. I asked, "Anybody hurt?" and found there were no casualties, so I said, "Cheer up, we have our trenching tools, we'll soon be out of here!" Directly we had been 'wrecked', the German gun had ceased fire, the observer evidently being satisfied that we could not have escaped being killed. As we were not deeply buried, it did not take us long to cut a way out through the soft soil. All this time we had wondered why none of the fellows, from the larger dug-out, a little distance away, had not come to our assistance, and we were greatly surprised to find that they had also been buried, but, like us, they had escaped injuries, except for one who had struck his head against an iron girder. What lucky lads we were! Fourteen buried and all alive and kicking at the end of the 'funeral'.[46]

    Lance Corporal John Jackson, 6th Cameron Highlanders

When they had a bit of time on their hands, they could really go to town, celebrating a single unexploded shell as if it represented a kind of triumph against fate itself.

In one case a German shell, which had lodged in the parados and failed to explode, was made the object of an elaborate wooden cross, with the inscription, "In memory of one of Kaiser's pills. RIP." And underneath:-

Here lies the body of a German shell,
It hoped to send us all to Hell.
But it didn't explode and did no harm,
So, we covered it up to keep it warm.[47]

    Captain Randolph Chell, 10th Essex Regiment

However, unexploded shells exerted a strange – and occasionally fatal – fascination on some men. Indeed, some idiot visitors to the Western Front still take their lives in their own hands by taking liberties with live ordnance they find on the battlefields.

The surrounding fields and remains of orchards were inundated with shell holes, smashed trees and outbuildings. There were many unexploded shells lying about, some of large calibre. I saw one stupid man trying to remove the brass nose-cap from one with a chisel. We gave him and the shell a wide berth. Perhaps he was fed-up with life![48]

    Private John Tucker, 2/13th London Regiment (Kensington Battalion)

The average 'Tommy' took an unalloyed pleasure when the British artillery scored a direct hit on any German target.

> One unfortunate Boche having run the gauntlet of our rifle fire was getting away, apparently only slightly wounded, when one of our shells burst on him as though aimed, and he went up – blown to pieces. Well, we cheered and laughed at the happening as though it was the funniest thing in the world.[49]
>
> Corporal Moorhead, 5th Australian Battalion

One of the more amusing reactions to German shellfire was shown by the Mother Superior of the Locre Convent, which was not far behind the front line, but still occupied by the nuns.

> The Boche threw over some shells which fell just outside the convent walls. During the performance, which lasted some time, the Mother Superior stood at an upstairs window calmly looking on. A captain of the Rifles expressed his surprise that she did not take cover, to one of the nuns. "Ah well," replied the latter, "she has not many excitements in her life!"[50]
>
> 2nd Lieutenant Frank Laird, 8th Royal Dublin Fusiliers

One consequence of the shellfire was the introduction of the tin helmet, or 'Brodie'. When they first arrived, they were often disliked or considered to be useless.

> Last of all came the new steel helmet, the battle bowler, handed out sparingly to be kept as trench stores. These early fruits were doled out first to the snipers; and, as fate would have it, Gerrard, a charming intelligent boy in No. 3, was at once killed. A fragment of shell tore through the steel and pinned his brain. Thereafter the helmet was condemned with one voice. No man would wear one, except under the direct orders and observation of an officer, and the trench store was gradually put to other uses: they were found to make admirable washing basins, were not to be despised as cookpots, and could be put to all kinds of uses not contemplated by their designer, often of a nature not to be recorded.[51]
>
> Captain Guy Chapman, 13th Royal Fusiliers

Gradually, the men learnt that although they did not give full protection, the helmets did save lives. But disparaging remarks were common over their appearance, which many felt gave the soldier a slightly Chinese aspect.

The British helmet now appeared, and was generally voted, as it first seemed, a hideous flat object, though some humourists admitted that it might have distinct possibilities as a washing basin. A few soldiers of the vainer sort thought they looked more 'becoming' with a 'tin-hat' over one eye, but the vast majority hated them, and it was with the greatest difficulty that those to whom they were issued, could be persuaded not to throw them away. This aversion, however, soon passed.[52]

Lieutenant John Hills, 5th Leicestershire Regiment

Others recalled their childhood nursery rhymes.

We have all been served out with the new shrapnel helmet, and now we look like so many Tweedledees. It was Tweedledee, wasn't it, who fought a battle with a dish cover as helmet? Anyhow the tin hats are about the limit in ugliness, just like an inverted dish cover or tin basin, and when it comes to wearing them they are about as uncomfortable as they can be. They are all made in one size, presumably what the maker thought was the average size of Tommy's head, but he can't have had much admiration for their brains, or he would have made them a trifle larger. Mine would only just balance in a sort of 'Charlie Chaplin' way on my head, until I took about half the lining out, and now I can wear it perched well on one side of my head in a manner which makes jealous generals stop and reprove me for trying to look too 'doggy', but, as I tell them, it can't be done any other way. Everybody looks so entirely different in them that sometimes you want to sit down and shriek with laughter, instead of which you have to stand bolt upright and salute, your inside rocking and all but splitting with pent-up merriment![53]

Lieutenant Norman Down, Headquarters, 8 Brigade

*   *   *

Not all shells were shrapnel or high explosives. Gas shells had been developed as a more efficient and accurate method of 'distribution' than the cloud gas attacks employed by both sides in 1915. The chlorine and phosgene gases were dreadful weapons of war and there are few if any 'amusing' stories of men being gassed. But that certainly did not stop men laughing at the threat of gas – and indeed the precautions it necessitated.

One afternoon at tea-time we were sitting round the C.O.'s dugout, and he said to me: "Have you heard about the new gas?" "No!" I replied. "What is it?" "It gets into your pay-book and kills your next-of-kin!" The name and address of his next-of-kin was in every soldier's pay-book.[54]

Sergeant Edgar Rule, 14th Australian Battalion

The early gas helmets were of the hooded P.H. type, which would continue to be the standard gas mask until the advent of the small box respirator in the summer of 1916. It was an ugly, barely functional piece of kit which had one basic design flaw that prevented there being any chance of the British soldier taking it seriously.

> The gas mask was a grey flannelled hood, saturated in an evil smelling chemical and uncomfortably sticky. It was drawn over the head and the base was tucked under the collar of the jacket or shirt, as the case may be. The hood had two large eye-pieces of metal rimmed glass. A rubber mouthpiece within the hood was gripped tightly between the teeth, through which the heavily impregnated disinfectant air, inhaled through the nose, was expelled through a rubber 'flipper' outside the mask, which opened and closed as one breathed. After a while, the excess saliva in the tube coagulated – for want of a better word – causing the 'flipper' to sound like a raspberry blower each time one exhaled. It is not difficult to imagine the cacophonous effect of thirty odd 'flippers' performing at the same time![55]
>
> Signaller Dudley Menaud-Lissenburg, 97th Battery, 147 Brigade, Royal Field Artillery

There was even a shocking 'amusing' slur on the supposed lack of intelligence of the Irish soldier. As is often the case, this story is probably apocryphal in the specific nationality attributed, but perfectly feasible if applied on less discriminatory grounds – men did at times do stupid things.

> We were once serving next to the men of an Irish regiment, some of whom had characteristically bored a hole in their gas masks so that, should it be necessary for them to wear their masks for any prolonged period, they might while away the time by having a smoke. Unfortunately, before their device was discovered, a gas attack did necessitate the use of masks, and it is feared that no one will ever be able to find out what they thought of their experiment.[56]
>
> Captain Joseph Goss, 7/8th King's Own Scottish Borderers

As gas shells became more and more of a threat, so the precautions were ramped up, with gas sentries appointed to warn of any danger.

A certain brigadier, a sleuth for discovering any irregularities whatsoever, was touring the front line near Givenchy Church. He came upon a man, who, whilst obviously a sentry, was at the same time in skeleton order and without a rifle. Scenting a flagrant case of indiscipline, the brigadier sternly demanded: "What are you, my man?" He received the reply in broad Lancashire, "O'm th' gas sentry, sir!" This explained the situation as gas sentries mounted "In light order without rifles". To the further question, "What are your duties?" the sentry still standing smartly at attention replied with a deliberate jerk of his thumb over his right shoulder. This action drew the attention of the brigadier to an empty shell case and a short iron bar hanging from the side of the trench. Underneath hung a board on which in rough lettering was the following inscription: "When the German gas you smell! Bang this shell like bloody hell!"[57]

Captain Charles Potter, 2/6th Lancashire Fusiliers

Gas also promoted an outbreak of levity at the highest level due to an unfortunate choice in the adoption of various codewords for gas supplies. One gas specialist officer was not paying sufficient attention when called upon to contribute.

The general in the chair was taking routine business and asking for code words for various things connected with gas defence. I was nearly asleep when he suddenly addressed me and asked me for a code word for divisional gas stores. He must have heard me snoring! I must have wakened very quickly for I said at once, "Drawers!" No one remembered that the code words for divisions were girls' names. More than a year afterwards, a signal arrived for me, Chemical Advisor (Second Army), from Chemical Advisor (Fourth Army). "Understand Nancy is coming to you – do you wish her to travel with or without drawers?" This went all round the headquarters and straight up to General Plumer, who hooted with laughter. He at once sent off a signal to General Rawlinson commanding Fourth Army, "The following signal has been sent to my chemical advisor from yours, do you allow such indecent code words to be used?" Rawlinson sent a signal back saying, "The code word was perhaps a trifle unfortunate, but Nancy feels the cold!"[58]

Lieutenant Leslie Barley, Headquarters, Second Army

* * *

Patrols and raids were a dangerous necessity. The Germans could not be allowed to 'settle', they must be harried at every turn to establish domination over no man's land, while raids would occasionally be launched with the aim of grabbing a prisoner and gaining intelligence to establish exactly which unit was in the line opposite them. From this, British intelligence officers could track German movements and judge whether they were planning anything 'untoward' in that area in the near future. Getting a grip on No Man's Land was considered very important, and there was much discussion within battalion order groups as to the best methods of inconveniencing opposing German patrols who were also intent on gaining the same degree of control. Some of these plans were in the realms of fantasy.

> Rather a joke at headquarters this evening. All officers commanding companies were there, and we had been having a most serious discussion about various ruses for strafing Boche. In the end the C.O. evolved one. No less than to dig a deep pit, cover it with turf and brushwood and then entice a Boche patrol on to it! How it was to be dug without the enemy seeing it and how the chalk was to be removed he did not say. I could not help it. I said, "Sir, if only you would put a man-trap in the bottom and bait it with a sausage, I feel sure all would be well!" There was a deathly stillness for a moment, but then came a wild burst of laughter, the C.O.'s being the loudest of all. On the whole, it was really fortunate for me that his sense of humour is well-developed.[59]
> Captain Charles May, 22nd Manchester Regiment

Patrols would creep out at night, with silence a very important consideration for obvious reasons. Any noise would usually lead to a series of German star shells and lashings of machine-gun fire. Sadly, many officers did not have confidence in their charges when it came to maintaining the degree of silence required.

> 'The dear, old English Tommy only has, and I expect, will ever only have, one idea of warfare. That is, to walk up to a 'Johnny' and stick a bayonet into him. In the aggregate, that is his sole aim and object. He cannot dissemble, has no cunning and only a canteen interest in strategy and only then as an excuse to blither with a friend over a can of beer. He cares nothing for the idea of stealth. He is not really built for quietly stealing on an unsuspecting foe. As proof you need only put one tin can in a 60-acre field and turn two Tommies loose in that field to do a silent night march. I will guarantee that in 3 minutes one has stumbled over the can and that in a further 3 both have kicked it. There must, I think, be some magnetism between ammunition, boots and odd cans which unknown people have discarded in out of the way places.[60]
> Captain Charles May, 22nd Manchester Regiment

But to be fair, it was not only the men that were noisy. Here is an account of two officers marauding around No Man's Land like drunken sailors on shore leave. Mind you, they were from the Royal Naval Division, and at least one of them was indeed at least slightly tipsy!

> Just as I was dozing off, I heard Freyberg's voice calling me. I jumped up and climbed to see him outside the dug-out. He said that Kelly had reported my having been out alone, and he wanted me to take him out and show him where I had been. The whisky had begun to take effect and I was full of Dutch courage, so I climbed over the parapet and walked straight over No Man's Land, kicking empty bully tins and tearing my clothes on old wire and swearing each time, exhibiting as little care as though walking through a field at home. After we had been out some time, stopping dead when star shells went up, Freyberg whispered, "Where are we?" As if I knew! I was quite happy! There in front of us was the German parapet – we heard them talking! Cautioning me to be quiet, Freyberg indicated we should start to return to our lines. Just at that moment shrapnel burst overhead and we heard bullets whizzing all round us, but we threw ourselves flat and in doing so I cut my hand. Needless to say, we arrived back at a different place to where we left and one of the sentries challenged us. Not hearing our reply, he started to fire at us, thinking that we were an enemy patrol. Luckily for us he missed, and we gave a loud shout to cease fire. In we scrambled and dropped down into the trench. Freyberg immediately scolded the sentry for not being a better marksman![61]
>
> Sub-Lieutenant John Bentham, Hood Battalion, Royal Naval Division

Passwords were used by the various patrols and working parties out in No Man's Land, although this too could lead to confusion.

> I had to take a message to the officer commanding 'C' Company in the valley. The night was quiet, there was no moon. Everything was peaceful. Too peaceful really! I was in No Man's Land and suddenly I was checked by a hoarse whisper, "Halt, who's there?" I also replied in a whisper, "Signaller QUJ!" 'QU' meant Queens and 'J' meant Tenth – Signaller 10th Queens. I'd come across one of our patrols out in front. "Give the password!" I said, "I don't know the bloody password!" "The day of the week!" said a voice![62]
>
> Private Fred Dixon, 10th Queen's Royal West Surrey Regiment

The men knew what they required from an officer on a patrol, and if he played his part then they would in turn try to protect him and keep him out of trouble. After all, casualties amongst junior officers were excruciatingly high and if they got a 'good' officer they wanted to keep him.

> The main duty of second lieutenants was to lead rather than direct on patrol – to set an example to others. Many of us, scared stiff at times, could screw up our courage to take the lead only because we knew the men were watching us, knowing this was our job. When a new officer proved himself in this way, the men were extraordinarily loyal, and he might find they were looking after him. Once, waiting in the dark to go out into No Man's Land, I overheard my platoon sergeant say to two men known as 'Smash' and 'Geordie', experienced toughs, "Ye two, mind ye look after wor little platoon officer!" They replied, "Ye're reet theor, sergeant, we'll keep close by the little bugger all the time!"[63]
>
> 2nd Lieutenant Basil Peacock, 22nd Northumberland Fusiliers

Often the patrols would be given a particular task, to examine some irregular feature that daylight observation, previous night patrols or the new science of photographic interpretation of aerial photos had uncovered.

> The commanding officer wished to find out if one particular crater post of the enemy's was part of his front line or merely a sap joined to it by a communication-trench. In the latter case he thought it would be an easy matter some night to surprise and capture the garrison. He accordingly detailed the scout officer, Lieutenant L.B. Mill, to go out with his corporal and reconnoitre the position. The night chosen for the patrol was rather too clear for comfort and, thanks to a sharp frost, the ground had a thin hard crust on it and crackled loudly as the two crawled round the crater. When they got near the German line, they were startled to hear a voice say, "Very good indeed, but if you keep to your left a little you will find the going easier!" All the men in the post were standing up and watching the patrol's progress with the greatest interest. What could one do with enemies like that? Mill and his corporal did the only possible thing. They burst out laughing and walked back to their own trenches.[64]
>
> Lieutenant Archibald Gilchrist, 10th King's Liverpool Regiment (1st Liverpool Scottish)

Not all the Germans encountered whilst patrolling were so cooperative. Often they were disconcertingly rough!

On the 10th January, 2nd Lieutenant Creed, with a mixed party of scouts from all Companies, while reconnoitring suddenly found that a party of the enemy was in their right rear and close to our wire, where four of them could be seen. Our patrol turned at once and ran straight at the four as fast as they could, coming, as they ran, under a heavy fire from a Boche covering party lying some 50 yards out. Private A. Garner was killed outright, but the remainder, led by 2nd Lieutenant Creed and Private Frank Eastwood of 'C' Company, rushed on and wounded and captured one of the four, who was found to be the officer. The remainder of the enemy took the alarm in time and made off. The officer proved to be an English-speaking subaltern of the 55th Regiment – our old opponents of Hohenzollern in October, 1915. He was led down to the aid post to have his wound dressed, much to the disgust of Captain Terry, the medical officer, who would have liked to have killed him outright, though Sergeant Bent, the medical orderly, took compassion on his shivering prisoner and fed him on hot tea, and actually gave him a foot warmer![65]

Lieutenant John Hills, 5th Leicestershire Regiment

The reaction of the medical officer, his Hippocratic Oath forgotten for the moment, is strangely amusing.

Patrols were small-scale affairs, but raids could be quite considerable operations of war, involving whole battalions and heavy artillery and mortar support. As such they were planned out in detail, with orders running to several pages delineating the exact theoretical timetable and resources allocated to the attack. There was also often a 'pep' talk as to what was expected from them. Raids were all about speed and domination, employing the maximum of violence, intended to shatter German confidence. Consequently, there was little clemency once the required prisoner had been secured.

When we went on the bombing raids this general came round to give us a talk. He said, "If you see a German, and he pleads for you to spare his life, he'll say he's got a wife and four children – you make sure he don't get five!"[66]

Private Harry Hall, 13th York and Lancaster Regiment

Many men dreaded being chosen for a raid. They were, after all, bloody dangerous. However, some men sought to actively test and prove themselves.

One of the volunteers for the raid, Private Rattray, was found to be underage and on that account was told by the commanding officer that he could not be allowed to take part in it. He was bitterly disappointed and, boy like, burst into tears. During the raid, however, he miraculously turned up in the German trenches and had the satisfaction of bringing back a fine large prisoner who, when Rattray fell headlong into a shell hole in No Man's Land, politely helped him to his feet and handed him his rifle.[67]

Captain Archibald Gilchrist, 10th King's Liverpool Regiment (1st Liverpool Scottish)

Raids were sometimes successful, sometimes abject failures, but the reaction of one brigade intelligence officer to a particular 'damp squib' of a raid was simply priceless.

This peaceful period was also interrupted by a raid carried out by our 8th Battalion. An officer of the Intelligence Corps came down to us that night in the hope of interrogating a prisoner, but no prisoners were taken; in fact, no Germans were seen. Warned presumably by our preliminary bombardment, they had apparently vacated their trench. This was very unfair on their part, especially as our bombardment had cost £10,000, and we badly needed an identification, but as a distinguished Socialist politician once said to me, "What makes internationalism so hard is the absence of the British spirit abroad."[68]

Captain David Kelly, Headquarters, 110 Brigade

Of course, as might be expected, the Germans were more than willing to launch surprise night raids to sow discord and despair in the British trenches. But they too sometimes had failures, and it was such moments that the British treasured.

I had more excitement in an hour this morning than I've had all the rest of my life put together. Just before dawn the sentry at my end post gave a yell, "Stand to, they're coming over!" As a matter of fact it wasn't an attack in force, but only a small patrol with one officer which he had spotted. I grabbed my revolver and rushed up to find my Lewis gun going like blazes and shots coming flying in at us from the enemy at about 10 yards range. Their officer dashed round the corner of the trench at point blank range, and he dropped at our feet badly wounded. Some of my lot got started with bombs and I got in three shots myself, the joint result being that the Boche hit the trail for home, less one man, who at present is lying dead just beyond our post. We will get him in tonight and give him the order of the wooden cross. I had time now to turn my attention to the officer, who was dripping blood; when he saw me approach with my revolver, he got the wind up properly, and shrieked out, "*Kamerad! Kamerad!* Don't shoot, I'm German officer!" Which shows what he expected. I got the stretcher bearers to fix his wound up a bit and asked him a few questions. He was only twenty and had the Iron Cross; he was in the 3rd Regiment of Marine Infantry. He was moaning and groaning all the time, so I got him sent down the line to headquarters, first deducting as souvenirs his cap (just like the Crown Prince's), his Iron Cross ribbon, and his gas mask.[69]

Lieutenant Joseph Maclean, 1st Cameronians (Scottish Rifles)

Chapter 6

The Men All Loved Me!

The men treated a young officer in two ways, either generously and genuinely as their leader, or else, equally generously, as a sort of precious and slightly incomprehensible child to be taken care of![1]

2nd Lieutenant Harold Mellersh, 3rd East Lancashire Regiment

The relationship between the various ranks of the British Army has long been a matter of considerable interest, well worthy of tedious academic thesis by various strange people who seem to know a compelling mixture of everything and nothing. The most fascinating contrast exists between the perception the average officer has of his role and what his men think of him – and the very different state of reality from the other side of the 'pips'.

It is said the French general addresses his battalions as his children; a company commander thinks of them as such. And really men in a body under control have much of the helplessness of infants. Of a necessity they cannot do many things for themselves; they cannot provide their own food or clothing, make or arrange for shelter or baths, attempt to remedy troubles, and in a hundred and one ways are dependent on the care and solicitude of their officers. Their very happiness is often in their superior's keeping.[2]

Major Claude Weston, 2nd Wellington Battalion

One splendidly pugnacious officer was hard on his men but was still sure that they 'had his back'.

This morning I saw a fatigue party marching off, the men all over the place, no discipline, and the corporal in charge, useless. I called out to them, but one man took no notice, so I ran out and gave him two under the jaw. They pulled themselves together then and marched off something more like soldiers. On parade this afternoon I saw another man scrim-shanking. Had seen the company parading but was "Just getting a

drop of tea hotted". I lifted him a couple of the best and kicked him till
he ran, and then I spoke a few well-chosen words to the men. Told them
that if they did not play the game to me, I'd lead them a dog's life, and if
they 'played up well', I'd look after them well. I am sure my little show
of firmness had its effect. All men like an officer who compels obedience,
and it's no use punishing a man on active service as one does in peace
time; the only thing is to hit him at once and hard, and if the men see
their officer takes a real personal interest in them, as I think I do, or at
least try to do, well these Irishmen of mine will follow me, I am sure.
It's the sort of discipline they're used to in civil life, and which they
understand; any appeal to their better feelings they regard as weakness.
On the whole, I like all my men and I think they like me.[3]

Major Gerald Burgoyne, 2nd Royal Irish Rifles

Most officers grew fond of their men, although few had much pretence of
understanding them. Many treasured certain caricature-type individuals they
encountered.

A typical Tommy of the 'Arf a Mo Kaiser' type. I never found out his
name, but his friends called him 'Woodbine', and the company sergeant
major referred to him as 'That Nuisance'. He was a weedy-looking youth
and had been out since Mons. A lock of raven hair struggled out from
his cap-comforter, on the top of which his cap perched at an angle of
forty-five degrees to the vertical, peak over the left ear. His eyes were
small, but twinkled, and his mouth was simply great. In fact, when
he grinned it stretched from ear to ear. He was always singing – you
could tell it was singing by the words. Early one morning, just as the
German trenches were becoming visible, he was found sitting on the
parapet, chanting gloomily to the tune of 'Little Brown Jug':

Ha! Ha! Ha! He! He! He!

Old fat Fritz, you can't see me!

But apparently, he was wrong, for with a splutter of earth a bullet
plonked into a sandbag not a foot from him. Undismayed he changed
his dirge to:

Ha! Ha! Ha! He! He! He!

Poor old Huns, they can't hit me!

And continued until he was dragged down by his sergeant amidst a storm
of bullets. Such men are a curse back in billets, but a heaven-sent blessing
in the trenches.[4]

Lieutenant Norman Down, 4th Gordon Highlanders

Officers admired the phlegmatic approach of the men. As most 'Tommies' would say, repeatedly, endlessly, over and over again, they never complained.

> Sergeant Ingham of 'B' Company was typical of Lancashire. He was somewhat diminutive of stature, but full of vigour, stout of heart, and of unfailing cheerfulness and good humour. One miserable night when it was as black as pitch and raining in torrents, we two were groping along a disused trench up to our knees in water. We were seemingly the sole representatives of our side in an evil world with 'Fritz' lobbing over 'Minnies', apparently for the purpose of our destruction. All at once there was a terrific burst of firing in the distance from the British guns, which up to then had been silent. Ingham slipped off a broken duck board and appeared above the surface of the water clinging to the board as if to a piece of wreckage. His face, lit by the numerous rockets and flares sent up by the enemy, was a picture. As the writer helped him out, he said, "We're all right now, Sir! The bloody British Fleet is coming up to help us!"[5]
>
> Captain Charles Potter & Lieutenant Albert Fothergill, 2/6th Lancashire Fusiliers

Looking the other way, there was an underlying formal tinge to the association. There was a great emphasis on 'the proper channels' and the appropriate formalized methods of address.

> There was a great insistence on the proper way to address an officer. If you are standing in the ranks and you are addressed by the officer you must be careful to say, "Sir!" after every ejaculation. You never start a conversation with an officer; if he speaks to you, you answer him – once when the officer asked me a question I answered and I didn't say, "Sir!" This sergeant major shouted, "SAY, SIR!" So, I had to say, "SIR!" That satisfied him I suppose.[6]
>
> Private Reginald Johnson, 1/4th Norfolk Regiment

This is not to say that officers and men could not converse in a relatively normal manner when there was no-one else around.

> It was always a tricky old valley. Going round the posts one day with our only Hibernian, things were quiet, the day was fine, and we strolled along the tow-path of the canal engaged in cheerful and improving discourse worthy of 'The Compleat Angler'. Suddenly old 'Fritz' let go at the landscape, one shell landing in the muddy swamp which had

once been the opposite bank of the canal. I hastily embraced a large poplar tree on the side away from the enemy, while showers of mud descended everywhere; and then I discovered that I could see no sign of my companion. "Where are you?" I sang out. "Where you'd be yourself, Sir, if you had any sense at all!" came the reply from nowhere I could see. Much struck by the respectful and practical nature of this reply, I at last detected the top of his tin hat in a neighbouring shell hole, and promptly joined him there: Jerry giving us a quite unsolicited encore, and my colleague a spasmodic lecture to me on the advantages, under such circumstances, of shell holes over poplar trees. And he was quite right too, he knew his natural history well.[7]

Major David Rorie, 1/2nd Highland Field Ambulance, Royal Army Medical Corps

Sarcasm was a potent weapon in the hands of an experienced NCO. For them, the verbal 'tics' that marked formal deference were just a veneer, beneath which bubbled all sorts of disrespect.

Nights were dark; the ground was covered with shell-holes, some of them of great size. Once Major Griffiths, going out with Grogan, his runner, suddenly disappeared from view in an enormous hole which had apparently amalgamated itself with some well or sewer. The major was almost drowned, but came to the surface in time to hear Grogan say, "You haven't fallen in, have you, Sir?" He was fished out and scraped down![8]

Lieutenant John Hills, 5th Leicestershire Regiment

The more intelligent officers were aware of what lay beneath such formalized interactions. They knew that a subaltern was in essence an officer under training, allowed to think they were in charge, with the real authority provided by the platoon sergeant.

All they expected of me was to lead them, put them in the right places and tell them what to fire at; they did the rest. I used to call them my "pirate crew". My sergeant, Bolt, was an ex-professional boxer and a good leader of men. Once when digging-in all night against time, I came up unnoticed in the dark and heard a newly-joined recruit complaining about the officer (me) who was driving them to this heart-breaking labour. The recruit threw down his shovel and swore. "Get on with your digging, or I shall report you to the officer!" said Sergeant Bolt! "Fuck the fucking officer!" "Pick up that bloody shovel, or I'll knock your block

off!" The recruit picked it up. Me, he did not fear, but Bolt's fist was another matter![9]
     2nd Lieutenant Eric Bird, 144th Machine Gun Company

Napoleon is reputed to have regarded luck as the most prized asset amongst his generals. In this he was certainly followed by the average British soldier, who soon noticed if their officer was lucky or not. Some apparently took it too far!

> I was sitting in a hole in the ground in the front line, things were very quiet. And I suddenly found my servant sitting in a little hole in the ground just nearby. I said, "Hello, what are you doing here? Why don't you get under cover and get a bit of rest?" "Well, Sir," he said. "You never seem to get hit and the nearer I am to you, the more likely I am not to get hit either! So, if you don't mind, I'd like to stay out with you!" He was wounded while I was away on leave![10]
>   Captain Sydney Firth, 26th Royal Fusiliers

A good subaltern would form a rock-solid relationship with his platoon sergeant. At times an NCO may have been a figure of fun to the dilettante officer, but at least they generally knew what they were doing.

> Some sayings by Sergeant Dyke, "I love ferrets. I love a ferret better than a wife!" "I never sneaks anything except from where it can be spared. I am like Robin Hood and if he had been alive today, I should have mucked in with him!"[11]
>   2nd Lieutenant Frank Warren, 17th King's Royal Rifle Corps

It was best not to strain too hard for popularity with the men, but Captain Guy Chapman seems to have got it just about right, at least judging from the conversation he overheard as some men were discussing the relative merits of various officers. However, at least in retrospect, some of them probably would have been mortified by his patronizing attempt to mimic their accents in his popular post-war memoir.

> "'E's not a bad little chap!" said a voice. "Little, all right," replied my own batman, Johns, "why 'e don't come even as high as my Titch even." I mutely thanked him for the comparison. The voice of the mess cook took up the discourse. "That there young Knappett, y'know, 'e's too regimental, making us all come up for the rum every night. Now young Brenchley, 'e knows 'ow to treat us. The other night, when the Sarn't wants us all one by one, 'e says, 'All right, Sarn't, I can trust the servants!'

See. Trusts us 'e does, remember when we was on the Menin Road, old Nobby an' me was lying in a shell hole – 'e comes over the top. "Ow are yer gettin' on,' 'e says; 'would yer like a drop of rum?' Would we like a drop of rum! And 'e brings it over 'isself. Oh, 'e's my ideal of an orficer, 'e is."[12]

Captain Guy Chapman, 13th Royal Fusiliers

The upper and middle-class officers undoubtedly found the men's accents a subject of great amusement. For them it marked out and confirmed what they took to be their mental and educational superiority. They *were* different.

I heard two men arguing outside. Said the first, "So I throws it into the destructionerator!" "You don't know what you're talking about!" broke in the other. "What you mean is the inspectorator!" They kept at it until my servant came in with my boots, so I asked him what all the trouble was about. Nothing at all it seemed, except that they were both trying to say "Insinuator!" "Insinuator?" I asked in amazement. "What's that?" "Don't you know, Sir? The thing they burn the rubbish in!"[13]

Lieutenant Norman Down, Headquarters, 8 Brigade

Some officers were staggeringly inconsiderate, often without meaning any overt malice. Their own comfort often seemed the priority, with little consideration for the situation of men who might have to risk their lives to satisfy a casually expressed whim.

Now was the time for the colonel to light up that well-seasoned pipe of his, which never seemed to burn without frequent resort to the matchbox. Safely ensconced in front of the Dammstrasse in the battered pillbox which now served as battalion headquarters. The colonel produced matches and pouch – and felt for his pipe. A fervent ejaculation announced that it was missing. "Signaller!" he shouted. "Sir?" replied the signaller, from the scant cover where he and the runners were crouching low to allow the machine-gun bullets to pass on instead of through. "I've lost my pipe. I think I left it in the shell-hole where Captain Fraser had his company headquarters early this morning. You know the spot?" "No, Sir, but I'll try to find it!" What a hope! To discover one certain shell-hole in a wide area absolutely pitted with them! However, off went our little signaller, not giving a thought to the fact that for so small a thing as a pipe he was running considerable risk of making a widow of that young wife of his. It was a case of dodging from one shell-hole to another, for the Boche was still sniping from the left. Time after time he found it necessary to lie doggo as the bullets skimmed the edge of the shell-hole or went with a thud into the earth nearby. For 5 hours this sort of thing went on and still there was no trace of the particular spot where the erring pipe was supposed to be. At last, he plucked up enough courage to go back to the colonel and report failure. While he was delivering this carefully worded sentence, designed to soften the blow to the C.O. and to alleviate the wrath which might possibly fall upon himself, he was interrupted with, "Oh! It's all right, Signaller, you needn't have worried; I found that I was lying on it!"[14]

2nd Lieutenant Reginald Russell, 11th Queen's Own Royal West Kent Regiment (Lewisham Battalion)

And then again, some officers achieved a level of vicious stupidity that seemed to sum up a trade unionist or socialist perception of their class. At times it could earn them a dangerous degree of hatred from the men who served under them.

'Our Number 3 Company was under the command of Viscount Lascelles. Tall and slim, with sandy hair and moustache and a fresh complexion, he was extremely elegant even in battle attire. His breeches were of a subtle pastel shade, his Sam Browne and high boots were superbly polished, and he brought an atmosphere of Mayfair into the grimy trenches. His most pronounced characteristic was a distinct lisp which the lads inevitably mimicked. When we assembled on parade, he would command, "Call the woll! Pawade, thand at eathe!" Patrolling the front line one day, attended as usual by Sergeant Langley, he pointed to a sagging parapet and complained: "Thergeant, thith ith monthrouth! That ith more like a jellyfith then a thanbag!" On a tour of inspection one morning the Viscount wisely kept his head well below the level of the parapet. Dawn came up slightly earlier than usual and he noticed that a sentry, whose duty it was to keep watch over the top at night, had lowered his head. "Thergeant, that man thould be looking over the top," he exclaimed. The boy heard and obeyed, a shot rang out and he fell dead. "Thergeant, put another man on there!" ordered the Captain and passed on.[15]

Private Norman Cliff, 1st Grenadier Guards

At the very least this story proves that the lower ranks too could satirize the speech impediments and accents of their 'betters' whom they considered ludicrously affected. Major George Lascelles, later to marry Princess Mary and thus become the son-in-law of George V, as well as the 6th Earl of Harewood, was wounded three times in action during his couple of years at the front. As such, he was clearly a brave officer, particularly as some of his worst enemies lay behind him rather than in the German trenches!

The officers' mess was a changing environment as the war progressed. Less packed with the sons of senior officers, the wealthy middle-classes or aristocrats, they took on a rather more egalitarian nature as the educated lower middle-classes and battle-experienced veteran NCOs were, of necessity, given commissions to fill the thinning ranks of officers. Casualty rates were such that relatively senior ranks got younger and younger, with a truly exceptional officer – such as Roland Bradford – even managing to be promoted to first colonel and then brigadier at the age of 25. Pre-war conceptions of what a major looked like, i.e., essentially middle-aged and 'crusty', were no longer an accurate indicator of an officer's rank.

> The colonel went on leave and we had an amusing incident. The second in command was pretty young, probably about twenty-six or twenty-seven. He was a rather cheerful, chubby faced man, Major 'Tubby' Walton, fair, very healthy looking, who looked even younger. He was for the first time left in command of the battalion. It was very hot weather, and we were going about with shirtsleeves, usually with no badges of rank showing. We were going to be relieved by another battalion. What happened was that the colonel with a couple of people, might come up by day beforehand when the battalion was going to take over by night. This other battalion, their colonel was also on leave – and their second in command was also quite young – and also in shirtsleeves with no badges of rank showing. He came in, he didn't particularly introduce himself, and started talking to our second in command. Neither of them knew that the other was second in command of their battalions. When they got to talking, they mentioned their names, but they didn't mention any rank at all! Each of these majors thought he was talking to a 2nd lieutenant – and was a little on his 'dignity' you see! Both thought they should be addressed with rather more respect! This went on for a little time to my vast amusement – I knew who he was. Then the truth about their identities came out![16]
>
> 2nd Lieutenant John Mallalieu, 9th Cheshire Regiment

New officers faced a real baptism of fire within the officers' mess, starting with their introduction to the august – and intimidating – figure of the colonel. This could indeed be terrifying.

> Most of his officers will remember the first time they reported for duty. Those keen eyes, gleaming forth beneath those beetling brows, seemed to look right through into one's mind. One felt that the C.O. had

summed up one's character and abilities within a few seconds. "Well, I've three kinds of officers in my battalion. There's the one who does his best and it's a damn good best; there's the one who does his best, although it's not very good; the third kind is the fellow who's not much good to me or anybody else – and I don't have anybody here long in that class. Now don't forget that's the class *you* start in!"[17]

> 2nd Lieutenant Reginald Russell, 11th Queen's Own Royal West Kent Regiment (Lewisham Battalion)

A young officer's contemporary subalterns could be equally judgemental, although Lieutenant Norman Down deserves some kind of posthumous award for the vicious nature of his character assassination of some hapless young 2nd lieutenant with whom he was forced to share a dugout:

> We've had a new subaltern posted to the company, and to me has fallen the honour of instructing him in trench warfare. He was a pleasant addition to a dugout I can tell you. His mouth is large and admirably suited to the method of mastication favoured by him. His hair is of a nondescript shade, best describable as 'dirty sandbag', and his eyes are small and pig-like. When he walks his hands flop about like washing in the wind, except that washing is generally clean. His conversation centres round the abnormal percentage of casualties among officers, and every sentence is rounded off with an "Eh?" only to be equalled by the bleat of an epileptic lamb![18]
>
> Lieutenant Norman Down, 4th Gordon Highlanders

Snobbishness was never too far away, even later in the war. The august personage of Captain Charles Dudley-Ward was discussing a dangerous future operation with an officer who did not meet his criteria for social acceptability:

> 'Broncho' was very serious, not a smile on his face, but at the same time he was suffering as he does most days from most violent indigestion and so he made strange noises from both ends of himself and once stopped to piss in an open field – but he never ceased talking. And when you consider that he had probably never been more earnest you realise on what a slender foundation good behaviour as understood in a drawing room is built on.[19]
>
> Captain Charles Dudley-Ward, 1st Welsh Guards

Burping and farting were not, it seems, socially acceptable. At least Dudley-Ward was reasonably subtle in his condemnation, but Captain Charles May was possessed of wonderful powers of invective in describing a senior major who had aroused his ire:

> Until I met him I always cherished the idea that the name 'English officer' was synonymous with that of 'gentleman'. I am reluctantly compelled now to admit that it can mean 'bully and cad' also. It has been somewhat of a shock to me, as a disillusionment always is, and I wish with all my heart that he would go away from us and make room for some decent, mannered gentleman whom we would look up to and follow. Perhaps a few characteristics to begin with. He is of the genus fox, weasel, stoat, ferret, and rat. Whether these creatures are of one genus or not I don't care. But combine all their more unpleasant qualities and you have him. He is cunning, smooth-faced, double-tongued, uncertain in temper, ferocious, predatory and given to burrowing underground. He is a born intriguer rejoicing in pulling secret wires, striving to undermine other people's reputations, gloating over their mistakes, making the worst of their errors, always imagining evil, always eagerly searching after vicious motives, stooping to wilful invention to cover up any mistakes of his own, and piling up damnation for others if thereby he can save his own face. He gets in the ear of the powers that be, and by subtle suggestion and deference worms his way into their confidence – and having won his way maintains his position by deliberately artless flattery, constant court and persistent attentions. In fact, my dear, he is the rankest poison I have ever met.[20]
>
> Captain Charles May, 22nd Manchester Regiment

To cheer you up after such a dressing down, here is a favourite story of the interaction of officers presented in all its glory:

> It was a dry night, no rain. In the early morning, when we all gathered shivering round a small fire, trying to get a cup of tea, Jones, the second in command of the company, arrived and said, "My word, it was cold last night, it affected my bladder! It was too cold to stand up, so I just turned over and let fly where I was!" We thought nothing of this until the company commander came in and said, "It must have been wet last night, I was lying next to Jones, and I woke up and my trousers were completely soaked!" We all said, "But there's been no rain!" He didn't realise what had happened![21]
>
> Lieutenant Norman Dillon, 14th Northumberland Fusiliers

Amusing incidents in the officers' dugout were treasured, especially when no-one was hurt.

There was a bang outside, and suddenly we were in the midst of a great hissing, roaring inferno. Everything seemed to be going round, and from the door came an overpowering red light and wave after wave of acrid smoke. "Bombs!" cried my servant, who was in the act of laying the table. And here I regret to say that no one dashed to the rescue and flung himself upon the box of ignited hand grenades. No one was out for the VC! And, besides, it wasn't bombs at all, but our rockets. A red-hot piece of shell must have swished downstairs and landed up in our box of SOS rockets standing at the foot of the stairs. The show lasted for about 5 minutes, during which time the dug-out seemed to be full of flying, screeching red rockets and blazing green stars. We put our hands to our mouths to try and keep out the smoke – and resigned ourselves to fate. As it so happened nothing did hit us, for the box which held the rockets was on the lowest step of the stairs and out of sight of the far corner of the dug-out. But only by a few inches. People who were outside say that it was a grand sight, long tongues of red flame and clouds of smoke issuing from the dugout and visible for miles. They seemed to think it was rather a joke. And so may we. After the war.[22]

Lieutenant Norman Down, 4th Gordon Highlanders

These were young men, desperate to find amusement in their surroundings, and it should be no surprise that stupid practical jokes abounded.

During dusk stand-to I was fooling about behind the trench where I found a dump of German stick bombs, close to where a hole in the ground acted as a ventilator to our dugout. I was prompted to perpetrate a little joke, and later, when Johnny Teague entered the dugout to talk to Ewing, I unscrewed the canister of a bomb, removed the detonator, then pulled the fuse and dropped the stick just inside the ventilator shaft. With a fizz the fuse burnt for five seconds, growing louder and ending in a sharp dull spurt. Putting my ear to the hole I heard Ewing say, "Good God! That was a near one!" "Blinking good job it was a dud," replied Johnny, whereupon I chuckled hugely and prepared half a dozen more. I waited a few minutes until they had settled down, then I dropped them in rapid succession. There was a faint groan from Ewing and I heard Johnny say in a puzzled tone, "They can't all be duds." Then I pictured Ewing's horrified face as he yelled, "They're GAS! Can ye no smell them?" I heard the rustle of their gas masks and thought it was time to end the comedy, so I jumped into the trench just in time to meet them as they rushed out to warn the Company. "Hallo!" I said. "Have you joined the Ku Klux Klan? Or are you doing a little badly needed gas drill?"[23]

Lieutenant Edwin Vaughan, 1/8th Warwickshire Regiment

When the fuss had died down, Vaughan was grabbed by Johnny Teague, who was by this time more than suspicious – he knew Vaughan was to blame!

> Little Teague, however, was not satisfied and I saw his eyes wandering round the walls until they were arrested by the ventilation hole. Then they switched to my face in a searching scrutiny. "How did you work it, Vaughan?" "Stick bombs without detonators!" I gurgled and my pent-up mirth escaped in a shriek of laughter. We both leant against the trench side and howled at the memory of Ewing's stricken face.[24]
>
> Lieutenant Edwin Vaughan, 1/8th Warwickshire Regiment

A rather more subtle practical joke was brilliantly countered by the intended victim, who managed to completely turn the tables on the two jokers who claimed – falsely – to have uncovered some new German weapon.

> Lieutenant Hammond, one day, sent a note to the intelligence officer (I.O.) enclosing in a sandbag a bright tin canister containing a liquid. The note stated that a shell had burst near 'A' Company's headquarters, and the tin canister had been found nearby; it was supposed to have been part of the contents of the shell, and to contain some atrocity in the gas line. The note and canister were brought by Lovell, who gave a vivid description of the bursting of the shell and the finding of the canister. The I.O. looked very wise and said it was undoubtedly a new type of gas shell, and that he would have it sent to Division immediately. This did not suit Lovell, who saw trouble ahead. He suggested that the matter should wait until the brigade gas officer called. The I.O., however, said that the find was too important to leave over and that he must see the colonel about it at once. The C.O. stated in very definite terms that the battalion had something else to do than to play practical jokes – and decided that Lovell and Hammond should be severely strafed. A note was sent down to Hammond in the afternoon saying that division considered the matter very important – and a staff officer would call and interview him with a view to getting details. Hammond immediately consulted his company commander, who sent him up to the I.O. to make a full confession and see if by any chance there was a way out of the mess. The latter said he would do what he could. In due course the staff officer arrived and went to see Hammond, who, after a bit of prompting, made a full confession. The staff officer waxed very wrath and said that he must report Hammond to the divisional commander. It was some

hours before Hammond got to know that the staff officer was a company officer from a neighbouring unit borrowed for the occasion.[25]

Captain Charles Potter & Lieutenant Albert Fothergill, 2/6th Lancashire Fusiliers

The following quote demonstrates an almost 'modern' sensibility in the attempt to record an amusing moment for posterity:

One of the communication trenches is called Pear Tree Walk from a fruit tree that grows at the bottom end of it, on its higher branches are a few pears. Yesterday, just before we were relieved, I decided to climb up this tree and discover whether the fruit was ripe, as if it was it seemed a pity to waste it on the unappreciative palates of the incoming battalion. Accordingly, I scrambled up and was just reaching for the nearest pear when bullets started to whistle all round me. Then it struck me that though the bottom of the tree was out of sight the top was in full view, and I lost no time in trying to come down, but in my haste, I let my kilt catch in a branch and found myself suspended in mid-air, an 800 yards target to the Hun. I yelled for help, and the signal officer came round the corner. He looked at me for a moment and then dashed off for help, or so I imagined. The bullets were whistling all round me, and I was making frantic efforts to escape, but nothing I could do was of any use, and it was with a sigh of relief that I saw the signalling officer coming back at the double. Then I noticed to my dismay that he was alone, but just as he arrived under the tree the branch gave way – and down I came on top of him. When he had recovered sufficient breath to swear, "You fool," he gasped, "couldn't you have managed to stay up there another minute after I had run all the way to battalion headquarters and back for my camera?"[26]

Lieutenant Norman Down, 4th Gordon Highlanders

*   *   *

Overall, the men enjoyed a warm comradeship amongst themselves. But they too were very fond of stories of pratfalls, personal discomfort and practical jokes that inconvenienced, injured or embarrassed their comrades. One example is when a soldier tried to improve the variety and sophistication of their diet in his dugout. Sadly, his efforts went unappreciated.

A Camembert cheese he had bought, proclaiming that it was an 'epicure's dream', but his comrades did not agree, so it was decided to drop the delicacy into the stovepipe sticking through the roof of No. 4 Section's dugout. Our stoves were homemade affairs consisting of a large drum, with a pipe made of biscuit tins hammered round a pole let into the top and leading straight up through the surface of the ground. Anything dropped down the pipe dropped into the fire below. After dark we scouted the position and finding no one about the cheese was dropped down the pipe, with a turf put over the chimney-top so that the inmates below would get the full benefit of the aroma! The resulting stench and smoke compelled the No. 4 Section men to put their gas-helmets on![27]

Sapper Arthur Sambrook, Royal Engineers

One nameless unscrupulous 'hero' excelled himself in a practical joke that gave him a worthwhile financial gain.

We were all playing cards at the bottom of the trench and there was quite a little pile of filthy old notes and odds and ends of French coins and that – quite a pile of it, as a matter of fact. And this chap came round, he was watching us playing cards and that. We saw he'd got in his hand a Mills bomb and he was messing about with this bomb and letting the lever come up. Of course, once the lever sprung away, that detonated the bomb and you'd got about 5-seconds before it went off. All of a sudden, the lever flew off, we saw it go – and we all scattered. Some went over the top, some went round the other way, the bay, but this chap, he didn't. He scooped up the money and put it in his pocket and off he went. What he'd done, he'd already taken the detonator out of the bomb and of course we didn't know that! When he let the lever go, we thought the bomb was going off![28]

Private Walter Grover, 2nd Sussex Regiment

Chapter 7

Friends and Enemies

They were a Saxon Regiment opposite us, they seemed to be friendly people – seemed to be friendly! A sign of their friendliness was that they put up a sign, "*Got Mit Uns!*" God is with us! We put a sign in English! "We've Got Mittens Too!"[1]
    Rifleman Francis Sumpter, 1st Rifle Brigade

The ability of the British soldier to vilify those of any other nations whom he met was a very evident trait. The old enemy, France, was now a friend, but that did not stop a sustained campaign of denigration as to their military incompetence, scatological habits and generally insanitary character. 'Tommy' also enjoyed an abusive relationship with the soldiers of any – and all – British colonies. A cliched caricature figure was often allowed to stand for the personal characteristics of a whole nation under arms.

We were, being in a passive sector, the frequent host of our allies' representatives. These resplendent figures would clank into our white-panelled chamber, and we would match our mutually indifferent French. I recall an overwhelming bevy of four exuberant Russian colonels, all magnificent animals, jingling with orders. One was very fair with a wide fan of blond beard: he bowed and smiled, and I think kissed the staff officer, while another, a swarthy Tartar, wore a scarf across his forehead where a bottle had cut it open. There followed two harassed-looking Portuguese generals, led by a long-nosed and voluble gunner brigade major who whispered, "They've given me the Order of the Aviz, which, I'm told, means the bird!" The Portuguese were succeeded by a plump little partridge of a Romanian army commander. His gold-laced jacket could scarcely restrain his pouting chest, while his ADC wore a glorious sky-blue cloak down to his ankles. This lad carried, loosely tacked to his chest, the Military Cross ribbon. When questioned about it, he said it was given to him on his arrival in England, and deftly turning it up, showed the words 'for valour' scrawled in indelible pencil on the reverse.[2]

Captain Guy Chapman, 13th Royal Fusiliers

Simple generalities were applied beyond all reason. Of course, these various insults were returned with redoubled intensity. Thus, the British were widely accused of being unimaginative, lacking in drive and vigour, buttoned up and unable to think on their feet.

> The British Army has certain shibboleths, one of which, and it has cost the lives of scores of thousands of soldiers, is that when you are attacked in overwhelming force you mustn't run away. The French who are much more logical than we, and who consider results and not prestige, invariably run away under such circumstances, and when the right moment comes run back again and deliver a counter-attack.[3]
>
> Captain Charles Miller, 2nd Royal Inniskilling Fusiliers

Things got even more complicated when the French handed over to the Australians.

> We got orders to take over part of the line south of Villers-Bretonneux which was being held by the 2nd Tirailleurs and Brigadier Herring and I went to see the French brigade to make arrangements for the relief. The French general was an oldish man with only one arm; but spry in spite of his disability. With the aid of his interpreter, who spoke very colloquial English, we studied their dispositions on the map and then went up on foot to look at the forward area. The Germans spotted our party and got on to us with whiz-bangs. One salvo burst right overhead and we all flattened ourselves on the ground. When I recovered my breath, I said gallantly to the interpreter, "I hope your old general will not be hit!" to which he replied ungallantly, "Bugger him! I hope I don't get hit myself!"[4]
>
> Captain Thomas Louch, Headquarters, 13 Australian Brigade

The French were reputed to leave their trenches in a terrible mess, but a closer approximation to reality is that most troops have a tendency to leave trenches in a poor state.

> This morning we went to our new trenches to see what they were like. They really are awful, but, of course, we saw them at their worst in the rain and wet. We take them over early to-morrow morning. The Canadians

had them, and for dirtiness and beastliness commend me every time to the Canadians. They are filthy brutes.[5]

Lieutenant Edward Underhill, 8th Loyal North Lancashire Regiment

Troops of a non-European ethnic origin were widely supposed to be 'mad' or 'primitive', reflecting the prevalent prejudices of the day, with stories – usually without much foundation – spreading to reflect those beliefs.

There are some Algerian troops on our left and they are awfully amusing. They shoot at any blooming thing that moves. One day they got tired of sitting in their trenches, so they arranged an attack on their own without saying a word to their officers, so at dawn they sallied out and of course suffered enormous losses but, I believe, gave the Germans something to chew. One of them came back to our lines with a bayonet wound in his leg and one of our officers noted his haversack was bulging very much and also very 'jammy'; so he asked what he had got in there. The Algerian said "Souvenir! Souvenir!" and displayed in his haversack a German helmet and head! Although I didn't actually see this, I only saw the chap come in and I believe it's absolutely true.[6]

Private Edward Packe, 1st Somerset Light Infantry

Some legends are still given some credence to this very day, such as the idea that all Australians are drunken oafs.

I was astounded to come across the Australians – they were dead drunk – so drunk you wouldn't bloody well credit it! They'd found carboys of whisky and they were rolling! I must say they could just stagger – that was about all! They'd captured a very nice Boche field cooker, with some nice horses. I was offering to take one of them away, when one of these Aussies said, "No you don't!" And pulled out his gun – there was a moment – I thought better of it and so I backed off.[7]

Lieutenant Ynyr Probert, 'O' Battery (Rocket Troop), Royal Horse Artillery

It is certainly the case that many Australians did not seem to respect some of the British officers they encountered.

Debonair Tommy officers on back area duties, all pink and white, strolled round blithely with gloves and canes. They moved me to dark thoughts of murder. I would not salute them. Blast 'em anyway.[8]

Private George Mitchell, 48th Australian Battalion

Such attitudes were harboured in turn by British officers, but few took the robust approach adopted by Lieutenant Jim Davies.

> I called out, "Halt, who are you?" He said, "Fucking Australian! Who the fucking hell are you?" I realised he was drunk, and I said, "You realise you're talking to an officer?" And he told me to go and fuck myself! My troops were watching this, and I wondered how to handle it. You can't say, "Fall in two men, take his name and number!" So I hit him! I knocked him down. I can see him now sitting with his knees up and his head at the back. I never saw him again; I didn't want to. He probably had a vague idea he had been hit, that somebody had knocked him into the mud. It was the only thing to do.[9]
> Lieutenant Jim Davies, 9th Royal Fusiliers

Even in action, there could be disgraceful, but very amusing, incidents. One typical story involved Lieutenant Adrian Ball and his platoon from the 24th Australian Battalion, which had just captured a German pillbox. Upon entering, they discovered some German cigars and several bottles of wine – enough to allow a bottle apiece. After they were suitably 'primed' and looking for mischief, they happened upon two crates of carrier pigeons. A series of cheery messages were despatched back, ranging from '*Deutschland Uber Alles*! Ha! Ha!' to 'Hock the Kaiser, I don't think!' but culminating in a request from Ball himself for certain information of an 'obscene and personal nature'. Having had their fun they pondered what to do with the remaining pigeons. The answer was obvious and soon they were settling down to a nutritious pigeon stew! Truly those pigeons 'also served' in providing sustenance to hungry Australians![10]

Even the more sober Australian soldiers could tire of the excesses of his countrymen when they were behind the lines.

> The more I see of the Australians the more I am convinced that they are the most foul-mouthed, bragging, malingering crowds in this war and all they think of is food, women, drink and to see who can curse the worst. My honest opinion is that they are mostly a damn lot of wastrels always talking about how to get to 'Blighty' or hospital.[11]
> Private Herbert Harris, 55th Australian Battalion

In fact, the Australians proved to be excellent soldiers and a very great asset to the British Army. Taken as a whole, their discipline may have been a tad 'looser' – and there was a self-conscious celebration of the 'wild Australian boy', which even extended to the tales recounted in their battalion histories and memoirs. Thus, one story commemorated a real Australian larrikin signaller named Lucas, who, imbibing too well, decided – for complex reasons that need not detain us – that his colonel needed his very own German servant to tend to his every need:

> One that would clean his boots, hold his horse, and do a goosestep. In short, Lucas decided that he would go back to the line, advance upon the enemy, and pluck from their midst one of their number. This amazing fellow turned about and walked through our outpost line and then into the German position until he came upon a large dugout. Standing boldly at the entrance, he called out for the occupants to come up and surrender or be blown to pieces in their lair. Eight Germans came sheepishly up the steps with their hands above their heads. Lucas lined them up, entertained them with a wild demonstration of bayonet-lunging, called out to an imaginary patrol behind him to keep down behind the parapet, and then beckoning a young Fritz to his side, chased the others below with threats that if they came up again, they would be cut to pieces. With his prisoner he returned through both the German and our own lines of posts without being halted. In festive mood, and having conceived a liking for the young German, Lucas decided that a holiday in the back areas would do them both an immense amount of good. So, crossing the Somme at Corbie, he and his prisoner became for five days and nights lost to the ken of men. Meanwhile Lucas was reported missing by his battalion and was thought to have been blown to pieces by a shell. On the sixth day a strange pair walked into the battalion horse-lines at Corbie – a young German carrying the web equipment of an Australian soldier and a boltless Lee-Enfield rifle on his shoulder and, beside him, flourishing a walking-stick with the air of a showman parading a rare exhibit, the mourned signaller Lucas. Lucas was, of course, placed under arrest. His story was not believed at first, but the German when examined confirmed it. Lucas would, no doubt, have received a decoration but for the reward in the shape of a holiday jaunt which he took unto himself.[12]
>
> Corporal Harold Williams, 56th Australian Battalion

However, for all the scorn poured on them from their colonial friends, one story shows that at least some elements of the British Army were well and truly capable of keeping their end up:

If evidence of our high spirits and virility was needed, I record the following for posterity. I was with a covering rear-guard party and was passed by a small detachment of Gordon Highlanders. Hastening to catch up with my own unit, I surprised one of the kilted Jocks who had dodged his own column and was well and truly seducing a French girl in a pile of stones – and he had not even removed his pack![13]

Sapper Frederick Cook, 78th Field Company, Royal Engineers

*   *   *

With the various animosities raging amidst the ranks of the Allies, perhaps it should be no surprise that at times the relationship with the men in the trenches opposite was sometimes more friendly than you might expect! Although amicable contacts such as had occurred in the Christmas Truce of 1914 were rare, nevertheless the two sides did often communicate with each other, often by means of noticeboards erected above the trenches.

During the daytime, 'Fritz' did his best to dishearten us by sticking up boards out of his trenches on which was written, in English, bad news such as 'A great defeat on the Ypres sector; thousands of Tommies taken prisoner' or news that we had lost a great naval battle and half our navy had gone to the bottom on the sea. Of course, we did not believe any of his lies and we were forbidden to write anything at all on boards for Fritz's information. But one day during ration issue a corporal of ours stuck up a loaf of bread on the end of a bayonet and raised it high for Fritz to see. Almost instantly two bayonets with loaves of bread on them were thrust up out of the German line.[14]

Corporal George Ashurst, 1st Lancashire Fusiliers

Sometimes, quiet sectors of the line drifted into a kind of 'Live and Let Live' attitude. The motivation was clear: to improve their own living conditions in circumstances when there was little military value in stirring up more trouble.

In the old Loos sector conditions were so foul and the trenches so close together that we tried to help each other, when we could. One of these local arrangements operated at Givenchy. Life in those flooded holes was miserable for both sides. Fellows needed a moment to enjoy their grub and both sides respected that. Neither side sent over mortar shells or grenades at breakfast time. The regiment opposite us were Saxons, decent fellows. The trenches were so close that we could hear them talking or singing, Jerry was a great one for singing and the Saxons set up little impromptu choirs. One of these choirs was so talented that he always earned a round of applause from our chaps.[15]

Private Lionel Renton, 16th Middlesex Regiment (Public Schools Battalion)

Many apocryphal stories circulated amongst the men imagining exaggerated versions of this 'harmony'.

There is rather an amusing story going about just now about another part of the line where things have been very quiet for months past and where the lines are very close together. The story is that an engineer walked across to the Germans one night and borrowed a mallet to drive in some stakes with. The story is very like that of another part of the line where our engineers are reported to have put up part of a barbed wire entanglement only to find in the morning that the Germans had finished it off as it was as much use to them as to us.[16]

Lieutenant Walter Coats, 1/9th Highland Light Infantry

It is often forgotten that Britain was then one of the great 'melting pots' of the world, with a number of Germans having worked or lived there in the pre-war years. Pork butchers, businessmen, students, seamen and waiters had all frequented the streets of our major cities. This led to some interesting banter shouted out between the trenches.

"Hallo Tommee!" cried a German voice. "Are you soon going home on leave?" "Next week!" the Englishman shouted. "Are you going to London?" was the next question. "Yes!" "Then call at 224 Tottenham Court Road and give my love to Miss Sarah Jones!" "I'll go round all right and I'll jolly well …" The fate of the lady was eclipsed in a roar of laughter from our side and the angry splutter of a machine gun from across the way.[17]

Captain Guy Chapman, 13th Royal Fusiliers

This kind of cheery banter often led to much laughter – and a burst of fire just to keep things 'honest'. These men were not really friends.

Weird sounds floated across from the German trenches: the strains of an accordion and the refrain of a song very popular at the time of the Boer War 'Goodbye Dolly Gray'. Waiting until the singer had finished, we signified our approval by shouting "Hooray!" and "Encore!" but ceased abruptly when a voice hailed us from the other side, "Hallo, Tommy! Hallo, Tommy!" Thoroughly intrigued by this development, we called, "Hallo. Give us another song!" Whereupon, after several false starts, we were treated to 'Down by the Old Bull and Bush'. We hoorayed again and clapped. "What's your name, Jerry?" one of us shouted. "Charlie, you bloody English bastards!" came the voice of that worthy instantly, which mouthful rather nonplussed us! We were racking our brains for a suitably fruity reply when Charlie called, "*Gut nacht!*" and several bullets in quick succession smacked into the parados above our heads. "He likes us!" remarked Freddy Smith with some feeling.[18]

Private Dick Read, 8th Leicestershire Regiment

Norman Dowie remembered an unusual communication attached to a mysterious object which initially caused some alarm as it looked like a bomb! This too triggered an amusing riposte.

We all scooted round the corner for a few seconds, and then as there was no explosion we went back, to discover an old jam tin lying on the trench boards. We picked it up and found inside a message. "Dear Jocks, I have a wife in Falkirk. What would happen if I came over to you tonight?" "There would be another widow in Falkirk!"[19]

Lieutenant Norman Down, 4th Gordon Highlanders

There were also cases of combatants whose families had emigrated from Germany and now lived in Britain or one of the colonies. An obvious example was the British House of Windsor – or Saxe-Coburg, as they had previously been known. One Australian soldier in the trenches realized he might be a little closer than he might really have wished to his father:

In the ranks of 'C' Company was a man named Schaffner; he was born in Australia from German parents. Prior to the outbreak of war, his father had gone on a visit to the Fatherland and found himself trapped; the son believed that he was serving in the German forces. One night, as I was standing on the fire step beside Schaffner, watching the white flares rise gracefully from the Hun line, he said quite casually, "Well, I wonder if my old pop is over there; it would be interesting to meet him!"[20]

Sergeant Edgar Rule, 14th Australian Battalion

It was generally believed that the Saxon units were more friendly than the Prussian 'real' Germans.

> The people over the way are Saxons. The other day at stand-to in the morning we discovered that during the night they had put up a notice on the parapet of their trench. As it became light, we were able to make it out. Here it is:
> "WE ARE SAXONS
> YOU HAVE KILLED OUR MAJOR
> HE WAS A PRUSSIAN
> THANK YOU"
> They do love each other, don't they?[21]
>   Lieutenant Norman Down, 4th Gordon Highlanders

Many of the men rejoiced in an amusing account of the progress of a German officer who appeared in their divisional newspaper. This was quoted in several diaries and post-war accounts.

> The gem of the season appeared today. It was a collection of extracts from the diary of a Hun captured at the crater. It read as follows:
> June 3. Lieutenant Reinaker is drunk.
> June 7. Lieutenant Reinaker is drunk again.
> June 13. Once again Lieutenant Reinaker is drunk.
> June 21. To-day we attacked. As we advanced Lieutenant Reinaker could be heard shouting "*Vorwarts!*" from a dugout in the support line.
> July 15. Lieutenant Reinaker has received the Iron Cross.'[22]
>   Lieutenant Norman Down, 4th Gordon Highlanders

Sometimes the friendly overtures from the Germans opposite were misunderstood or led to confusion from those British units not directly involved in the initial exchanges.

> It was the custom to pull the Boche's leg. On November 5, an effigy of the Kaiser was displayed in German uniform with a large cardboard iron cross complete. There was one unfortunate incident. A Polish deserter who came over to us said that many of his comrades wished to do the same. A large board with a notice in Polish was put up in No Man's Land. This caused many of the enemy, probably Poles, to collect in the trenches and expose themselves. The Light Trench Mortar Battery, who had apparently not been warned of the notice, seeing an excellent target,

let fly in their midst. It was from certain points of view unfortunate, as we might otherwise had had a large number of deserters.[23]

Major William Lowe, 18th Durham Light Infantry

And perhaps we should remind ourselves that these men were generally bitter enemies. However, not all interactions across No Man's Land were well-meaning.

The Boche is a poisonous blighter. They have got hold of a dead Scotsman, propped him up with his backside towards us, and turned up his kilt in mockery; and there he stands, with one of their sentries beside him so that we can't get at him, though we try night and day. Ugh![24]

Lieutenant John Staniforth, 7th Leinster Regiment

A soldier never complains;
he observes – a lot.

Sexism was quite common in the Great War.

It may not be tasty, but it was nutritious!

Safe as houses!

Come in the water's lovely!

Nothing like a good chat!

Sometimes it was all too much.

Cheers, it will all be over one day!

You should 'ave seen the Prussian I took it off! Ten foot tall he was!

No laughing matter. Sometimes nothing could help.

If he cheats again shoot the bastard.

An attack was never funny, but humour helped them soldier on.

The newspaper view of British morale.

Grub's up!

After the battle.

Dogs didn't last long in the trenches – what they needed was armour plated tortoises!

Making the best of it.

Chapter 8

Gunners

Things were certainly pretty bad at the guns, the air still reeking of gas, the ground saturated with mustard gas liquid and the men all half blind and covered with mustard gas blisters. Every order had to be given in writing, as neither I nor the NCOs could articulate a word, and to complete the humour of the situation everyone was sick at every possible opportunity.[1]

Major Neil Fraser-Tytler, 'A' Battery, 150 Brigade, Royal Field Artillery

T he gunners were the masters of the Great War battlefields. Of this there was little doubt. They wielded unimaginable powers of destruction. Collectively, the Royal Horse Artillery (13-pdr guns to support the cavalry), Royal Field Artillery (armed generally with the 18-pdr or 4.5in howitzers) and Royal Garrison Artillery (armed with a range of medium and heavy guns) grew exponentially in size throughout the war. Their guns smashed down defences, broke up attacks, created walls of shells that prevented the arrival of reserves and fired the gas shells that affected anyone within range. It has been estimated that the guns caused far more casualties than any other weapon. Throughout, they fought a ceaseless war of counter-battery fire with the opposing gunners. And that was the problem – the German gunners wielded weapons of equal power.

The Royal Artillery guns may not have been located in the front line, but as a natural focus of German artillery fire they were carefully dug in, if the situation allowed it.

The gun emplacements, set at 20 yards intervals, closely resembled the tumuli frequently seen on Salisbury Plain and had at the 'business end' an aperture large enough to allow for elevation and a sweep of 80 degrees. Well dug in and each skilfully camouflaged and protected by an overhead half-barrel shaped roof, supported by strong beams of timber on which was heaped several layers of sandbags covered with turfs of green grass. It was difficult, even at close-quarters to detect that concealed here was a formidable unit of destruction. On either side of the spade of the trail, four steps led down to, on one side the sleeping quarters of the detachment and, on the other, a recess for storing ammunition. The battery staff and signallers' pit was positioned 20 yards south of No. 1 gun-pit in line under the trees. It was certainly a masterpiece of engineering ingenuity – a holiday chalet in fact. Six steps led down to a spacious floor above which heavy crossbeams of timber supported layers of sandbags and turfs similar to the gun pits. The interior was well appointed with tiered bunks along the walls, a space on the floor for the equipment and a frame holding the blanketed gas-screen for placing over the door, if necessary. The command post, which was connected to the signallers' pit by a communication trench, was a deep pit, 7 foot by 7 foot by 7 foot, provided with a small rough table sufficient to accommodate a message pad and a D3 telephone, an empty ammunition box as a bench, and two sleeping bunks, tiered – one for the officer on duty and the other for the signaller at rest. A ladder led from the floor up to the command post above, up which the officer would shin when alerted, to shout his orders to the guns, through a megaphone from an aperture facing the guns.[2]

Signaller Dudley Menaud-Lissenburg, 97th Battery, 147 Brigade, Royal Field Artillery

Menaud-Lissenburg was lucky in his battery positions, as few were so well-ordered and supplied with comfortable dugouts. In sharp contrast is this gun position:

In front of our guns ran a little gully and as the weather worsened the overflow from the shell holes turned this gully into a little stream with the result that a number of old corpses became exposed showing all their bones as white as snow as this rainwater had been flowing through for almost 3 years. There was one body that lay exposed right in front of my gun and the rains had washed the skeleton's bones like ivory. As a matter of fact, his ribs formed a kind of trap which filtered the brushwood that flowed down the gully and left a clear space in the middle of clean rainwater into which I used to dip my 'enamel mug' for a clean drop of water for a shave.[3]

Gunner Austin Heraty, 241 Brigade, Royal Field Artillery

The Royal Artillery had had a lot to learn at the start of the war, but by 1916 had amassed the trained gunners, NCOs and officers who knew their grim business. A few still clung to the idea of a 'gentleman's war', where maths and gunnery could be ignored, but they were already relics of the past.

The senior subaltern said, "I'm going to the major in his dugout, to ask him if I can put on the 'meteor' corrections on the gun!" When he got there the major, who was a regular mark you, an Irishman, said, "My boy, this is war, this is practical stuff, forget all that nonsense they taught you at 'The Shop' – if it's cold cock her up a bit!"[4]

Lieutenant Murray Rymer Jones, 74 Brigade, Royal Field Artillery

The regular major spouting his 'common sense' was in fact a fool. Accurate meteorological corrections were essential to accuracy of the guns – and accuracy was essential if they were to hit the German trenches and gun batteries. This was a technical and scientific war.

Huge barrages would be fired when the infantry went over the top, but they were also responsible for firing defensive barrages to protect the infantry during German attacks.

Recently the infantry sent up 'SOS' rockets, and for such contingencies our guns have definite points to fire on, points constantly checked by us each time we man the observation posts. On this occasion, Gunner Clarke, who is a real soldier, was on duty at the gun-pit, and who, without a moment's delay, after we passed on to the gun position the message, pulled the firing lever of his gun which roused the other gunners to man the guns. The following day, [Captain] Sabaston, inspecting the gun, asked what had become of the muzzle cover, a leather cap, strapped around the muzzle between bouts of firing. Clarke promptly replied, "It's in the Jerries' lines, Sir."[5]

Gunner Ivor Hanson, 311 Brigade, Royal Field Artillery

The number of shells fired was extraordinary; the logistics of feeding the guns were staggering. Even taking away the empty shell cases was a challenge, one that a wise officer could evade with a little thought.

We heard we had once more changed our divisional Royal Artillery commander and that the new arrival, whose name is General 'B', was coming to inspect the brigade in action. He is an individual well known for having a 106-fuse temper and 'non-delay' language far in advance of any other general in the regiment, and worst of all it was reported that his pet mania was the immediate clearance of all empty cartridge cases from gun positions. The careful return of empty shell cases is no doubt very necessary, but on some positions it must pay the tax payer best to let them lie until the next advance. Casualties to horses and men, while performing the slow job of loading them up into wagons, may thus be avoided. But this was no excuse in the general's eyes and he slated two batteries of the brigade unmercifully on account of them. It was to be our turn next day. Just behind our guns were two huge craters filled to the brim with shell cases, at least 10,000 of them. All seemed lost; however that night came 'Inspiration'. At dawn I arose, found an old notice-board and swiftly the battery painter covered its face with the following legend:-

C. 28. C 53. Dump.

All 18-pdr and 4.5 cases to be dumped here.

Result, much kudos for our very neat position and a broad smile on the face of our colonel, standing behind the general.[6]

Major Neil Fraser-Tytler, 'A' Battery, 150 Brigade, Royal Field Artillery

Although the gunners handed out rough punishment to the Germans, they were a much-coveted target in themselves if their gun positions were identified by German aerial reconnaissance or flash spotting. This led to many close escapes, as for instance with Major Neil Fraser-Tytler earlier in the war.

Our few shells brought on a sharp reply from a 77mm 'Whizz-Bang' battery, which made us beat a hurried retreat into the nearest dugout. At the critical moment, while diving down the trench towards the shelter, one of my great feet, clad in trench waders, got wedged between two duckboards. Two would-be 'Victoria Cross' signallers, however, emerged from the dug-out and gallantly pulled me in – all somewhat helpless from laughter.[7]

Major Neil Fraser-Tytler, 'D' Battery, 151 Brigade, Royal Field Artillery

However, not all were so lucky. Even if they were not killed, a German shell could mark the end of a sportsman's hopes and dreams. A sad little story appeared in the *Cockney War Stories*.

'Spider' Webb was a Cockney, from Stepney, I believe, who was with us on the Somme in 1916. He was a splendid cricketer. We had had a very stiff time for 6 or 7 hours and were resting during a lull in the firing. Then suddenly Jerry sent over five shells. After a pause, another shell came over and burst near to Spider and his two pals. When the smoke cleared, I went across to see what had happened. Spider's two pals were beyond help. The Cockney was propping himself up with his elbows surveying the scene. I said, "What's happened, Webb?" The reply, "Blimey! What's happened? One over – two bowled!" And, looking down at his leg, "And I'm stumped!" Then he fainted.[8]

Lieutenant George Franks, Royal Garrison Artillery

Some gunners would be rendered 'mad' by the thunderous detonations of German shells. Stress had built up, and then just one shell could trigger a near-total mental collapse.

> The cruellest blow of all was yet to come. Thirty minutes before dinner a 5.9in [shell] landed near our kitchen, and the cook went 'loony' from shell-shock. After rushing wildly about he went to ground in a covered-in sap. No one could get him out. I tried to coax him out by crawling in with a biscuit, a sergeant grasping my legs to pull me out in case he bit me. Eventually we had to take the roof off, and he was tied up and sent off in a passing ambulance.[9]
>
> Major Neil Fraser-Tytler, 'D' Battery, 151 Brigade, Royal Field Artillery

Although gunners were not in the front line, it is often forgotten that every day they would send forward a gunnery observation officer, gunnery specialist assistant and a signaller to form an observation post from where they could observe the fall of shot from their guns and send back wireless corrections to ensure the shells hit their targets. These teams shared the discomforts and dangers of the infantry. If there was a suitable building surviving – a farmhouse roof or church steeple perhaps – they would use that, but the Germans were always on the lookout for likely observation vantage points and would often target them with extra shellfire. Hence, the party would usually be forced to set up the post amidst the trenches.

> The forward observation post would be an enlarged shell hole, probably with some sandbags round it and duckboards to keep you a little bit out of the wet. You'd get your head below the level of the sandbags, you couldn't build them up far or you'd be spotted, but you could get a little shelter from them. You used your binoculars to look though the gaps. Sometimes you couldn't do that and there was nothing for it but to look over the edge. That wouldn't last long if the Germans were near! You couldn't get much range of vision because we never really had the dominating ground, but I could see 400–500 yards inside the German line from one of our posts. I could see two ruined farms from one post I was in they must have been 300 yards in [the other side of No Man's Land]. I very rarely saw the Germans – they were no chaps for exposing themselves. I used to think sometimes our people were a bit careless like that. But the Germans were pretty careful. Once, I saw some Germans labouring along behind the line, evidently carrying a latrine bucket. The temptation was too strong for me and I let go two howitzer shells. I'm glad to say I missed then but it seemed to me

afterwards that it was a shit's trick! It was totally irrational [as] they were enemies; they'd have shot me as soon as they possibly could, but they were engaged on this humble task, I had a feeling that I shouldn't have done it.[10]

2nd Lieutenant Cyril Denys, 212th Siege Battery, Royal Garrison Artillery

The journey up to the observation post was often fraught with danger.

As bad luck would have it, just as we were going to the observation post the Huns started firing salvoes of 5.9s right on to it. However, by making rushes between the salvoes we reached my tunnel entrance, and all seven of us crawled in. It was pitch dark, one of the previous shells having upset the only candle. To ease the intense congestion of packed humanity, I told Macdonald that he should crawl up the emergency exit tunnel. The next salvo came, one shell blew in the mouth of the emergency exit and the blast sent Macdonald on to me and me backwards on to the colonel. At the same time another shell exploded near the main entrance, causing the last two officers, who were only a few feet in the tunnel to make desperate efforts to push further up. By this time, I was helpless with laughter. Imagine seven of us on our hands and knees in a narrow tunnel, rather damp and very dark, all pushing towards the centre![11]

Major Neil Fraser-Tytler, 'D' Battery, 151 Brigade, Royal Field Artillery

Officers on duty in the front-line observation posts were not above making stupid jokes to amuse themselves and while away the dreary hours.

At about 5 o'clock on a dreary, drizzly morning, when I was at the observation post, I suddenly realized it was 1 April, so thought of a ruse to get the adjutant out of bed by sending him word of a juicy target on a bogus map reference that sounded like part of our sector. After a moment's thought, I called to the signallers below to send this message to brigade, "Can you get heavies to fire on armoured train derailed at X38 Central!" Unless he was very wide awake, he would jump out of bed and try to look up the reference on his map and so become an April fool. Instead of this, he passed the message straight through to divisional headquarters, where our brigade major, who is a bit of a fire-eater, rang up our heavy artillery to engage the target forthwith. They 'stood to' for nearly an hour in the rain, ready to fire, while their officers puzzled over the map reference and asked for verification of the square's number, etc. When it was finally realized that there was no such square, the fun began. The first I knew about it was a wrathful call from the colonel himself, demanding an explanation. He finally ended with, "Did you see an armoured train?" When I replied, "No, Sir," he shouted, "What the hell do you mean by it? I am coming to see you!"[12]

Lieutenant Julian Tyndale-Biscoe, 'C' Battery, Royal Horse Artillery

When the fuming colonel got into the front line, he took Tyndale-Biscoe to one side and interrogated his errant subordinate.

"Now, what is the meaning of all this?" All I could reply, and very submissively, was that it was 1 April. He sort of exploded at this and rushed out, saying over his shoulder, "You should not make a fool of army matters!" An hour or so afterwards, I got a phone call from Lennox at the battery saying somewhat diffidently, "I have just had orders to put you under arrest!" To which I asked, "Open or close arrest?" He seemed a bit confused at this, and then said, "Open!" "Then I shall continue to command the battery!" It began to dawn on me later that Lennox had been trying to pull my leg. I was never very anxious about the outcome of a court martial, if there was to be one, because, since the map reference did not exist, no ammunition could have been fruitlessly expended. And what is more, it showed that the staff folk were a bit hazy about their maps![13]

Lieutenant Julian Tyndale-Biscoe, 'C' Battery, Royal Horse Artillery

The relationship between the gunners and the infantry was of a mixed nature. Most of the infantry were aware that they depended for their lives on the guns to protect them, to take out German artillery, prepare the way and then chaperone them forward with creeping barrages during an attack, and to break up German attacks. Yet there could be a degree of jealousy, or even bitterness, evident as the infantry often imagined the gunners lived in luxurious safety several miles behind the lines.

The people I have conceived a thorough dislike for are our own heavy gunners. They have a hearty lunch in their princely chateau about 6 miles behind the lines, and then stroll out smoking big cigars. On the velvet lawn they catch sight of their gun. "Oh, I say," says someone, "this jolly old gun, what?" "Suppose we let off the bally thing, dear old chaps?" suggests another. So, they whistle up a fellow and order a couple of fine, old, crusted shells, and ram them in and poop them off, and go back to finish their cigars. Then for about 5-hours the infuriated

Hun hammers our front trench madly in revenge, and a fat blooming gunner asleep in an armchair hears the strafing, cocks a drowsy eye, and remarks lazily, "Poor old gravel-pushers; coming in for some more hate, what?" And off he goes to sleep again! At least, that's how I picture it.[14]

Lieutenant John Staniforth, 7th Leinster Regiment

Far more serious to infantry was the endless bitter dispute over the question of Royal Artillery shells dropping short into their own front-line trenches. As gun barrels got worn, so they lost accuracy, and this could have a calamitous impact. There were also mistakes in gunnery calculations; after all, the opposing trenches were not far apart.

One day, an order was sent to the front line troops to withdraw from all posts and trenches to a position 250 yards in rear, because the heavies were going to bombard 'Fritz's Folly' a small sharp salient just to the north of Gueudecourt. The troops were withdrawn, and when the time came the heavies did their worst – and that is no figure of speech – for eyewitnesses who might certainly have been a trifle biased, stated that not one shell reached the German position. The boys had the mortification of seeing their own miserable trenches pounded with heavy shells for an hour and a half. If ever any troops were cursed heartily it was the artillery engaged in the operation. The only bright spot in an otherwise depressing afternoon was when the Germans, thinking that they might assist in the demolition of the Australian trenches whilst the going was good, started a return shoot. The first enemy shell fell right in the middle of the Folly and was evidently a bull's eye, for duckboards, sandbags and other trench furniture flew high in the air, and the "Diggers" managed a faint cheer. They felt that things had been evened up somewhat.[15]

Lieutenant Walter Belford, 11th Australian Battalion

The gunners generally denied that such things ever happened and demanded solid proof. This caused further unrest.

Complaints were frequently sent to the artillery units concerned. These only brought the usual response that, if the troops would send back a piece of one of the shells, or preferably a whole shell – for there were many 'duds' – then the matter would be inquired into and steps taken to find out the guns, if any, that were doing the short shooting. Naturally, there was a snort of indignation from the front-line troops, and one officer savagely remarked: "What the hell do the bastards expect me to do?

Catch one of the bloody things?" Naturally there was not much chance of finding any shells or fragments in the soft, rain–sodden ground.[16]
    Lieutenant Walter Belford, 11th Australian Battalion

Men like Belford found the whole thing extremely frustrating. They knew guns were firing short, but they could not seem to get anything done with the intransigent gunners to stop it.

> It was always very hard to get the artillery to admit that the short shooting was caused by any of the batteries engaged, although it is a well-known fact that a sudden drop in the temperature would affect the range of guns to a great degree. In very cold weather 18-pounders would lose 500 yards in 2,500, and heavier guns were affected correspondingly. Many troops in the 'Poor Bloody Infantry' knew these things, and yet all complaints were treated with contumely and disbelief. A good story is told of some infantry who had been shelled quite a while by their own artillery. At length one of the officers made [it] back to the battery that was doing most of the short shooting and offered to surrender to it if only it would stop firing.[17]
>   Lieutenant Walter Belford, 11th Australian Battalion

Most of all the front-line soldiers enjoyed it when senior artillery officers sent to the front line to investigate found the shells falling short all around them.

> Tudor, our Commander Royal Artillery, was nearly killed here by one of our shells. We had repeatedly complained of short shooting on the part of the 4.5in howitzers – nothing very original in that! It was difficult to bring it home to any particular battery, because every group always assured us that they were not firing at the time we complained of. Tudor was up one day when our howitzers were indulging in their nasty little habits. Making us clear the trench he went forward into a sap; the next shells buried him. He was then perfectly satisfied that our howitzers were shooting short![18]
>   Lieutenant Colonel William Croft, 11th Royal Scots

Chapter 9

You Can't Eat the Wireless!

Hunter-Weston was commanding a battle in this area and he was most anxious for the first news to come in – and he was haunting the pigeon loft. Presently, in flapped a pigeon – it was pounced on and the message was taken out of its little case. It read, "I'm fed up of carrying this bloody bird!"[1]

> 2nd Lieutenant Ralph Cooney, 4th Battalion, Heavy Machine Gun Corps

Communications were crucial to the British Army on the Western Front. In the early days, wireless was too 'new' to be widespread, but telephone lines gave nightmare problems. Because of the threat from German shellfire, it was soon realized that they would have to be duplicated, or triplicated, to form a virtual 'ladder' that would give them hope of keeping open a line between the front line and the headquarters well behind the lines. Wires were here, there and everywhere. They could be a bloody nuisance for men passing through the communication trenches.

On the way to the observation post, we have to pass a place known as Suicide Corner which is subject to frequent bursts of shrapnel. After a dash along there, one continues in a trench which is even more of a trial to one's temper, especially at night, as telephone lines are laid across it in most ingenious ways. First, there is a wire just at a suitable distance from the ground to trip you up into an especially filthy pool of wet mud. After getting up and walking carefully, picking your feet well up, a wire knocks your hat off, and manages to detach the badge, which entails a hunt of several minutes according to how far the badge had sunk in the mud, and the distance that the hat has rolled. One proceeds again, and next runs hard up against a wire stretched tight across just at the height of your neck![2]

> 2nd Lieutenant Julian Tyndale-Biscoe, 'C' Battery, Royal Horse Artillery

The signallers were constantly checking and rechecking the wires, fixing breaks as best they could. However, sometimes the breaks were not down to the Germans alone.

> It was on the Somme; we were out in the open and we made a dugout for ourselves. I'd been doing some washing [of] shirts and for the want of a line I was looking round. There were hundreds and hundreds of telephone lines in the trenches, obsolete lines. I got a pair of pliers and cut a few dozen or so yards of telephone line to use as a clothesline thinking it was obsolete. Quite innocently, I cut this line. I should have known better of course! Later on in the day, there was a hell of a commotion, they couldn't get through to headquarters down in Albert! Some swearing signallers came up, walked all the way to find the line cut! Who the bloody hell had cut the line? I said nothing of course! I kept doggo! If they'd seen the clothesline out there, they would have recognised it – it was the headquarters telephone line I'd cut! The battery was out of touch with the headquarters for 6–8 hours. I thought I had a lucky escape that time – I might have been court martialled.[3]
>
> Private J.W. Mortimer, 115th Heavy Battery, Royal Garrison Artillery

They usually used plain speech over the telephone, but increasing worries as to the ability of the Germans to intercept messages via induction led them on occasion to use a simple code. This in turn could cause embarrassment all round.

> One afternoon, after a perfectly quiet and uneventful day, in which there was absolutely nothing to put in the intelligence report, which was then due, the company commander in the front line decided, in order to save a runner the journey back with the report, to send it over the telephone by code. This consisted of groups of figures representing sentences in general use. For instance, the sentence, "Our rum has not yet arrived!" might be represented by the figures "528", and "Please expedite" by "172". In this case the message selected was "Situation normal!" which was duly dispatched to battalion headquarters. A few minutes later the company commander was rung up on the telephone by the battalion intelligence officer. He gathered that his message had caused considerable alarm and despondency at battalion headquarters. He was able to reassure them until the report could be sent down by hand, and he then discovered that the message as deciphered read: "Tanks are approaching!" which had not unnaturally caused a considerable stir, and the commanding officer was already on his way up armed with field glasses, to investigate.[4]
>
> Major Herbert Wenyon, 8th Royal West Kent Regiment

The choice of code words could also lead to amusement when they were combined.

> The next stage was the introduction of codes and code names. At first these were very simple, we were 'John' after Colonel Jones, while 'gas' became the innocent 'Gertie', and to attack was 'to tickle'. One very famous message was sent when an expected gas attack had to be suddenly postponed, "John can sleep quiet tonight; Gertie will not tickle!"[5]
>
> Lieutenant John Hills, 5th Leicestershire Regiment

One old-fashioned method of communication pressed back into use was the employment of homing pigeons to carry messages back. The system was simple – at least in theory.

> The signal section had attached to it a 'pigeon man'. Wakelin was a very quiet person, he looked after our birds which were for emergency use only. He had two pigeons and every morning at nine o'clock he freed one and it flew up into the sky from the slight clearing in the wood and usually flew around once or twice to get its bearings and then set off for the brigade pigeon loft. It had been kept unfed and so flew straight back. Not long afterwards a despatch rider brought up another one, fed before he had set off with it. The next morning, the other one, by now hungry, was freed. If a message had to be sent, it was first made out in triplicate. One copy was kept in the signal office in the 'sent out' tray and the other two copies were put into a very light aluminium container which had two soft catches attached to it, and these were put round the pigeon's leg.[6]
>
> Rifleman Gerald Dennis, 21 King's Royal Rifle Corps

But things could and did go wrong. The first problem was the edible nature of pigeons in a world where soldiers endured a monotonous diet. A tasty treat was sometimes difficult to resist.

> On two occasions, when he arrived from the brigade pigeon loft, the despatch rider reported that our pigeon had not arrived back at the loft. Could a German sniper be such a crack shot that he had been successful in hitting our birds as they circled above the trees before turning away from his lines? If so, where were the bodies? Why had not we, who watched it set off, noticed its fall? What was to have been a well-kept secret was later disclosed. It seemed that at a company mess one evening an officer had said in fun more than anything else to his cook batman, "Can't you do better than this with the bully beef?" The batman, who

had been a gamekeeper in civvy life, took the remark as a challenge. The next evening and the evening after that the officers' dinner was supplemented with pigeon pie, a rare delicacy and much enjoyed. However, after the second tasty dish, the batman's own officer gave him a hint that he had better not produce another titbit like those pies. Our pigeon service continued normally after that.[7]

Rifleman Gerald Dennis, 21 King's Royal Rifle Corps

However, a general ignorance of the noble art of pigeon handling also interfered with the efficiency of the system. Apparently, pigeons had feelings too.

We received our first basket of pigeons. Some of the higher staff being anxious to see that their release, etc. was carried out properly, visited battalion headquarters to observe the results. Unfortunately, those in charge of the pigeon-loft some miles in rear did not then know all there was to know about pigeons, and instead of sending two cock or two hen pigeons, sent one of each. On their release with the messages clipped on their wings, the amative couple, disregarding their military duties entirely, proceeded to fly over to Serre and, lighting on an old ruin, perched there, billing and cooing, wholly oblivious of business. Whether they ever were pricked by conscience and returned to their own pigeon-loft is unknown, as the staff lost patience and went home to tea.[8]

Major William Lowe, 18th Durham Light Infantry

As a 2nd lieutenant in the Signal Service, Royal Engineers, Arthur Hemsley was surprised to be tasked with organizing the ANZAC Corps pigeon school to ensure that people knew how to handle pigeons and also to make the Australians appreciate the importance of the messenger service.

The colonel turned to me and said, "These Australians, we keep getting pigeons to send to them and they keep eating them instead of using them for messages! We shall have to have a pigeon flying signal school! Go and do it!" I said, "I don't know anything about pigeons!" He said, "Well, now's your chance! You'll soon find out! Go to one of the pigeon lofts and get some information!"[9]

2nd Lieutenant Arthur Hemsley, Headquarters, I ANZAC Corps

After getting himself a little up to speed, Hemsley set up a building which would house the training sessions for Australian officers and key signal personnel. He did not get off to a good start.

My first lesson had been rather terrible because I had a basket of pigeons, I took a pigeon from it, put the message on the pigeon, showed the troops how to do it. My first pigeon didn't like it and left me! It flew round and round the room. I said, "Well open the window and let him go!" So, he went! I had to do it all over again![10]

2nd Lieutenant Arthur Hemsley, Headquarters, I ANZAC Corps

He had a huge sign erected in Bailleul on which was written 'Australian Corps Signal Service'.

That was rather a dangerous thing because, I'd only just got going with it when Major General White of the Australian staff, was driving by and saw my impressive board – so he came in to listen to me giving my lesson on pigeons. I was in great style with my pigeons. He said, "I must get General Birdwood to come round and see this – this would please him, I'm sure!" The next morning, sure enough, General Birdwood drove up in his car – and his staff, they came stamping in. He looked at me and I said, "This, Sir, is one of our messenger birds!" He took it from my hand and said, "Oh, yes, a very nice Blue Pigeon – I've been a pigeon fancier for years!" He knew far more about pigeons than I ever did![11]

2nd Lieutenant Arthur Hemsley, Headquarters, I ANZAC Corps

Overall, Hemsley thought his school performed well; at least there were fewer reports of the Australians eating the pigeons.

There was one popular story regarding pigeon messages, so popular it was told and retold time and time again.

As soon as the attack was well under way the major general went to the loft to await the first news, but no pigeons arrived. The morning dragged on but still there were no pigeons. At last, a tired-looking bird entered the loft and an orderly was despatched to get the message and bring it to the general. The general opened it, read it, crushed it in his hand, dashed it to the ground and strode away with a face like thunder. One of his staff, wondering what calamity had occurred that could bring such a cloud to the Great Man's brow, carefully smoothed out the crumpled message and read, "I'm sick of carrying this bloody bird!"[12]

Lieutenant Archibald Gilchrist, 10th King's Liverpool Regiment (1st Liverpool Scottish)

* * *

Pigeons were not the only animals employed to carry messages. Dogs were also pressed into service. Once again, it was the hapless Arthur Hemsley who found himself required to become an 'instant' expert.

> The colonel turned to me and said, "It's dogs this time! Headquarters are going to send forty-eight dogs, three dogs to a man, and you've got to deal with them!" I went to a little village, found some ground there, had it wired in. Put my 'dogmen' in there with their dogs. The dogs were taken from Battersea Dogs' Home of all shapes and sizes! Not little ones, but a collie, or a retriever, any large dog was good enough! They were lovely animals. When I visited them there was complete bedlam – all forty-eight of them barking at once. Whereupon the village mayor came and complained bitterly because they barked all night and kept all the village awake. So, I had to uplift them from there and put them well away in the woods, where they were no trouble to anybody! They fed these dogs on fresh-cut horsemeat, well they gave the dogs the odd bits, but actually the steaks they all ate themselves! The dogs were quite useful, they were taken up the line, a message put on them – and off you go home, then they come back to their handler who was waiting for them at the headquarters. They had a blue and white collar – and the orders were quite strict that no one was to touch them, but it was terribly difficult. One of the big problems was the Englishman's love of dogs. They would try to stop the dogs on their way back passing through the gun lines. The gunners would come out and give them meat – and delay them.[13]
>
>   2nd Lieutenant Arthur Hemsley, Headquarters, I ANZAC Corps

Then he had an inspection visit from a very senior staff colonel. Hemsley's dog team had been out on a mission visiting a nearby brigade headquarters. Sadly, on their way back his men had fallen prey to temptation.

> On their way back they went through one of the towns that had been very severely battered. The men's outfitting shop had been shot right out into the street. This dog group – about six men and eighteen dogs – stopped, and they all helped themselves to bright coloured velour hats! I said to this very senior colonel standing beside me, "The lorry's just coming in, Sir! The men will be taking the dogs out!" They dropped the back of this lorry and out came this group of clowns, with these funny coloured hats – purple hats and so on! This colonel was very offensive to me about it! "Is that the way you train your men!" They were quite

incorrigible these chaps – their one job was dogs! They were not much good for anything else![14]

2nd Lieutenant Arthur Hemsley, Headquarters, I ANZAC Corps

All in all, there were a multiplicity of methods to get messages back to headquarters, but in a heavy German bombardment, none of them could be relied upon. Signaller Bert Chaney discovered this to his utter horror when all his careful 'failsafe' preparations had been rendered useless by a combination of the shelling, the prevailing mist and the eternal problems of working with dumb animals.

One by one our telephone lines were smashed. We endeavoured a number of times to repair them, going out into the barrage, creeping down communication trenches trying to find the ends of the wires, but in that mist and in that barrage, it was a hopeless task, and we had to get back to our dugout thankful to be in one piece. Looking across in the direction of our visual communication system on the mound we saw that it was impossible to see anything: the Aldis lamps were unable to penetrate the mist, even the telescope did not help. Dashing down into the dugout I scribbled two similar coded messages on the special thin paper, screwed them up and pushed them into the little containers which clip onto the pigeon's leg. I and one of my boys, each carrying a pigeon, crept up the steps and pushing the gas blanket to one side, threw our birds into the air and away they flew. We watched them as they circled round a couple of times and then they swooped straight down and settled on top of our dugout. We retrieved them and tried once more, but those birds refused to fly. So down into the dugout again and another message was written and put into the small pouch attached to the dog's collar. Leading it to the entrance, I gave it a parting slap on the rump, at the same time shouting firmly, "Home boy! Allez!" I watched it for a minute or two as it trotted off, then dropped the gas blanket back. Even while we were still sighing with relief a wet nose pushed the blanket aside and in crawled the dog, scared out of its wits. All our efforts could not budge him, we pushed and shoved him, pulled him by the collar to get him moving, but he just laid down, clamped his body firmly to the ground and pretended to be asleep. He was a lot smarter than we were. All we could do was swear a lot and give him a kick. So ended all our wonderful preparations for keeping communications going during the attack.[15]

Signaller Bert Chaney, 1/7th London Regiment

What a story to cherish!

Chapter 10

Donkey's Bollocks!

"Good morning, good morning!" the general said as he passed down the line with a wound in his head. Now we knew he was wounded by the way that he bled, and when he got to the base, the poor bugger was dead.[1]

Soldiers often didn't much like their generals. They made fun of them and laughed at their idiosyncrasies. This did not make them bad generals; it just meant that they were authority figures surrounded by men who were – for very good reasons – fed up and in the mood for a moan and a laugh. But it wasn't just the generals who acted as 'lightning conductors' to the men in the front line. The staff were widely disliked, considered to be gilded lilies who were woefully inefficient in everything that mattered like battle plans – but all too keen to busy themselves with pettifogging details – to the absolute distraction of stressed officers who were up to their eyes in mud, blood and Germans!

I am very much annoyed by memos sent round from headquarters that come in at all hours of the day and night; they stop me getting a full night's rest and some of them are very silly and quite unnecessary. When I am very tired and just getting off to sleep with cold feet in comes an orderly with a chit asking how many pairs of socks my company had a week ago; I reply "141 and a half"! I then go to sleep; back comes a memo: "Please explain at once how you come to be deficient of one sock?" I reply, "Man lost his leg!" That's how we make the Huns sit up.'[2]

Captain Alexander Stewart, Cameronians (Scottish Rifles)

The 'red tabs', so called because of the red insignia worn on the uniform of staff officers, were often perceived as lazy and stupid.

Lloyd George claims that silver bullets are going to win the war. According to Lord Northcliffe it is high explosives which will at last enable us to blast our way to Berlin. Others mention the Navy, the Russian steam-roller, the liquor restrictions, and what not. I once heard a man say that the brains of the staff would be the deciding factor, but I am not such a pessimist as he. I still hope for a favourable issue![3]

Lieutenant Norman Down, 4th Gordon Highlanders

Such perceptions were generally unjustified. The staff were responsible for an enormous range of functions, without which the larger formations – from a brigade through to an army – would simply fall apart. They not only planned the battles, issuing the detailed orders to everyone concerned, but also dealt with the mass of logistical arrangements without which an army could not move and would certainly starve. It was hard work, as the cynical Lieutenant Norman Down soon found when he got a staff position.

> There seems to be quite a lot of work to do. It appears that you do work on the staff after all! Of course, it isn't considered correct to be caught out working, and that's why, when you enter the brigade office, you may find the brigade major peppering the staff captain with paper balls. It's only done so that you may think that they don't work. If it was once discovered that the staff worked as hard as other people, the chief grouse of the British Army would be taken away, and it is well known that the British Army without a grouse would be heartbroken.[4]
>
> Lieutenant Norman Down, Headquarters, 8 Brigade

That is not to say the staff did not make mistakes, although in truth some were made by attached front-line officers who were simply helping out. Perhaps it wasn't that easy after all.

> I spent the month of November with the neighbouring 64th Brigade, acting as their brigade major in the absence on leave of the real one, being attached for that month as a 'staff learner'. At that time, I had not yet become an expert in the interpretation of aerial photographs and when on one occasion an artillery brigadier called at the brigade headquarters, and asked for suggestions as to targets, I showed him some photographs I had studied and indicated some obvious centres of activity, tracks and works suggesting battery positions, headquarters, etc. We identified these on the map, and he departed in great good humour promising to strafe them like blazes, but after he had gone, I found to my horror that the obvious targets I had shown him were all on our side of the line, as we had been looking at the photographs upside down! I left to General Headlam (commanding 64th Brigade) the task of explaining this to the gunner.[5]
>
> Captain David Kelly, Headquarters, 110 Brigade

At the higher levels, the staff dealt with 'after-action' reports assessing the impact of new weapons and tactics – on both sides. They planned the next offensive down to the last detail, disseminating the plans to the hundreds of units that would be needed. They monitored basic field security to make sure the Germans remained in ignorance of their plans. They tracked the movements of every German division through a variety of intelligence sources. They arranged the movement and distribution of millions of tonnes of stores, making sure weapons, ammunition, uniforms and foodstuffs were all where they were needed, when they were needed, in the quantities needed. It was a huge task.

At General Sir Douglas Haig's General Headquarters, they also had to cope with visits from civilian politicians. The borderline – or actual – alcoholic, Prime Minister Herbert 'Squiffy' Asquith, found Haig's rather austere hospitality to be less generous than he might have wished.

> Douglas Haig has some excellent old brandy, which, however, he only sends round once at each meal; after that it stands in solitary grandeur in front of him on the table. The Prime Minister obviously appreciated it very much and wished for more but did not feel that he could ask for another glass. His method of achieving his aim was to move his glass a little nearer the bottle and then try and catch D.H.'s eye and draw it down to his glass and then to the bottle. The glass advanced by stages as small as those of our attack, until, last of all, it was resting against the bottle; then, overcoming all his scruples, the Prime Minister, with a sweep of the arm, seized the bottle and poured himself out a glass. I was sitting opposite and the by-play was indescribably funny. D.H. did not notice it at all. When I told it to him afterwards his comment was, "If he has not enough determination to ask for a glass of brandy when he wants it, he should not be Prime Minister."[6]
>
> Brigadier General John Charteris, General Headquarters, BEF

The ignorance of British politicians seemed unbelievable to Haig's staff, who had to explain slowly and repeatedly that there was no 'easy alternative' magic war-winning strategy. This was very frustrating.

> Sooner or later they, one and all, bring the conversation round to the Eastern versus the Western Front problem. That is [an] easy argument but leaves an uneasy feeling that there is some very strong leaning at home towards easy victories in unimportant theatres, with small casualties and no real results. How on earth one can hope to beat Germany by killing Turks or Bulgars passes comprehension. It is like a prize-fighter leaving the ring to trounce his opponent's seconds.[7]
>
> Brigadier General John Charteris, General Headquarters, BEF

Politicians, then and now, always look to avoid the real issues for the sake of 'easy' victories.

* * *

One bane of every soldier's life was inspection by the 'great and the good'. In or out of the line, these were a distraction to their real work, but they had to conform to every possible requirement of the inspecting general, or the consequences could be painful indeed. But there was also a great deal of humour in these occasions.

> Brigadier General Douglas-Smith said to the colonel, "Davidson, I can't understand your battalion; the men are such a curious mixture. Most of them are obviously gentlemen, but you seem to have a number of absolute toughs as well. Now look at this ruffian!" Indicating a lance corporal in a goat-skin walking towards them, mud to the eyes and with a three weeks' growth, "I shouldn't care to meet him alone on a dark night. Do you know who he is?" "Yes, Sir!" said the colonel. "He's my brother!"[8]
>
> Lieutenant Archibald Gilchrist, 10th King's Liverpool Regiment (1st Liverpool Scottish)

Somehow, ludicrous things always seemed to happen under the eye of a visiting general, probably because men were slightly distracted by his presence.

> Simon Ord – aged about 50 – was one of the industrious 'young' platoon commanders at this time. Few who have witnessed it will forget the ceremoniousness of his salute. And when on one occasion the general passed by his platoon drawn up by the side of the road, Ord was so occupied with the salute that he disappeared into a 4 foot ditch of water. But the salute remained intact. "A zealous 'young' officer that!" said General Higginson.[9]
>
> Captain Randolph Chell, 10th Essex Regiment

Many stories were told of a hapless officer, watching aghast as the general unerringly picked the doziest individual in his unit to question.

> On the occasion of a tour of the line by General Lawford, it so happened that this visit followed a few days after the issue of the voluminous divisional defence scheme, the gist of which was ordered to be communicated to all ranks. This particular sentry was not one of

our brightest and best, and this individual was somewhat hesitant in the presence of one so highly placed as a divisional commander. The general fired the following question at him, "What would you do if the Boche came over?" There was no reply. "Come on, my boy," said Colonel Corfe. "Tell the general what you would do, if the Boche came across!" More hesitation and then, "Stick 'ere, and fight like 'ell!" No answer could have pleased his colonel more, and the latter turned to General Lawford and remarked, "There you are, Sir, there is the whole of your defence scheme in a sentence!"[10]

    2nd Lieutenant Reginald Russell, 11th Queen's Own Royal West Kent Regiment (Lewisham Battalion)

There was also the case of a general inspecting a 'Bantam' battalion, a unit made up of men of small stature who were below the 'official' height for enlistment. There was considerable concern that these men would not be able to stand up to the physical trials of trench warfare, as related in this wonderful tale told by Thomas Chalmers in his history of the 16th Highland Light Infantry.

There is a warm tear lurking in the story of a conversation between a general, himself of small build, and one disconcerted 'Bantam'. Peremptorily, the general asked, "Could you fight a Boche?" The little fellow looked appealingly at the staff officer and then said, "Yes, Sir, but he would need to be a wee yin!"[11]

It is sad to say that sometimes generals were thoughtless in the extreme in the demands they made on tired troops.

We were back at rest in a very pleasant little French village. We were due to go back into the line on Christmas Eve, which we didn't look forward to at all! A few days before, my excellent young batman, who looked after me, he woke me up and said, "Sir, we've got orders from the general – we've got to go!" Very unwillingly we got ourselves up as quickly as we could, fell in the troops and we set off to make a rendezvous with the general about 4–5 miles away. We were greeted by the news that he'd been and gone! He'd left behind his Christmas cards, which was a photograph of himself on his white charger![12]

    Lieutenant Alex Jeffries, 2nd Berkshire Regiment

On the other hand, some generals made every effort to put the men at their ease, recognizing the dangers of their situation in the front line.

The general did visit us in the line, arriving at our company headquarters dugout having crawled the last 20 yards, since the trench had been blown in. We were a little shy, we were unaccustomed to receiving such VIPs in our home, and we felt inferior and scruffy. His first words relieved the tension, "By Gad, you chaps, I thought a sniper would get me crawling those last few yards as my bottom's too big and sticks out a bit!" When he had sipped a mug of tea, laced with a tot of rum, and chatted amiably, we began to think him a grand chap, although he did not tell us how we were to win the war, and when he had departed, we agreed that it was damn decent for an elderly grey-haired man to crawl through all that mud to pay us a call.[13]

2nd Lieutenant Basil Peacock, 22nd Northumberland Fusiliers

As the war went on, generals got younger and younger as the British Army expanded and promising officers were promoted at a speed that was unimaginable in peacetime.

Just after dark the commanding officer came round with a youngish-looking officer, whom I took to be a Royal Engineer. He began to criticise a sandbag traverse which my men had built, and which I was rather proud of, and as I was feeling fed up at the time I suggested that the people who lived in the trenches ought to be the best judges of how to build them. "Perhaps you're right!" said he, and went off with the C.O. Soon after the adjutant rang me up, "Well, what did you think of the new general?"[14]

Lieutenant Norman Down, 4th Gordon Highlanders

Many stories are told of the Australian and Canadian perspective of their generals. There are several versions of the following apocryphal tale, all much loved and cherished.

The Army staff under Plumer had a conference on discipline at which dissatisfaction was expressed at the saluting of the Canadians. 'Plum' let it go on for a while and then broke in with, "Well, gentlemen, I don't think there's very much wrong with the saluting of the Canadians. Nearly every Canadian I salute returns it!" That brought it to an end.[15]

Major Rory Macleod, 'A' Battery, 240 Brigade, Royal Field Artillery

The following story sums up the Australian attitude to authority.

Along came General Birdwood and staff, all well mounted, and gleaming with red tabs, gold and polished buttons. The general passed along the scattered line of troop, nodding and smiling and speaking as was his wont. Some of the troops acknowledged his greeting and grinned in return, but many only stood and glowered in silence. After the corps commander had passed an officer of his staff came up to two fairly recent arrivals in the battalion, who were standing silent and glum, and asked them, "Don't you know who that was?" The two 'Diggers' shook their heads. "Why!" the officer said, "that's General Birdwood – the Soul of Anzac!" "Oh, is 'e?" said one of the "Diggers". "Well, I'm Private Smith – the mug of Fricourt!" The officer hastily spurred his horse to overtake his party.[16]

Lieutenant Walter Belford, 11th Australian Battalion

There was a widespread dislike of being forced to bull their uniforms, march miles and often stand in the pouring rain for some visiting dignitary. This could lead to resentment, even when it was to be inspected by the very man whose uniform they wore – the King himself!

It started to rain. The whistle blew and we fell in. Then we were given the most peculiar order, "Fall in and look as if you're out at rest!" We did our best. There were detachments from every other battalion in the division all down the street. Then Captain Girling said, "Now, in a very short while, round the corner of that side street will come a car and King George will be in it! When he drives past us, when I put my cap up in the air, I want you to give him a cheer!" Well, it was raining and we were all miserable. We waited a little while then the car came round the corner. Up went Captain Girling's hat – and not a man cheered! It was a proper flop. King George sat in an open car and he looked as miserable as sin! Girling was a bit annoyed and he said, "When the King comes out from headquarters in about three quarters of an hour's time, I want you to put up a better show!" Again, the King came past and Girling threw up his hat – and nobody cheered! I considered that we were being buggered about! It was all eyewash![17]

Private Fred Dixon, 10th Queen's Royal West Surrey Regiment

Generals often made speeches to their men, usually blather, laced with a cheery optimism that normally had no basis whatsoever in fact. One such was made by the distinguished figure of Lieutenant General Sir Richard Haking to some of the officers of his XI Corps.

His address was cheery and optimistic. He told us that on his corps front our troops had established a moral superiority over the Boche, and that he looked to us to keep up this satisfactory state of affairs and pointed out that the only way to do so was by means of frequent patrols and trench raids; the main point of trench warfare was to make things lively for the other side. In conclusion we were asked to remember that there was no such thing as No Man's Land. No Man's Land belonged to us, and the Boche were only there on sufferance. All this sounded very interesting and reminded one somewhat of the man who owned a dog of which his friends were in perpetual fear. To reassure a particularly timid friend the owner of the dog said, "You needn't be afraid of him; he doesn't bite!" To which the timid friend replied, "That's all right. You know he doesn't bite and now I know, but does the dog know?" Similarly, in spite of all that had been said, we were not quite certain that the Boche knew his place in the order of creation.[18]

Captain Charles Potter & Lieutenant Albert Fothergill, 2/6th Lancashire Fusiliers

Captain Guy Chapman long cherished the memory of a formal inspection by Haig, where his benighted company commander had lost control of his horse, which had bolted, carrying him far from the parade.

We had only just time to stiffen and present arms before the commander in chief was upon us. Not until he had reached the last of No. 2 Company did I realise that I was now the commander of No. 3! Darting round to the front, I was met by a kind smile and Sir Douglas's soft padded hand. "And how long have you been in command of this company?" "About 2 minutes, Sir!" was all my scatterbrain would allow me to say. "He's only temporarily in command, Sir," put in Major Ardagh anxiously, frowning me down, while I blushed and stole away to the rear.[19]

Captain Guy Chapman, 13th Royal Fusiliers

The visits by Haig were often dreaded by the troops. Not through some visceral hatred of Haig, but because of what a visit from the commander in chief entailed. It meant an attack was scheduled for the near future.

Field Marshal Sir Douglas Haig inspected the division. We were informed afterwards that he was much pleased with our recent performance and so struck with our present appearance that before long we should be given occupation suitable to our mettle – or words to that effect. Naturally, inspecting generals invariably presuppose that troops in reserve are burning for the fray and that the only reward of service is to be at it once again. War can only be waged upon this thesis. All the same, there is a certain element of humour in the supposition. What would have happened on the occasion of inspections if a general obsessed with an opposite idea had said, "This division has done well and as a reward for its service, and as a tribute to its efficiency, I will see that it is placed for three months on Lines of Communication!" It is probable that ranks would have been broken and that strong men would have stooped to kiss his stirrup leather with broken cries of, "God bless you!"[20]

Captain Charles Potter & Lieutenant Albert Fothergill, 2/6th Lancashire Fusiliers

Stories multiplied about many of the generals, but a few stand out. Head and shoulders above these for the range of tales regaled of their foibles is Lieutenant General Sir Aylmer Hunter-Weston, who commanded VIII Corps on the Western Front from 1916–18.

The ubiquity of General Sir Aylmer Hunter-Weston was phenomenal. He was fond of touring the front line, and on coming to a sentry post, to mark his estimate of the importance of that duty, he would stand in front of the bewildered sentry, saying, "I, your corps commander, salute you!" and, suiting the action to the word, did actually give the sentry a most ceremonious salute. He was keen on researches on the roofs of and behind cookhouses, while at battalion parade inspection he made men take off their boots, and exposed officers' ignorance of the 'innards' of a water-cart. That legend should gather round his name is not surprising. He was a fine officer.[21]

Lieutenant James Crossley, 1/4th King's Own (Royal Lancaster Regiment)

There are many versions of his interactions with hapless private soldiers.

He was a very theatrical type of chap, who always liked to play up to the gallery. He was going round his troops in the front line, [when] he came upon this soldier standing there as a sentry, next door to a Belgian sentry. The corps commander said to the soldier, "Who are you?" The soldier said, "Private Buggins, Middlesex!" The corps commander said, "Oh no you aren't, you're much more than that! Do you realise, my man, that you are the left-hand man of the left-hand platoon of the left-hand company, of the left-hand battalion, of the left-hand brigade, of the left-hand division, of the left-hand corps of the whole of the British Army!" And the fellow looked at him and said, "God Almighty, if you gives, 'Right wheel!'"[22]

Lieutenant Maurice Laws, 30th Siege Battery, Royal Garrison Artillery

Did this really happen? Probably not, but it sums up the typical reaction to Hunter-Weston's bluster. His popular nickname, 'Hunter-Bunter', was far too obvious to be neglected – and he was in many ways a vainglorious buffoon. But there was another side to Hunter-Weston. He had been a bright and heroic young sapper officer during the Boer War, described as a 'slashing man of action'. He had been rapidly promoted on clear merit from colonel to lieutenant general from 1914–15, far too quickly to gain the experience required at the different levels of command. This was hardly his fault. His physical courage was also unquestioned.

> During the morning light, I was up in the front line standing beside one of my sentries, to talk to him, when suddenly, Hunter-Bunter with a whole train of generals, *aides de campes* [*sic*] and people behind him, came up to me and started asking me questions about the line and what was in front of us! That was the first time I had ever met him. With him there was a divisional commander, a brigade commander, all these people who followed him around, they were obviously anxious to get the thing over with as quickly as they could. They kept on 'nudging' Hunter-Bunter, saying, "Sir, I think it's time we moved on!" Nobody really in their sense would like to dwell in that sort of position too long! To which he replied, "Go away, I want to talk to this boy!" Hunter-Bunter had no sense of fear at all, he was obviously as brave as a lion! Which in some ways compensated for his rather strange personality! He was bombastic to a degree![23]
>
> Lieutenant Alex Jeffries, 2nd Berkshire Regiment

Another general who suffered a great deal of denigration but for rather different reasons was Major General Sir Cameron Shute, who was appointed to command the 63rd (Royal Naval) Division in 1916. This fine body of men had a very high opinion of themselves and did not take kindly to Shute, who, in turn, kicked hard against what he saw as the prevailing laxness and ludicrous naval affectations of his command. In some sense, both sides had right on their side. Shute was experienced in Western Front conditions, with a far better grip on what was required to survive in the trenches facing the massed artillery and fighting power of the German Army, in contrast to the RND's previous experience at Gallipoli, which had been a tough but different challenge. He demanded that basic duties of trench life were carried out properly, that trench repairs, stores, sanitation and basic disciplines were important. On the other hand, Shute was an officious bastard, who lacked the sympathetic tactful personality that might have got the lessons across without friction. The result was that he was hated and despised by the officers of the RND.

I was standing in a communication trench talking to George Peckham about everything in the world except the war, when we were surprised by the general's arrival. Foolishly, we were standing in a blind corner and there was no avenue of escape. A rain of questions descended, which we were fortunately able to answer, and all seemed to be going well. Alas, the general had a habit when standing still of striking the ground rather forcibly with the point of his walking stick. Our trenches were innocent of duckboards and more than ankle-deep in mud. The general's stick went in deeper and deeper, till suddenly it struck something hard. Instantly there was an ominous bristling. After much kicking and scraping a perfectly good box of small arms ammunition was revealed. "Ammunition boxes lining the communications trenches," the general exclaimed, drafting out loud another report to corps headquarters on the iniquities of the Navy. "Good God, Sir," cried George Peckham, with a credible imitation of pietistic, but tolerant horror, "I believe you're right!" He stood looking at the general, who was now quite white with rage, as if he were a lunatic to be humoured and then, on some pretext or other, shown off the premises. "And you were deliberately standing there trying to conceal it from me. It's a dammed disgrace!" "Good God, Sir," says George with a broad smile, "If I'd known you were coming, this is the last place on Earth where I should have been standing!"[24]

Captain Douglas Jerrold, Hawke Battalion

Time and time again, Shute reported the RND failings to higher command, pointing out their failure to achieve the standards required on the Western Front. Unfortunately for him, the RND had several officers of a poetic bent, one of whom responded with the following devastating broadside of scatological doggerel:

The general inspecting the trenches
Exclaimed with a horrified shout
"I refuse to command a division
Which leaves its excreta about"
But nobody took any notice
No one was prepared to refute
That the presence of shit was congenial
Compared with the presence of Shute
And certain responsible critics
Made haste to respond to his words
Observing that his staff advisors
Consisted entirely of turds

For shit may be shot at odd corners
And paper supplied there to suit
But a shit would be shot without mourners
If somebody shot that shit Shute.[25]
    Captain A.P. Herbert, Hawke Battalion, 189 Brigade, 63rd (Royal
Naval) Division

Although there was blame on both sides, in the final analysis, the RND officers
were in the wrong. Shute saved the lives of many of his officers and men by
insisting – despite their moaning – on the men digging assembly and jumping-
off trenches prior to their attack during the Battle of the Ancre on 13 November.
They may have cursed him, but they were grateful as they sheltered by the self-
same trenches during a barrage of German shells that fell on them before they
went over the top. Generals and staff officers may be annoying, but they did have
a role to play.

Chapter 11

Out of the Line

On leaving the trench we saw a man stuck in a shell hole. "Give us a hand, mate. I can't move in this fucking mud!" he shouted. It took two of us, one on each arm, to move him at all. "Something's caught!" he yelled. Just then he came away from the mud causing us to fall over. We roared with laughter. Poor devil. He had left his breeches, pants, and everything else in the mud; he stood in his shirt. "What are you going to do now?" "Don't you worry about me, Sir," he replied. "I shall get back to billets if I have to crawl the whole fucking way!"[1]

Captain Geoffrey Dugdale, 6th King's Shropshire Light Infantry

Days in the trenches stretched out like weeks. The British regular rotation system was designed to maintain the morale of the troops during periods in the front and support lines, to give the lads something to look forward to, restricting a stint to usually about three days. Although it involved a great deal of staff work and shuffling of the units, it was seen to be worth it, in contrast to some of the problems suffered by other nationalities, who left troops to 'rot' in the front line for longer with no hope of relief. People can endure a great deal if they can see a light at the end of the tunnel no matter how dark and grim that tunnel may be while you are in it.

The men are as cheery as crickets tonight with the thought of being relieved tomorrow. They are at present singing and making the most fearful noise. What they like is to get a sentimental song and sing it like a dead march. The more sentimental, the deader the march. I have been fearfully tickled with them since I came here. There is only an open door between their cellar and mine, and I hear all that goes on. Three nights ago, I heard one team composing a French song and nearly died of laughter. The song seemed to consist chiefly of a list of different French foods strung together and put to music, with a 'S'il vous plait!' and 'Mademoiselle!' stuck in every here and there.[2]

Lieutenant Walter Coats, 1/9th Highland Light Infantry

The process of a battalion being relieved was also complicated: the trenches could not be left unguarded, so the troops had to filter in, with 'in' and 'out' routes predefined to avoid the communication trenches becoming blocked with men. There were also last-minute briefings to be passed on as to new threats, parts of the trench needing repair after a bombardment, dangerous fixed machine-gun lines, active snipers and the exact state of German trenches. The visit of an innocent young officer also proved the ideal opportunity for one light-fingered soldier to replace some missing kit.

> On the early evening of the Fusiliers' relief, one of our Middlesex friends, an out-and-out Cockney, was getting his kit together and was searching – unsuccessfully, we noted – for his greatcoat. At length he exploded, with justifiable annoyance, that, "Some lousy bastard had half-inched it!" Thoroughly disgusted, he was fixing his almost empty valise to his equipment, before donning the same minus greatcoat, when a youthful lieutenant of the Fusiliers advance party came along and inquired of our corporal the whereabouts of the company bomb store. As the latter prepared to show him, the officer placed the trench coat which he was carrying on the firestep of our bay and followed the corporal round the traverse. As he disappeared, the Middlesex man seized the coat and stuffed it into his valise. Adjusting the straps, he made a respectable looking pack as he patted it down and then donned the complete equipment, leaning on his rifle as he waited for the relief to commence. We were just venting our feelings of mingled astonishment and admiration when the owner returned, "Have you seen a coat lying about here?" he inquired, running his eye along the firestep and obviously nonplussed. The Middlesex man looked the picture of innocence as, standing to attention, he countered, "Why, Sir, have you lost your'n, Sir?" Muttering something unintelligible, the lieutenant passed on.[3]
>
>   Private Dick Read, 8th Leicestershire Regiment

The journey back to the billets was often a nightmare. In the pitch-dark, they would stumble through the communication trenches, with all sorts of pitfalls trying their patience.

> The night was absolutely inky, and everything was slippery from the incessant rain. The first part of the journey is from the fire trench back to the road, three-quarters of a quagmiry mile, the first half of it in full sight of the flare-loving Hun. The ground is peppered with shell holes, and seamed with little ditches, all of them full of ice-cold water. We clambered out of the trench and started on our homeward way. I led,

advancing by inches at a time, and probing the ground in front with the long pole I always carry at night for this purpose. Following me were the men, the foremost gripping me by the coat, and the remainder hanging on to the equipment of the man in front. Can you imagine us, stumbling along through the dark, and falling flat in the mud every time the star lights went up? There was something in our antics which reminded me vaguely of a beauty chorus at its best – you know the way they dance across the stage and then bob down all together, and then up and on again. Of course, our beauty was slightly soiled, but what of it? There is one great disadvantage, too, in being the leader. Sometimes your pole misses a shell hole. You don't, and there you are in a cold bath, with a muffled scream of merriment travelling down the line, "The officer has fell in!"[4]

    Lieutenant Norman Down, 4th Gordon Highlanders

On the way there might be the classic Cockney wag to lighten the journey.

Our division was on its way from the line for the long-looked-for rest. We were doing it by road in easy stages. During a halt, a pack animal – with its load of two boxes of .303 – became restive and bolted. One box fell off and was being dragged by the lashing. Poor old Nobby Clarke, who had been out since Mons, stopped the box with his leg, which was broken below the knee. As he was being carried away one of the stretcher-bearers said, "Well, Nobby, you've got a 'Blighty' one at last." "Yus," said Nobby. "But it took a fousand rahnds to knock me over."[5]

    Private Harold Krepper, 5th Northumberland Fusiliers

As they emerged from the trenches onto the open road, there was an opportunity for yet more humour.

For once we found ourselves marching along curling, instead of monotonously straight, roads, and this offered a chance to grouse that could not be missed. "Why the Hell can't they make their ruddy roads straight?" pessimist Plaice demanded. "By the time we've finished turning all these corners and twisting round in circles we shall have doubled the distance!"[6]

    Private Norman Cliff, 1st Grenadier Guards

The men would often start singing. Their sophisticated lyrics were often complex evocations of their hopes, their dreams, their aspirations for a future free of the niggling irritations of army discipline! Something like this:

When we were on the march some wag would start up a bit of doggerel:
"We won't be buggered about! We won't!
We won't be buggered about! We won't!
We won't be buggered about! We won't!
We won't be buggered about!"
That would be taken up by the whole battalion![7]

  Private Fred Dixon, 10th Queen's Royal West Surrey Regiment

Once clear of the German shellfire, they might be offered a lift in motor transport. Here is another example of the poetic soul of a young officer and the ready wit of his men.

> We snuffed the damp autumn wind and looked with glad eyes at the mottled sunset and the black line of the Monts Noirs, crowned with trees and windmills. Once more our feet were free and our minds unshackled. The lorries at Bus House were no longer tumbrils. As we slid and rattled towards Locre, we allowed ourselves to notice and marvel at the rich phenomena of the war. Half a mile short of our destination, the lorry shot across the road, hit the hedge and then canted sideways into the ditch. "Mother told you ridin' on buses was dangerous!" said a voice behind.[8]
>
>   Captain Guy Chapman, 13th Royal Fusiliers

In the later years of the war, they might even travel on a Decauville railway. However, things did not always work out as they would have wished.

> The return to the camp after the first tour in the line was accomplished by means of a light railway. This was felt to be soldiering in luxury. The little open trucks, crowded with men in full marching order, were hauled and pushed by two diminutive engines, one fore and one aft. After a great puffing and emission of smoke these sturdy locomotives got the train under way, only to come to a standstill on the first slope. No amount of puffing enabled them to proceed. The two drivers dismounted and held a conference amid the ribald remarks of the troops. It was even suggested that perhaps they had been pulling in different directions. By unloading and pushing, the train was ultimately got under way again and triumphantly reached the camp. The end of this noble attempt to lighten the burden of the infantryman was inglorious, for, on a later journey to the line, the speed down the slope was permitted to exceed the customary 6 miles per hour, and at the bottom the train overturned and shot the surprised Kensingtons

into the embankment. After this the troops marched in the usual manner!⁹

> Sergeant Oliver Bailey, 1/13th London Regiment (Kensington Battalion)

By the time they got to their billets, many of the men were not only tired but stressed. This may have contributed to one officer's disgraceful loss of temper, which did at least cheer up his fellow officers.

> Parry told us a delightful story about Captain Alexander, the officer commanding the brigade ammunition column. The column had just dismounted in a village street in front of brigade headquarters where the colonel and several others were, when they heard a muffled expletive from one of the drivers – a horse had probably trodden on his foot – followed by a mighty roar from Alexander, which could be heard right down the street. "Stop that swearing, damn you! Can't you speak like a gentleman, you foul-mouthed BUGGER!!"¹⁰
>
> 2nd Lieutenant Julian Tyndale-Biscoe, 'C' Battery, Royal Horse Artillery

Upon arrival, many must have wondered what kind of accommodation they would find.

> Troops coming out of action for a short spell in reserve had to be content with living in the open, sometimes in the remains of old battered trenches and shell-holes, often under long range shell-fire. In wet muddy weather this can be a miserable hell. Often the so-called 'rest' would only be for a few hours, or a night or two, orders coming for a return to the front line, either to the same or a nearby sector, until at last relieved for a spell in the back areas, sometimes in an evacuated village, or if lucky where there were a few civilians and an estaminet or two. I would sometimes think of my parents at home and be glad to believe that they were snug and warm, and wonder if they ever imagined what we were enduring over here. The plaintive wail of our fat little Bantam exclaiming "If only my Muvver could see me now!" seemed very appropriate and afforded some comic relief, in spite of the pathos.¹¹
>
> Private John Tucker, 2/13th London Regiment (Kensington Battalion)

The troops were often billeted in farm buildings, with the officers ensconced in the farmhouse itself, while the men would be in a mixture of ramshackle outbuildings and barns.

The Flemish farm in 1915 was probably much the same as the Flemish farm 200 years previously, and at both periods it was occupied by British soldiers. There was the farmhouse with its stone floor, quite clean, but very cold and damp to sleep on; there was the Dutch stove, which stood like a fortress at the end of the room, from which *cafe au lait* could always be procured at a moment's notice, and on which something was always cooking. There was madame, the stout and portly custodian of the stove, in a white apron and felt bedroom slippers, with a wooden spoon in one hand and a pudding basin in the other. The stove was the centre of all the activities of the place; it might have contained the sacred fire and madame might have been one of the Vestal Virgins (though assuredly she was not) from the amount of attention she paid to it; but then madame paid attention to everything. She saw that the major had the most comfortable bed, she made an unimpeachable omelette for the company mess, she did a roaring trade in *cafe au lait* with the rank and file, she understood the French of the quartermaster sergeant, she warned her daughter against the blandishments of enterprising lance-corporals, she chained the big black dog into the wheel that churned the cream, she comforted her weeping hysterical neighbour who was half-demented by the war, and she tucked up the grinning telephone orderly in two chairs and a blanket before shuffling off to bed candle in hand. She ruled the household with a rod of iron, but it was the one with which she raked the stove. Outside was the midden on which anything and everything was thrown; it supported a few fowls, a pig or two wallowed in it – and occasionally private soldiers who walked across it suddenly found themselves up to their waists in filth – and had to be extricated by hilarious comrades with poles.[12]

Captain John Milne, 1/4th Leicestershire Regiment

The midden and the dung-heaps were a focus of constant debate, with the Belgian and French farmers regarding them as a sort of birth right and resisting any efforts to clean it out for reasons of hygiene.

Dear, old, tax-ridden, law-abiding England! How I would delight to see one of your wolf-nosed sanitary inspectors turned loose in this! How you would sniff, how snort, how elevate your highly educated proboscis! How you would storm, how shriek and how summons! And how masterly indifferent would our grubby people be of you, how little would they be impressed, how hopelessly insane they would think you, and what grave danger there would be of a second revolution if you or any untold number of you essayed to remove from them their beloved dung-heaps.[13]

Captain Charles May, 22nd Manchester Regiment

As they gazed at the draughty barns that were to be their home for the next few days, the soldiers often responded in the manner which a keen observer of the typical soldier's behaviour over the centuries might well have predicted.

> The boys were at first rather shocked at the look of the rough billets that were allotted to them, and when one company was shown a large, bare shed, which was to be the temporary home of the troops, the faces of the boys registered first astonishment and then dismay. As the first of the disillusioned troops began to file in, some wag, thinking no doubt of the shearing sheds in far off Western Australia, started to bleat like a sheep, and soon there was the most wonderful chorus of 'Maa'ing' and 'Baaring' that ever afflicted the eardrums. The noise and clamour that they made soon restored the troops' good humour, but what madame thought of the mentality of the troops on that occasion has never been divulged.[14]
>
> Lieutenant Walter Belford, 11th Australian Battalion

The outbuildings were sometimes in a terrible state, not so much ramshackle as falling down, in which they were soon joined by men who trusted the strength of the attic flooring.

> The houses are mostly one floor, with hay lofts above. The outhouses, queer barns with mud walls and floors feet deep in straw. The first accident soon came, as ladders have to be used to ascend. There was only one ladder for five lofts, so struggles ensued. One lot captured the ladder, and one man ascended. The top rung broke and down he came, everyone hugely delighted. One loft was so bad that the men used to keep falling through the ceiling as fast as they reached their upper room![15]
>
> Lieutenant Lionel Sotheby, 2nd Black Watch

The men made the best of it and soon settled in. After all, it was a lot better than the trenches.

> Most of the chaps in our billet got out their playing cards and started a game of brag. One chap by the name of Sullivan had had several drinks before he joined in and luck seemed to be against him at the game. He lost what money he had, borrowed some more and was losing that when the orderly corporal came up with our rations for the next day. The food was issued out to each man and all of us, except for Sullivan, put it away in a safe place. He was so excited over the game that they were playing (anxious to get back the money he had lost, I suppose), that instead of

putting his rations away, he just placed them on a box behind him and went on playing. Meanwhile, some fowls came along and started eating Sullivan's rations without him noticing it. They had almost finished the bread and cheese, the butter was in the dirt and a half tin of jam had been knocked over and covered in dirt as well, before someone noticed what was going on. When Sullivan looked around and saw the remains of his rations, My! Didn't he swear! He chased the fowls around the yard and set us all laughing at the way he chased first one fowl and then another, swearing all the time. No more card games were played but we all stood around and gave advice to Sullivan, cheering him on in his efforts to catch the chickens![16]

Private Harry Stinton, 1/7th London Regiment

The officers' mess established in the farmhouse was a haven in comparison, and of course officers had the benefit of their servants to tend to their every need. Some of these men were possessed of great initiative – and extraordinarily light fingers.

Being a young officer, on arrival, I was told that I was to be the mess secretary – and that I was in charge of the cook and the cookhouse. I went to see the cook. To my astonishment, a charming man, apparently a good cook. He must have been educated at a very good school, he was a most interesting man, spoke beautifully too! The first dinner in the mess that I was taking over, I was pleased to note he marched in and put a nicely roasted chicken in front of the major! He then came back and he brought a dish of green peas, then another dish of new potatoes. The major seemed quite pleased with this and he congratulated me on the success of my taking over. I went out to the see the cook, Private Morton, to ask him how this had all happened, I hadn't understood we bought this kind of thing! He said, "Sir, if I go for an early morning walk at about six, and I see a missing chicken walking about with no owner, and if there's somebody left a place there with peas and potatoes not being touched – the only thing to do is to bring some back! I'll look after the cooking, Sir, you look after the village!" I don't know what he could have been in private life, but I think he must have a very superior burglar! Because whenever I took him shopping into St Omer, Morton always accompanied me with a sandbag over his arm. When I wasn't looking, he'd slip things in there without me knowing! Sometimes I had to stop him outside the shop and send him to put them back! Which he would do with great apologies to the chap, saying it was "All a mistake!"[17]

2nd Lieutenant Arthur Hemsley, Headquarters, I ANZAC Corps

Then again, some of them were utterly useless.

> My servant is none too good and I can scarcely say one good word for him.
> He is never punctual. He does not obey with alacrity. He is not smart or
> orderly in speaking and saluting which latter is his worst point. He is much
> too untidy, careless, and lackadaisical. He is also very skimpy and non-
> thorough in all that he does. I am most particular in having a clean room
> and everything in order, and his method is very jarring. Then again, he is
> apparently very hard of hearing although only the other side of the door![18]
>
> Lieutenant Lionel Sotheby, 2nd Black Watch

Even stern New Zealand officers could be amused by their servants at times.

> There are two servants on our premises who perform the duties of
> caretakers, and incidentally look after the owner's horses, parrot, three
> dogs, two cats and nine canaries. The parrot lives in the kitchen and
> talks a little English. Last week when Canterbury headquarters were
> in here, it called out, "Cook!" and the cook rushed in, clicked his heels
> and saluted in his very best manner. Then seeing only the parrot he
> turned away swearing to himself, whereupon the parrot swore at him
> too. The cook mentioned the incident to his mates, and later Colonel
> Young chivvied him about it. He replied "Well Sir, I thought it was
> you calling, Sir!" "What! Did you confuse me with the parrot, cook?"
> "A begging your pardon, Sir, but it spoke very stern!"[19]
>
> Lieutenant Colonel Herbert Hart, 1st Wellington Regiment

One amusing story of life in the billets was regaled of Robert Graves, a man
always willing to embellish a tale, but strangely reticent on this matter.

> 'A' Company headquarters was the cellar of a house. Among the occupants
> were two much made of kittens – and Graves. Graves had reputedly
> the largest feet in the Army, and a genius for putting both of them in
> everything. He put one on a kitten: it was enough! Not long afterwards
> he was transferred to the 1st Battalion.[20]
>
> Captain James Dunn, 2nd Royal Welch Fusiliers

The French and Belgian civilians had to share their lives with the interlopers,
who were a bloody nuisance, but at the same time they were there fighting to
save their country from the German jackboot. Despite a mutual interest in the
promulgation of a successful war, the two sides shared little else except a baffled
incomprehension.

Off parade we fraternised with the inhabitants and began to make our wants known in that delightful medium of intercourse which we fondly believed to be French – and which the inhabitants just as firmly believed to be English.[21]
    Captain Charles Potter, 2/6th Lancashire Fusiliers

The difficulties were inevitable, but the Tommies certainly left their mark on the language of their hosts.

Awakened by great shouted oaths below. Peeped over the side of the manger and saw a Belgian lass milking and addressing a cow with a comprehensive luridness that left no doubt in my mind that British soldiers had been billeted here before.[22]
    Private Norman Ellison, 1/6th King's Liverpool Regiment

Indeed, many Belgian civilians had learnt from the British.

He spoke sadly of everything Belgic, "Why, they can even speak our language!" he said indignantly. A few days before, while ambling in stately fashion through Locre, saluting with grave elegance the ladies of the place, he had offered a "Bonjour, ma petite!" to a small girl who was watching him with serious eyes. Swift as a bullet came the reply. "Garn, fat arse!"[23]
    Captain Guy Chapman, 13th Royal Fusiliers

There were countless grievances on both sides. The French and Belgians guarded their daughters, their livestock, their crops, their orchards, their woodpiles and their water as zealously as they could. They sold their food, beer and wine at what they considered a fair rate. The British railed against it all!

France is a fraud! Here have we been led to believe for the last 6 months that it is a land flowing with fair maidens, free wine, and flower-strewn paths. And what do we find? First of all, horrible cobbly roads that hurt your feet. You have to march on the wrong side of them too. The roads, not your feet. The free wine is in reality very bad beer, for which you have to pay the fair maiden (generally about 50 years old) a wholly exorbitant price. And they don't even seem to understand their own language.[24]
    Lieutenant Norman Down, 4th Gordon Highlanders

The British could not understand their attitude; were they not the 'heroes' fighting to defend these ungrateful wretches?

It is not our fault that we take the spare wood of the village in this clandestine fashion. One must be warm. That is unanswerable. Yet the people are so constituted that they will not sell their beloved wood! Then, what would you? To see an otherwise honest and respectable English gentleman, sneaking stealthily from one shadowy wall to another and flitting swiftly across the open spaces where the moonbeams flicker, with a large and cumbersome fence post under his arm, is not a sight one of a strict moral rectitude similar to my own, can look upon with equanimity, but when one is reduced to a choice between witnessing it or enduring the sensation of slowly freezing from the feet up, not to mention the other minor disadvantage of becoming the possessor of an enduring dew-drop, one is liable to find oneself weak. And certainly, I confess that as the flame leaps joyously upwards from our stolen fuel it thaws into non-existence the last ice of my own honesty.[25]

Captain Charles May, 22nd Manchester Regiment

Water was a particular problem. French wells were often limited in the amount of water that they could supply, but the troops simply had no appreciation of this. Feelings ran very high on both sides.

The farmer's wife, [is] furious because my company are bathing – the first time in two months – in a shed where a copper gives them a chance to have a hot bath. Apparently, she doesn't want the copper used – she's a grasping old body and wants money I fancy – so dashed in and emptied a cold bucket on the fire while the men were in their tubs, nearly scalding and suffocating them. When she tried to repeat it, the man in charge – a very civil fellow and ordinarily well-behaved – kicked her bucket on to the dung heap. She swears he caught her by the throat, but all the men say he didn't![26]

2nd Lieutenant Harold Mellersh, 7th South Lancashire Regiment

As might be imagined, not least from their own gleefully regaled stories, the Australians were some of the worst offenders when it came to scavenging extra food, pillaging the farmers' livestock mercilessly.

A tearful Frenchman came to the rough billet where 'C' Company's officers were having their frugal breakfast. He held the decapitated heads of several fowls as a kind of Exhibit 'A', and kept murmuring, "Les pauvres poules!" and something about "Guillotinees!" Black stood out and admitted that the boys had taken nine fowls, but that they were quite willing to pay for them. This was explained to the owner and he was somewhat mollified, and immediately fixed a stiff price for the slain birds; but he went off still shaking his head and moaning his password of "Guillotinees!" When Black came along with the money, he reckoned that the feed had been worth it, but he added, "We must have been half sozzled when we took the dam' birds, because we burned up all the feathers, but we left the bloody heads lying in the yard!"[27]

Lieutenant Walter Belford, 11th Australian Battalion

Even if the French were cooperative, they could never really satisfy the 'needs' of the soldiers.

It was by this time early morning, and the officers were feeling in need of a little refreshment. On being asked if he could produce anything drinkable, the old rascal winked and said: "Moi aussi, j'ai fait la guerre en soixante-et-onze" (I, too, went to war in 1871), and went off chuckling to find some wine. He came back still chuckling with a couple of bottles and helped to drink some of the very indifferent vintage. It was late next day when the troops were awakened. There was an unholy row going on in 'C' Company officers' billet. The lady of the house was accusing the old soldier of being up to some of his tricks, but the old rascal kept shaking his head and chuckling to himself. Possibly he had made a raid on the cellar to get the wine during the previous night, for the good Madame kept on saying, "Brigand! Voleur! Larron!" Truly, 'Old soldiers never die!'[28]

Lieutenant Walter Belford, 11th Australian Battalion

One trait of the French, much commented upon by the men, was their lack of embarrassment when it came to matters of bodily functions and nudity.

At one of the camps near a village behind Arras we had some rather embarrassing visitors. Our latrine was the usual deep trench surmounted by a pole supported by trestles, the area being screened by canvas. Two or three young women would arrive from the village and walk along the seated occupants selling chocolate from trays hung from their shoulders. This they did quite unconcernedly, joining in with the inevitable banter.[29]

Private John Tucker, 2/13th London Regiment (Kensington Battalion)

For some unfathomable reason, it seems that French women found the sight of young, virile British soldiers bathing in the nude to be of great fascination!

Throughout the whole battle of the Somme one of the greatest hardships had been the lack of water. The joy of endless water, clean, clear, fresh water, in which we could lie and bathe and at the same time enjoy quietness and peace, was a miraculous thing. Our bathing parties were always of the greatest interest to the inhabitants of the nearest village, wherever we happened to be. Many village mothers and children used to come out and stand stolidly to gaze at the two hundred naked men who romped like schoolboys under their eyes. Our battery clerk was a corporal, a rather senior man and essentially respectably British, and he thought it excessively improper that he should bathe naked in front of the admiring gaze of about ten girls or more from the village, so whenever bathing time was due, he betook himself some quarter of a mile away to a remote spit of land beside one of these large pools that were used as reservoirs of water for controlling the flow of the river. No sooner had he settled down to undress and bathe in a private manner than a girl, accompanied by her small brother, detached herself, walked the 400 yards, and plumped herself down beside him and almost on top of his clothes. Each time we bathed, the wretched corporal adopted the same procedure, and each time the same girl walked up and sat beside him.[30]

    2nd Lieutenant Richard Talbot-Kelly, 52 Brigade, Royal Field Artillery

There was a general belief amongst the British that the French never washed, which may or may not have been founded on fact. Certainly, there were numerous stories to that effect.

I said, "Look I want to have a bath!" "You want to wash all over?" I said, "Of course, I do!" "You English must be dirty people – we never do it!" I said, "What do you mean? You don't bath!" "Of course not, we're not dirty like that!" I said, "Can you give me that big wash tub?" I was sitting in the tub, singing away – and whistling. All of a sudden, I heard the door click! And there was madam and her three daughters in the door, giggling with laughter! I was stupid! I knew that directly a lady came into the room you have to stand up – I stood up! There were screams of laughter![31]

    2nd Lieutenant James Lovegrove, Loyal North Lancashire Regiment

The irascible Lieutenant Norman Down was also taken unawares in a makeshift bath, but at least could console himself with an excellent joke!

Here we stayed for a day or two in glasshouses, the largest in the world, so they say. In the parts where grapes are being grown the hot-water pipes are still on. My servant discovered this, and a tub, and procured me a hot bath. Just as I was getting into it along came a bevy of fair grape-pickers. Horrible confusion. Moral – those who live in glasshouses shouldn't have baths![32]

Lieutenant Norman Down, 4th Gordon Highlanders

The troops were given baths as often as could be managed, while at the same time their underwear and uniform would be steam cleaned to kill, or rather try to kill, the pernicious lice.

One day we marched in the sunshine to the army laundry which had been improvised on the riverbank opposite the sea-side township of Paris-Plages. Alongside the placid, somewhat characterless, estuary, the ugly army building, spurting steam from a regular Heath Robinson structure of pipes, supplied abundant hot water for washing our underclothes. On the far bank, against a frieze of pretty villas, a row of buxom Frenchwomen were using the stream, as is customary on the continent, as a laundry. The boys who were awaiting their turn at the tubs whiled away the time by conducting a long-distance love-making across the waters, a love-making that left little to the imagination, much to the delight of our friendly hosts, who were safely protected from this horde of predatory males by the wide band of water![33]

Private Norman Gladden, 7th Northumberland Fusiliers

Of course, there were exceptions that proved the rule.

Here, too, it was that a complaint came in from a supersensitive lady, living in a house at the canal side, to the effect that she could not look out of her back windows without having her finer feelings shocked by the sight of our uncostumed men bathing. We sent her a polite message that the difficulty could be met on all such occasions by her seizing the opportunity to enjoy the purely pastoral landscape visible from the front of her establishment.[34]

Major David Rorie, 1/2nd Highland Field Ambulance, Royal Army Medical Corps

A fine example of British tact and diplomacy.

* * *

Many soldiers had a limited range of interests they desired to pursue during their moments of leisure: to eat food that wasn't bully beef and biscuits, to consume alcoholic beverages and engage in sexual activity. Most of these requirements could be satisfied, at least in part, at the local *estaminets*.

> The Kensingtons were glad to partake of such hospitality as the village offered, and, following the day's training, they sought out the cottages where eggs and chips could be bought. These were plentiful in this rural area, and the poorest of linguists was able to demand, "Deux oeufs avec pommes de terre frites" and no matter how atrocious the accent was certain to be understood. For a modest sum, the hungry soldier sat in a warm room and watched with anticipation the expert efforts of madame to coax the charcoal stove into a blaze and cook the appetising dish. It was common ground between French cooking and English tastes – the men enjoyed it, and every French woman seemed able to do the required cooking.[35]
>
> Private Oliver Bailey, 1/13th London Regiment (Kensington Battalion)

The ubiquitous 'egg and chips' was much referenced in post-war accounts and interviews. Cheap, simple and satisfying, it was the perfect 'top-up' meal. Every street seemed to have an *estaminet*, competing for trade and flaunting their natural assets.

> The villages swarmed with troops. Every mother who possessed a pretty girl seemed to use her as an innocent lure to sell bad coffee or wine to the soldiers who crowded in to flirt with her and say things to her they could never have said to an English girl. I think the French girls who repeated and threw back at the men all the bad language they heard had little notion what it all meant.[36]
>
> Private Stephen Graham, 2nd Scots Guards

Sex was in the air, but not so much on the cards. This was more a matter of allurement than gratification, but the men were certainly keen enough.

> Pay day brought money for the first time for weeks, and a thirst accumulated over a like period. The village was studded with estaminets, and drink was cheap in those days. No. 3 Platoon passed from parade *en masse* to an estaminet close to our billet, and here we celebrated in great style, served by Madame and two buxom wenches, Jeanne and Marie. Each one of us must have asked the two mademoiselles about the prospects of spending the night with them. They did not destroy all hope for us but fixed the appointment for *apres la guerre*.[37]
>
> Corporal Harold Williams, 56th Australian Battalion

Even officers could fall prey to temptation, and they had the ability to travel a little further afield to a rather more sophisticated establishment, but really the agenda was just the same.

> It was enjoyable to jog into Bailleul on the company horse for a bath at the asylum and then go to tea at the *Faucon* or at *Tina's*. Everybody knew Tina; she was a very engaging young lady, and she kept a tea-shop with her mother and did a roaring trade. She talked to everybody, she joked with the gay ones, she took the shy ones into the garden and showed them snapshots of herself. She collected cap badges and stuck them in large sheets of cardboard; she had one of almost every regiment and a chaplain's into the bargain. One sometimes wonders what has happened to her, whether she has now settled down peacefully in the district as a godly matron. There were rumours that she was removed from Bailleul because she knew too much of the military situation from the gossip of the officers she met; there was a tale that she was shot as a spy. Who knows? But one thing is certain; she did much for the 'Brighter Bailleul' movement in 1915![38]
>
> Captain John Milne, 1/4th Leicestershire Regiment

Another young officer was able to convince himself that his relationship with an *estaminet* girl was somehow more real, although his assertions that she was 'nice' and hence not like most French girls is quite staggeringly offensive.

> The couple who keep the café have a very pretty daughter there who waits on you, and she is all the more pleasant because she is not like most other French girls I have seen so far, who smile and try to talk at once – and familiarly with you if you are in a kilt – especially! She is most demure and quiet and not like the fast French girls, indeed this one in her simplicity and neatness is far, far more attractive and would make a most excellent companion to talk to, as one could almost imagine she was English, and with the better views of an English girl.[39]
>
> Lieutenant Lionel Sotheby, 2nd Black Watch

Many of the young lads were innocent and somewhat bemused and flummoxed by these first contacts with friendly members of the opposite sex. This was all new to them.

> There I discovered a small village shop kept by a friendly French woman. She was older than I, with all the traditional fascination of the French woman, and seemed inclined to hold me in conversation. My French was

as halting as her English, but a native prudishness almost overwhelmed me with shyness and I saw gaping before me – quite unwarrantably no doubt – the most awful temptations. I beat a hasty and, I fear, in retrospect, a most unchivalrous retreat. As I walked back, still flustered by my unsatisfying encounter, my imagination surveyed in vivid terms the possible delights and almost certain dangers that could have lurked behind that shop counter.[40]

Private Norman Gladden, 7th Northumberland Fusiliers

The combination of drink and pretty women could have a devastating effect on men who were unused to either.

In Hazebrouck there were three quite pretty sisters, Blanche, Madeline and Biatre, and they ran a café in the corner of the square. I went in there and I'd been teetotal at home, all my life, I wasn't used to alcohol. I sampled all the different coloured liqueurs on the shelf at the back: Crème de Menthe, Benedictine, Carassius and all the rest of them! Well, you know the effect it had on me! I had one of these girls sitting on my knee – and I was feeding her with chocolate creams! And I passed out! They sent word to the headquarters where I was working and some of my mates came out and collected me![41]

Private Eustace Booth, 323rd Motor Transport Company, Army Service Corps

Drink has across the ages always been a besetting vice of British soldiers. The Great War was no different, and men often got very drunk indeed.

We paraded in the lane and Sullivan turned up the worst for drink. We hid his condition from the officer and the NCOs by holding him steady while standing still, but when we got on the march he couldn't walk straight and kept bumping into the men on either side of him. This wasn't noticed until an NCO told Sullivan to get in step. Sullivan couldn't manage and he told the NCO that he was in step and that it was the men in front who were wrong. The outcome was that Sullivan got a punishment and a stoppage of his pay.[42]

Private Harry Stinton, 1/7th London Regiment

The assortment of drinks available, and the differing strengths, often caused a variety of near disasters. The following story is a telling warning of the perils of drink.

I made a dash towards the latrine, which was in the rear of the estaminet garden. Getting in sight of it, I found it was already occupied, so breaking the buttons of all my trousers in my haste to relieve myself, I stooped down with a big sigh behind some bushes in the garden. What a relief! I was all of a sweat. It was now dusk and, after relieving myself, I looked up and found I was relieving myself right in front of the living room window of the estaminet, which was filled with several persons, staring at me. I didn't stop to count them but hurriedly adjusted my clothes and bolted inside. Evidently, the people did not recognise me and no one else saw me enter the garden, for the people made complaints to the orderly officer, and he sent out orders for the man to confess his guilt. Of course, seeing that they did not know who it was, I didn't volunteer the information – had I done so, I no doubt would have got into serious trouble.[43]

Private Harry Stinton, 1/7th London Regiment

Another story warns of the perils facing those who boast of their drinking capacity, proving that pride does indeed come before a fall.

Much amusement was caused here at mess one evening by 2nd Lieutenant Rainbow's effort to drink half a bottle of Cointreau for a wager of 60 francs; and this was after he had already done himself quite well at dinner with other drinks. He was successful of course; nothing would beat him in this line, but I was his unfortunate companion in billets. I managed to get him home and to steer him through madame's bedroom without any too suggestive a conversation with her but was not able to undress him; and down he flopped on his bed, dead to the wide world. A little after midnight 'crash' went the window, and, getting up with a start, I discovered friend Rainbow with his head through the broken window, groaning for all he was worth.[44]

Lieutenant Charles Lander, 10th Royal Warwickshire Regiment

It should be emphasized that often the officers were as bad, if not worse than their men. After all, they had a greater disposable income and more opportunity to seek out alcohol.

One evening three of us rode over to a little town, which had better be nameless. We dined quietly and then went out into the darkened and apparently deserted streets. We asked a traffic policeman if there was anything doing in the town. He directed us to the *Cafe de la Paix*. Outside, the cafe appeared quiet and uninteresting. As we pushed open the door, however, a roar of noise smote us. Through a thick haze of tobacco smoke, we saw that the place was packed with officers. A piano and a gramophone were both going full blast. At the bar, a group of officers were placing pennies on the marble until they were cold and then posting them down the front of the barmaid's blouse. As she wriggled and screamed, they betted on which leg of her knickers – obligingly displayed – the penny would come down. In a corner a very drunk senior officer was standing on a table making a speech. It was the town major – in charge of the town; supporting him with hand and voice was the assistant provost marshal, responsible for the maintenance of discipline. A jolly evening.[45]

2nd Lieutenant Eric Bird, 242nd Machine Gun Company

The temptation for the ill-judged practical joke is something few drinkers have avoided when in their 'cups'.

Among the many other parades which the battalion had to practise, were surprise alarms. Apart from the usual military object of these, there was the necessity for the troops to be turned out quickly into the open in case of the approach of Zeppelins. One such involuntary parade was the cause of much amusement and not a little annoyance. It so happened that 2nd Lieutenants C.F. Hall and Morley had had an enjoyable evening at the theatre. What caused him to do it he himself would probably be unable to explain, but as they mounted the steps into the officers' quarters, 'Cherub' – by which name Hall was always known – emitted a noise resembling the warning sound of a siren. The imitation struck him as so good, that he continued to repeat it as he passed upstairs to his room! Whether by accident, or intent, one such effort was made outside Colonel Townshend's room. The colonel immediately turned out himself and gave orders for the battalion to parade on its alarm post. This it did with commendable alacrity, and, in a short time, Colonel Townshend was able to report to brigade that the battalion was all present and correct – or, at least, apparently so. There were, in point of fact, two officers absent, keeping very quiet in their room. Brigade, somewhat naturally under the circumstances, expressed a certain measure of surprise that the 11th Royal West Kents should be parading at that late hour, and in due course the parade was dismissed. Reveille next morning found two young men somewhat worried and perturbed. However, they opened their hearts at breakfast time to one of their seniors, and on his advice made a clean breast of it. The colonel was, to say the least of it, decidedly indignant, and our friend, the 'amateur siren' was lucky enough to get away with no more disastrous a consequence than a good wigging![46]

2nd Lieutenant Reginald Russell, 11th Queen's Own Royal West Kent Regiment (Lewisham Battalion)

Battalions rarely had a formal mess dinner night during the war, but the 15th Welsh Regiment seemed to have made a special effort. Harold Hayward drank a little too much and committed an act of amazing *lèse-majesté* – and he got away with it!

> The battalion was going to have a 'Grand Night' and the colonel said, "Will you act as mess president?" I think I put on about a four-course meal and people were licking their lips. Everything was going quite well. Then the grub finished, and the drinks came on. We had one or two people in the band come into the Nissen hut where this was being held to play. All that they played was 'Bunny Hugging!' You had a partner and as the music struck up you got up and buggy hugged up and around with this one chap all the evening – between drinks. Apparently at about midnight there were only two 'wallflowers' – myself and the brigadier. I got up, staggered across the room, pulled him up and danced with him for 3 hours. People said to me the next day, "You've got a nerve!" I said, "I didn't – I can't remember!" He said, "It was, for 3 hours you and he were going up and down the room and everybody was getting out of your way!" That's when Jones turned up with a stretcher and a pal and carried me back to my tent![47]
>
> 2nd Lieutenant Harold Hayward, 15th Welsh Regiment

Drink helped men forget; after all, they had a lot to forget.

*　*　*

Sex was rarely freely available in the billeting areas. One way or another, men would pay, whether by a financial transaction, buying gifts or contracting a sexually transmitted disease. It is also true that for many men this all went on above their heads.

> We were, I suppose, very innocent by modern standards, right was right and wrong was wrong and the Ten Commandments were an admirable guide. There was no obsession with sex, drink and drugs. The approach to sex was perfectly normal, while the horror of venereal disease very real. A 'homosexual' was a bugger and beyond the pale. A drunk was a drunk and quite useless. A coward was not someone with a 'complex' – we would not have known what it was – but just a despicable creature. Drugs were unheard of, and I personally never heard of a lesbian until I was over forty. Frugality, austerity and self-control were then perfectly acceptable.

> We believed in honour, patriotism, self-sacrifice and duty, and we dearly
> understood what was meant by 'being a gentleman'.[48]
>
> Lieutenant Robert Money, 2nd Cameronians

Some men were lucky enough to encounter girls willing to sleep with them,
but this could cause terrible problems with the outraged families for this insult
to their family honour, as the following ludicrous story gleefully recounted by
Charles Dudley-Ward reveals. Picture the setting, so redolent of sweet romance:
a pig stye.

> My part in it was nil and beyond hearing a squeal and much screaming
> of angry women I know nothing beyond what Percy Battye told me. It
> appears he was wakened by an old man, who lives in the farm, and the
> two women I have referred to as strumpets – the latter in their night
> dresses. The old man could speak no English and was too frightened
> and excited to attempt French, so the women translated his Flemish
> into bad English and French. He was going round the farm locking up
> and had reached the pig stall in the stable, where he said he heard the
> pig grunting. He was about to lock up when the door burst open, and a
> man dressed only in a shirt ran out and disappeared into the night. He
> was sure it was one of our men. And then both women, shouting at once,
> accused one of our men of behaving indecently with the pig! Battye
> turned out the guard, the servants and some corporals and hunted high
> and low for the beast – but found no-one. All he discovered was that a
> wild figure had run past the sentry. He put out extra sentries to watch for
> the man and went to bed. This morning, the mother of the two women
> – a fearfully evil old hag – triumphantly produced a slipper which, she
> said, had been found in the pig house. Again, she urged Battye to find
> the wretch, who had sunk to such depths as to have an affair with a pig.
> To cut the story short, they discovered that the only man who possessed
> such slippers was the canteen man – of another regiment. This man
> was brought before him and then in an agony of nervousness the man
> conferred that though appearances were dead against him it was the
> girls he was concerned with in the pig house and not the pig! Then
> Percy, with true Sherlock Holmes perspicacity, remembered the night
> dresses he had seen these two creatures in and that they bore traces of
> the farmyard!!![49]
>
> Captain Charles Dudley-Ward, 1st Welsh Guards

This kind of 'free' sex still carried a very real threat of venereal disease (VD),
particularly gonorrhoea, syphilis and 'crabs', tiny insects that thrive on human

blood, especially around the genitals. There were written warnings and regular lectures warning of the perils of VD, but it did little good.

> The padre was raising his voice in order to attract attention. His subject was 'Angels' and he told the wonderful story about the 'Angel of Mons'. He spoke thus, "Yes! I believe in angels. I am better educated than any of you men, and I believe in angels. Angels do exist. I'll give you an example, one night two comrades, an old and a young soldier, were in a certain town, and the elder was trying to persuade the younger to go into a house of ill-fame; and just as the younger was about to agree he felt, as it were, a hand on his shoulder. Now, what do you think that was?" The padre paused dramatically. Instantly, a tired voice from the back drawled, "The sergeant of the picket, I suppose!" Not a sound! Then a ripple of laughter that rocked the whole battalion.[50]
>
> Lieutenant Walter Belford, 11th Australian Battalion

Barracking and laughter seem to have been a frequent reaction to the earnest warnings of the clergymen.

> The lecture was given by the brigade's bishop. At the conclusion he said, "Remember for 5-minutes of pleasure you'll get a lifetime's misery!" The sergeant major got up and said, "How the hell do you make it last 5-minutes?"[51]
>
> Private Edmund Williams, 19th King's Own Liverpool Regiment

In the larger villages and towns there were brothels, which later in the war were regulated by the British Army, hoping to reduce the number of VD infections. These initiatives inspected the prostitutes for disease and also sought to provide prophylactics to ensure that the soldier protected himself when having intercourse. One universal truth of oral history and personal experience accounts generally is that, while they may have known of, seen and even visited a brothel, they never personally availed themselves of the services offered. Indeed, many of the men were simply too inexperienced to be bothered.

> I was too young to worry about sex. The other boys used to line up for the prostitutes, there were licensed brothels to keep the men quiet! Those that were older, if they wanted sex, they were able to line up for it there. It didn't worry me at that time![52]
>
> Private Harry Wells, 'C' Battery, 175 Brigade, Royal Field Artillery

But many of the men were interested. They were in the prime of life, a life that might not last much longer, and they were keen to make the most of their chances.

> The Red Lamp, the army brothel, was around the corner in the main street. I had seen a queue of a hundred and fifty men waiting outside the door, each to have his short turn with one of the three women in the house. My servant, who had stood in the queue, told me that the charge was 10 francs a man – about 8 shillings at that time. Each woman served nearly a battalion of men every week for as long as she lasted. According to the assistant provost-marshal, 3 weeks was the usual limit, "After which she retired on her earnings, pale but proud!"[53]
>
> 2nd Lieutenant Robert Graves, 2nd Welsh Regiment

Although many jokes are made, it is chastening to think of the reality of these remarks.

> The first call for many was the 'Red Lamp', the brothel some distance up a side street, whence the queue stretched as far as the main road. On the further side stood several red-tabbed 'Brass Hats' of our divisional staff, watching the scene in amused amazement. Before 'lights out' that evening it was said that the general had been among those watching, and he was credited with the remark, "My God, if those Leicesters fuck like they fight, God help those poor women in there!" Probably a complete fabrication, of course, but amazingly morale lifting at the time! Judging, however, by the conversation before the candles were doused and the snores commenced, one of the women, by catering for the needs of about 80 per cent of our company, had earned the soubriquet of 'The Baby Elephant', an amazing performance by any standards![54]
>
> Private Dick Read, 8th Leicestershire Regiment

Private George Ashurst was adamant that while he visited the brothel with his mates, he was not at all tempted, although he seemed to have remembered the details of the 'procedure' in the bedroom for the best part of seventy years!

> Oh! So common! Oh no! No, I didn't fancy them at all! Tom said, "Are you going up there?" I says, "Nah!" Not with them things. The women were all sorts of ages. Fellows would tell you what it was like going in. She's there, the first thing she does is grab your five franc note – that's the first thing she does! Then she unfastens your flies and has a feel, squeezes it – sees if there's anything wrong with it! Then she just throws this cloak off and she's on the bed, ready for you! That's what happens.

Then when you've finished she has a kettle boiling there with some herbs in. She just gives you a bit of a swill with it – for safety's sake – for disease! But no, I didn't go up there![55]

Private George Ashurst, 2nd Lancashire Fusiliers

Ashurst does tell a wonderful story of how an evening of fun and games came to an abrupt end.

We were allowed out in the town in the evening and the boys were out to have the best possible time. Drink flowed freely in the estaminets and cafes, and as the music and singing went on the boys danced with mademoiselles in the flimsiest of dresses, or flirted with them at the tables, using the most vulgar expressions. All the evening Tommies could be seen either going to or coming from the girls' rooms upstairs, queues actually forming on the stairs leading to these rooms. During one of these riotous nights, when the queue of drink-sodden Tommies almost reached from the first girl's room to the floor below, a sudden command of "Attention!" rang out. As the boys did their best to stand upright, into the estaminet walked the battalion padre along with the sergeant of the military police. The padre glared at the queue on the stairs and then at the tables swimming in cognac and vin blanc. Then in scathing words he started to address us. He told us that the conditions under which we had lived for the last few months were no excuse for our beastly conduct. He asked us if we had forgotten that we were Englishmen, or forgotten our mothers and sisters and wives, or had no shame at all. During all this the queue on the stairs had disappeared; men left their drink and slunk out into the street, but the padre had promised to report to the commanding officer. He certainly kept his word, for the next day the battalion was formed up on parade to be lectured by the colonel. Angrily our commander rode onto parade, and away he blazed about our conduct the night before in the Rue des Bons Enfants, as reported to him by the padre. "The irony of it!" he said. "Do you know what 'Rue des Bons Enfants' means? It means 'The street of good children'." A low titter went round the battalion.[56]

Private George Ashurst, 2nd Lancashire Fusiliers

But VD was no joke. Tens of thousands of men fell victim to it.

We used to have a week's leave in Paris and some of the boys would return full of pox. On the train back, they used to have braziers to keep you warm, and one particular boy who'd been to Paris a few times said he'd sat too near a brazier with his legs open, that he had gone to sleep, and when he woke, he found his trousers nearly alight, and his privates burned. That's what he said had gone wrong, but it wasn't that. He'd come back with pox, and his penis was nearly falling away it was so rotten.[57]

 Private George Ashurst, 2nd Lancashire Fusiliers

The various treatments were no fun, and to catch VD was to be considered as a malingerer. George Ashurst recalled the medication required when an outbreak of 'crabs' got out of hand in his battalion.

We were supposed to have a bad dose of 'crabs'. I don't know what the medical name is. They were a tiny crab-like creature that attacked the lower parts of the abdomen and lived under the skin, so that if you happened to have these irritating little creatures, they were very hard to get rid of. A circular canvas compound was erected, about 15 feet in diameter and 4 feet 6 inches high, quite close to our tent. The men were ordered to go in the circle and take with them their shaving kit, then to strip off and shave their private parts thoroughly. If men could not do this awkward job themselves, then they had to shave each other. During this operation one can imagine the remarks made by the men. It was a bloody, painful, and still humorous performance, especially using a blunt army razor. After shaving, we were given lots of a dark blue ointment which we plastered all over our lower parts. The boys called the ointment 'blue unction', which we had to abide with for 3 or 4 days before washing it off. I think the shaving and blue unction did the trick. There was no further 'Operation Crab'.[58]

 Private George Ashurst, 2nd Lancashire Fusiliers

* * *

One relatively harmless pastime was the concert parties which were set up by several units. These were variety shows, redolent of the music halls, with singers, comics and, most wondrous of all, 'women'.

The officers in the front seats came in for a good deal of chaff from the men, some telling them they should be on the platform with the performers, but they got nearly as big a cheer when they came in as the entertainers themselves. The colonel was now firmly established as the 'Old Joker' and this title was heard a good many times that evening, one man actually asking him to sing amid general laughter. Hine, the adjutant, was also chipped a good deal, but save for his queer smile took it in good part. "Hi, mates, would you believe it? Look, they've sent us some girls from home!" And it did look like it. Some of the men began brushing their hair with their grimy hands, and some of the young officers were nearly as bad. Even Hine winked at the performers, though only just married. By Jove, they could sing and dance, lifting legs so high that the front rows got sunburnt, and each time the curtain went down the cheers nearly wrecked the hall. But the girls were boys, for at the last, there they all were standing with their wigs in their hands.[59]

Private Davie Starrett, 9th Royal Irish Rifles

Lieutenant Norman Down, always a miserable bugger, took a perverse pleasure in the sheer awfulness of some of the performers on offer in the shows put on within his battalion. The various comics were acceptable, but to Down the singers were truly beyond the pale.

The performer clears his throat huskily. His friends make encouraging remarks and offer useful suggestions. All power of song seems to have left him, as he stands there, a prey to stage fright of the most virulent kind. At last, he gathers up courage and starts a low moaning, gradually rising in tone until he has attained the desired key. This seems the favourite way of doing it in the absence of a piano. Once started, the song, which is of the ultra-pessimistic 'Cheild-your-father-has-gown-down-in-the-good-ship-Queen-Bess' type, seems unending, verse succeeding verse with regular monotony. You sit and pray for the end. When at last he does stop the applause is simply terrific, for there is nothing in the musical line which the British soldier prefers to a good old mournful dirge. Warmed up by the clapping, the artist breaks forth into another rollicking ditty of some fourteen verses. This time the 'poor child' has lost her mother, who has 'broken her veow', whatever that may be, and so the poor child, to make it rhyme properly, 'has no meother neow'! More applause greets this effort, but now that the child is both fatherless and motherless the singer seems to have lost interest, and jumps down from the wagon, and retires to nurse his grief![60]

Lieutenant Norman Down, 4th Gordon Highlanders

Of a far more even quality were the near-professional troupes of performers set up by several of the divisions, which toured behind the lines performing regular shows for the men.

A concert party, styling themselves 'The ABCs' were giving a show of the revue type to which we flocked for joyous relief. The company, we thought, was a mixed one, although at first, I had had my doubts, for it was strange to find so many Englishwomen in the battle zone. The actual performance immediately stilled such doubts, for the females of the troupe were so essentially feminine and had such dulcet voices that any idea of impersonation seemed out of the question. Could they be nurses from a not far distant hospital? It was a delightful entertainment which long before the conclusion had the entire audience in an ecstasy of collective emotion. No doubt a much less competent show would have had its failings masked by that upsurge of amorous feeling. Great was the shock therefore, and unrestrained the immediate laughter, when at the finale the wigs were removed to disclose the all masculine truth. Even greater was the generous applause which marked with appreciation, not unmixed with disappointment, the effectiveness of the subterfuge.[61]

Private Norman Gladden, 7th Northumberland Fusiliers

Some suspected that heads really were turned by the view of 'ladies' on offer.

The presiding genius of the battalion concert party was a wasp-waisted quartermaster captain. His soubrette was a miracle – he was rich and had his stage dresses sent over to headquarters from England – and to the sex-starved heroes he was a sight for sore eyes. What astonishes me now is the way 'females' engendered excitement among their rude and rough male audiences. Why did those Fusiliers, not long out of the line, fight for seats near to the improvised stage? To be near enough to detect the rouged and powdered cheeks that a few hours earlier had been shaved by an army razor? To decide that the swelling bosoms under the flimsy dresses were false, and that above those twinkling black-stockinged legs was a sex organ that could have differed from something they had only in size? Judging by the way they sat and goggled at the drag on the stage it was obvious that they were indulging in delightful fantasies that brought to them substantial memories of the girls they had left behind in London, Manchester, Glasgow, wherever. As the quartermaster captain lisped after performing before a particularly rapt audience, "I bet there were more standing pricks than snotty noses tonight!" Astonishingly, I suspect he was right![62]

Lance Corporal Eric Hiscock, 26th Royal Fusiliers

But it wasn't all sexual frustration; there was a very real enjoyment of these shows.

We were enlivened by the 5th Divisional Concert Party, 'The Whizz Bangs'. They gave an excellent show in the Municipal Opera House. Many of the items were topical and parodies on the songs of the day.

"If you were the only Boche in the trench,
And I had the only bomb!"
Was a delightful skit on "If you were the only girl in the world".[63]
Captain Charles Potter & Lieutenant Albert Fothergill, 2/6th
Lancashire Fusiliers

One of the experienced performers was Tommy Keele, who remembered with glee how the company got their own back on somebody who was stealing their drink, which was totally unacceptable to any decent thespian.

> Naturally, you like a little drink while the show is on, so we used to send out nearly every night for a bottle of plonk, cheap white wine. We used to have a little drop of it and save a drop for when the show finished. Every night for some time we noticed that the bottle, instead of being full, was about a quarter full! We came to the conclusion that somebody, while we were on stage, was drinking our wine! Which we didn't like! Somebody who had got a dirty mind, I should think it was me, said, "Well we'll finish the wine off tomorrow night, instead of leaving a drop left over for whoever is pinching, we will all 'widdle' in the bottle, and put it back where we usually do!" Which we did! Evidently, whoever it was had a swig at it, then spat it out, all on the floor, he must have had a mouthful of our 'wee'! We thought it very funny! Never afterwards did our wine go down![64]
>
> Private Tommy Keele, 'Ace of Spades' Concert Party, 12th Division

*   *   *

Another innocent pleasure was writing home to family, girlfriends and friends. The men were encouraged to write home, as it was a healthy release. It also meant they were more likely to get letters from home, which were much treasured, although not as much as the occasional parcels of assorted goodies and foodstuffs. The letters they wrote were censored by their officers, although they could get 'green envelopes' which they could use for more private communications and which then would only be censored at base. Thomas Chalmers summed it up in his history of the 16th Highland Light Infantry.

> Every officer must have scanned thousands of letters in search of military indiscretions. Mostly, as this source of information as to their contents reveals, letters were naive and simple, almost justifying the celebrated joke letter, "Dear Mother, please send me The Christian Herald and £5. Your loving son. P.S. Do not forget The Christian Herald." But in them

all, long or short, bald or loquacious, gruff or affectionate, there was little reference to the war. Some were amusing. "Dear Wife, you will be glad to know I am teetotal. The beer here is not fit to drink!" The Padre occasionally acted as amanuensis to those who had never written a letter in their lives. One man who had won a decoration asked him if he would write a note 'to the old man'. It was done and then read over to him. "Man, that's grand," was his admiring remark. "Wid ye mind writing the same to the wife?"[65]

There were many stories of these 'Cyrano de Bergerac' arrangements, where some poor woman was being wooed by letters penned by some literary silver-tongued Lothario, rather than her real-life monosyllabic dullard.

> A certain officer, who shall be nameless, was engaged to a fair young thing. He couldn't write love-letters for nuts but had in his platoon a certain ex-schoolmaster in the same way as himself. Accordingly, he used to copy out the best bits from his schoolmaster's effusions and insert them in his own poor missives. All went well till one day in a fit of absent-mindedness he forgot to change the girl's name. Some people never do have much luck, do they?[66]
>
> Lieutenant Norman Down, 4th Gordon Highlanders

However, even more amusing is a story from Padre Pat McCormick, who was censoring a letter from a man who was trying to establish contact after some fleeting romantic, or more likely sordid, liaison with a woman whose surname he had forgotten.

> Dear Molly,
> A Happy Christmas. I am sending this to my aunt to forward to you as I do not know the address. Please tell me your name when you write as I have forgotten it.
> Yours, Dick[67]

The censorship was to prevent the soldiers passing on details of their unit, activities and location that might prove of use to the Germans. There were many codes employed to circumvent this, usually to let the parents know where they were so that they could follow the generalized newspaper reports as to what was happening to their precious son. Private Leonard Davies was one such, and he was clearly not as clever as he thought he was as his ruse was soon spotted by an alert censor.

I did a silly thing. I thought I would let my mother know where I was. I wrote her a letter telling her all about what we were doing without mentioning the name of any place – which I knew was wrong. [Instead] I put a little dot under letters as they occurred. So, if it was a place like Bethune then B. E. T. H. U. N. E. She would read it through and see these dots – and she'd be able to find out where I was, so she wouldn't be worrying so much. Of course, this letter was censored. He [the censor] got hold of this letter and called me in – and told me I could have caused a very serious [effect] by letting people know where I was. He said, "Well, why didn't you try and get a little better system!" He said, "Well, rewrite the letter! And don't put any dots underneath letters!" It was very nice of him really![68]

Private Leonard Davies, 22nd Royal Fusiliers

* * *

Although out of the line, normal military duties and discipline continued. Any fantasies of a veritable paradise were swiftly disabused by the army.

The phrase six days' rest was really a snare and a delusion. In the imagination one looked forward to sleep unlimited, parcels from home galore, letters from at least half-a-dozen armfuls of delicious womanhood alluding affectionately to the joys of past and future leaves. One had visions of binges in Bailleul, razzles in Reninghelst, and perchance passion in Poperinghe. But in reality, six days' rest was an entirely different affair. Certainly, it began with parcels and sleep, followed by baths and clean clothes, but after that it was sadly tarnished by, "The commanding officer will inspect!" "The battalion will parade!" or "A working party will be furnished!" which meant that companies had to pull themselves together and remember that they were soldiers once more and not semi-troglodytes living in trenches and dugouts. And that as soldiers they had to stand smartly to attention, to fix bayonets, to keep the thumb in line with the seam of the trousers, and the feet at an angle of 45-degrees. And, after the morning had been energetically spent in drill and bayonet fighting, they would be gratified to hear that there would be a route march in the afternoon.[69]

Captain John Milne, 1/4th Leicestershire Regiment

Guard duties had to be done around the billets, stores and headquarters, which gave rise to this splendid story illustrating the cheery nature of the Australian soldier.

Unfortunately, one of the boys detailed for guard was about the most casual soldier in the whole Australian army, and his presence in the guard worried Fergie so much that he took him aside and gave him a lot of private instructions as to what he should do if he saw the commanding officer or a field officer approaching. The 'Digger' promised to do his best. When his turn came for sentry-go, it seemed as if the fates had heard Sergeant Ferguson's prayer, for hardly a leaf stirred in the village. But 'Jock's' coaching was not to be wasted, for Major Boyd Aarons, who was then temporarily in command of the 11th Battalion, appeared at a considerable distance away. The sentry immediately came to the slope and then gave the major a smart 'present arms'. There was no response, as the major had not noticed him. But the casual one was not to be baulked in this manner. He lowered his rifle, put his fingers in his mouth and emitted a piercing whistle. The C.O. stopped dead in his tracks and gazed in the direction of the sound. The sentry waved his hand, pointed to himself and then in his best style presented arms. The major, who was always a real sport, appreciated the situation and returned the salute.[70]

Lieutenant Walter Belford, 11th Australian Battalion

To maintain a balance, there is a story of insouciant British guards and a surprisingly tolerant commanding officer.

Some of the signallers were at one period detailed as part of the coal dump guard. After 'Lights Out' one night, the regimental sergeant major happened to be walking along the road, when he saw two forms, with sacks on their backs, making their way towards the camp. "Hi! You fellows! What have you got there?" "It's all right, Sir; it's only two signallers going back to the hut with blankets and kit after being relieved from guard." "All right, carry on, but don't mention that I saw you coming from the coal dump!" Even the colonel was human enough to shut one eye to the efforts of his men to keep out the wet and cold of that wretched winter. Entering No. 15 platoon's hut, he noticed how cosy the atmosphere seemed and remarked, "You all seem nice and comfortable here!" Then his eye caught sight of the cause of the homely warmth – a huge coke fire in a bucket. He asked where the coke came from, when up spoke one stout soul, "From the dump across the road, Sir!" "But there's a sentry there, isn't there? What is the use of a sentry if you go and steal coke like this?" "To hold the bag up, Sir!" The colonel went out laughing![71]

2nd Lieutenant Reginald Russell, 11th Queen's Own Royal West Kent Regiment (Lewisham Battalion)

A sad story was told by Robert Graves of two soldiers, Private Richard Morgan and Lance Corporal William Price, who ran into serious disciplinary trouble from which there was no way out.

> Two young miners, in another company, disliked their sergeant, who had a down on them and gave them all the most dirty and dangerous jobs. When they were in billets, he crimed them for things they hadn't done; so they decided to kill him. Later, they reported at battalion orderly room and asked to see the adjutant. This was irregular, because a private is forbidden to address an officer without an NCO of his own company acting as go-between. The adjutant happened to see them and asked, "Well, what is it you want?" Smartly slapping the small-of-the-butt of their sloped rifles, they said: "We've come to report, Sir, that we're very sorry, but we've shot our company sergeant major." The adjutant said: "Good heavens, how did that happen?" "It was an accident, Sir." "What do you mean, you damn fools? Did you mistake him for a spy?" "No, Sir, we mistook him for our platoon sergeant!" 'So they were both court-martialled and shot by a firing squad of their own company against the wall of a convent at Bethune.[72]
>
> 2nd Lieutenant Robert Graves, 2nd Welsh Regiment

On 20 January 1915, Morgan and Price had indeed shot Company Sergeant Major Hugh Hayes. Whoever they had meant to shoot, the sentence was death, and the hapless pair were executed by firing squad at Bethune on 15 February 1915.

*   *   *

Training was a priority that could rarely be evaded. The men had to maintain their basic fitness; there were new skills to learn, new weapons to master and new tactics to practice. After the first day or two, rest periods seemed to involve very little rest.

> The weather was not very good, but we managed to do many hours work, the usual physical training, bayonet fighting, steady drill, and extended order work, night compass work and lectures. The most exciting event was one of the night trainings, when Colonel Jones combined cross country running with keeping direction in the dark. The running was very successful, but the runners failed to keep direction, and ran for many miles, getting in many cases completely lost; far into the night the plaintive notes of the recall bugle could be heard in the various villages of the neighbourhood.[73]
>
> Lieutenant John Hills, 5th Leicestershire Regiment

Route marches were considered essential to revive the fitness of men who had been trapped in static warfare.

> This platoon had a sergeant who set an excellent pace and possessed only one man who could not keep step. There are always one or two men in a platoon who, unfortunately, have no sense of time or some other kindred mental defect, and who find it an impossibility to follow the regular pace of their fellows. The result is a conscious or unconscious irritation to all but the offender, as regularity would seem to be essential to our brains. To anyone riding behind the platoon, the head and shoulders of the one out of time with the rest were most apparent.[74]
>
> Major Claude Weston, 2nd Wellington Battalion

As usual, the men in turn seized on any opportunity to laugh at their officers.

> The whole brigade was in training like us. One regiment had a very small man as an officer leading and some of the men were amused by this. Jokes were made at the officer's expense who knew well what was going on but took very little notice until the joke went too far. Some of the men got up a song that ended with the words, 'And a little child shall lead you!' A day came when the officer led the men on an extra-long march, and they came back feeling tired and footsore. They had tea and were surprised at an order to fall-in for another march. When they formed up, the little officer said to them, "Men, we are going on another route march and a little child shall lead you on horseback!" The men came back exhausted and there were no more jokes about the officer being small after that![75]
>
> Private Harry Stinton, 1/7th London Regiment

Route marching was hard work and triggered a considerable amount of comment, not all of it positive!

> One heartily, and forcibly, agrees with one of our most apt Tommies, who remarked apropos of this continued route marching: "It's not the fucking marchin' I object to, it's the fucking about!"[76]
>
> Lieutenant Carrol Whiteside, 7th Border Regiment

They would practice their rifle shooting, but Private Norman Edwards was chosen to be part of a Vickers machine-gun team. It meant more training and a considerable amount of extra weight to carry into battle. But like soldiers then and ever since, they appreciated the sheer excitement of the increased firepower as compared to the humble Lee Enfield.

It was a rather heavy weapon: [a] water-cooled barrel and there was a separate tripod. No. 1 did the actual firing; No. 2 carried the tripod. Each section was four or five men. They had to carry the belts of 250 rounds. We inherited this song from the Regular Army:

'You can talk about your rifle,
You can talk until you stifle,
But it's only just a trifle,
To the gun we have now,
The Maxim of course is,
The pride of all the forces,
So just unhitch the horse,
And let the bugger go!'

You caught hold of two handles and with your thumb pressed the lever and the thing went, "Knock, Knock, Knock, Knock!" about as fast as that. You gradually traversed the thing on your target. We had a lecture by an experienced regular machine gun officer. He told us all about the elevations: how you turned the wheel to elevate it and for each degree of elevation the bullet would go so many feet further on and so on and so forth. When he had finished, he said, "Now carry on with the training, corporal!" The corporal said, "I'm sorry, Sir, I don't think I'd better take that on – I'm a greengrocer in private life!"[77]

Private Norman Edwards, 1/6th Gloucestershire Regiment

Bayonet fighting was regarded as an important component of trench warfare: the atavistic terror of 18 inches of cold steel was not to be underestimated. The men were taught to bellow out loud in the most intimidating fashion as they charged home.

Dummies made of sacks full of straw were made to look like Germans – and savagely bayoneted and concussed with the butt of the rifle. Special attention was drawn to the most vital parts of the body, and the rider was added that, "Four inches of bayonet would do the trick!" Stranger oaths than ever entered the fertile brain of 'Willy' Shakespeare were heard on the assault course.[78]

Captain John Milne, 1/4th Leicestershire Regiment

Specialist trainers rammed home the point, literally and figuratively.

The great exponent of the art of bayonet fighting was a Major Campbell, of the army gymnastic staff, whose lectures were already well known at the army schools, and who was now sent round the country to talk to all battalions. He had devised an entirely new scheme of bayonet instruction on very simple yet practical lines, doing away with many of the old drill-book 'points and parries', and training arm and rifle to act with the eye, not on a word of command. His powers as a lecturer were as great as his keenness for his subject, and for 2-hours he held the attention of a hall full of all ranks, speaking so vividly that not one of us but came away feeling that we were good enough to fight six Boche, given a bayonet. He was particularly insistent on not driving the bayonet home too far, and we shall always remember his "Throat 2 inches is enough, kidneys only 4 inches, just in and out!"[79]

Lieutenant John Hills, 5th Leicestershire Regiment

Going hand in hand with bayonet fighting in clearing a trench of Germans was the use of the hand grenade. Men were taught to throw them with an overarm cricket bowling action, but accidents were frequent.

Lance Sergeant Hart of 'A' Company took a bomb, bit the fuse and was waiting the usual 5-seconds before throwing it, when suddenly the fuse being defective burnt up quickly, and the bomb exploded – blew one arm off, and most of the stomach, head and face. He was practically killed but was supported by the sides of the trench. The explosion of the bomb set fire to his pouches and all his ammunition, about 150 rounds blew off, almost simultaneously. He received practically all these in him. Many bullets flew through him – and threw pieces of him yards away. He was quite dead now.[80]

Lieutenant Lionel Sotheby, 2nd Black Watch

Overall, the troops were not enthusiastic about the training. Many would have preferred to rest. One young officer was darkly mordant on their prospects.

We are continuing our usual training but have now got on to attack formations and tactics again, so there is certain to be some entertainment in the near future. I feel certain that the war will be over by about July 1925![81]

2nd Lieutenant Eric Marchant, 1st Essex Regiment

But they did have to train: there were new weapons and tactics being introduced and the men had to learn. But they could not be expected to enjoy it.

* * *

Worse than training were the working parties. The troops hated these; officers, NCOs and men were united in detesting the imposition of huge amounts of backbreaking – and worst of all lethally dangerous – tasks at a time when they were supposed to be out of the line. They may have been dog-weary or traumatized to the very soul by all they had experienced in the line, but fatigue duties dogged them like an avenging angel. It seemed they were nothing but beasts of burden to take up water, food, ammunition, barbed wire, telephone cables, duckboards and the veritable forests of wood and chicken wire required for revetting. There was always plenty of digging to do, building roads, improving trenches, dredging drains, laying pipes and burying signal wire; in fact, doing anything that anybody could think of. And this the British Army called 'rest'. There was minimal honour and very little credit for those carrying out these mundane tasks, as one cynical officer mused.

> The man who is going to win the war is the poor old lance corporal of the unpaid variety. General 'A' wants something done. He acquaints Colonel 'B' of his wishes. Colonel 'B' notifies Captain 'C', who in his turn passes on the good news to 2nd Lieutenant 'D', who skilfully shifts the burden to Sergeant 'E'. Sergeant 'E', intent on obtaining a disproportionately large issue of rum for his platoon and himself, details Lance Corporal (unpaid) 'F'. Lance Corporal 'F' takes six men, three shovels, and a tin of chloride of lime, and the job gets done. Then he returns and reports the completion of the job to Sergeant 'E', Sergeant 'E' steps up to 2nd Lieutenant 'D', salutes, and reports, "I've done that job, Sir!" 'I' mark you! No mention of Lance Corporal 'F'! Lieutenant 'D' wires to Captain 'C', "Have done job!" Captain 'C' sends a message by orderly to the effect that he, "he" mark you, has completed the allotted task. Colonel 'B' writes, "I beg to report that this work has been brought to a satisfactory conclusion by me!" General 'A', replete with a good dinner, receives the message. "Good fellow that Colonel 'B'!" he murmurs.[82]
> Lieutenant Norman Down, 4th Gordon Highlanders

Carrying parties were much detested. The quantities of material required in the front line were such that the garrisoning battalions could not carry everything they would – or might – need during their tour of duty.

> It is a very difficult journey from here to where we are digging, and the 'sailing' directions are like this: "Across field to haystack; bear half left to dead pig; cross stream 25 yards below dead horse; up hedge to shell hole; and then follow the smell of three dead cows across a field, and you'll arrive at exactly the right place!" The best of these landmarks is that you

can use them on the darkest night. I brought my lads back on a short cut
I devised for myself, including a couple of dead dogs and a certain amount
of one German. It is a much better way, and I got the bearing so well that
I walked right into the last cow without even smelling her, so strong was
the wind blowing the other way.[83]

Lieutenant Denis Barnett, 2nd Prince of Wales' Leinster Regiment

The loads to be carried were often heavy or of a shape that rendered carrying
them through a communication trench an almost impossible task. Private Arthur
Beatty revels in his adventures with a 12ft-long plank:

To the uninitiated who have only witnessed the carrying of a plank
along the King's Highway, plank-carrying may appear, at first sight, a
very humdrum occupation. But when two men endeavour to negotiate
the twists and turns of a tortuous trench bearing on their shoulders a 12
foot plank, the possibilities are endless. The diabolical malice of things
inanimate is well known. The propensity for bread and butter to fall
face downwards on the best carpet, and the elusive gambols of the wily
collar stud are everyday occurrences; but for absolutely fiendish cunning
commend me to a 12 foot plank. We had not gone more than 100 yards
along the trench before my rifle got between my legs and caught in my
puttee. I, naturally enough, leant the plank on the parapet and bent down
to unfasten my leg. This was the opportunity for which the plank, having
lulled us into a false sense of security by its apparent docility, was waiting.
With diabolical malice it leapt from the parapet and smote me on the back
of the head. As there were no stretcher-bearers in the neighbourhood I
quickly recovered, and we proceeded on our pilgrimage. 'Ere long we
arrived at an exceedingly sharp turn, the projecting piece being made of
sandbags. We were just thinking of sitting down to discuss the matter when
one of the men in the traverse came to our aid. Poor lad! He didn't know
that plank. "We'll shove it over the top!" Seizing one end, [he] leapt lightly
to the top of the pile of sandbags 'ere we could warn him. His retribution
was swift. The pile of sandbags collapsed, our good Samaritan was hurled
through the air, the plank swung round and hit him on the head, while the
avalanche of sandbags buried 'Ebo' Smith. I dug 'Ebo' out. We thanked
our friend, hoped we hadn't upset him, and left him seated and thinking
deeply amidst the debris of this ruined traverse. Whether the plank had
satiated its lust for blood or whether it was again a case of the triumph
of mind over matter, I know not, but it gave us no more trouble.[84]

Private Arthur Beatty, 15th London Regiment (Civil Service Rifles)

General working parties were sent forward to attend to a variety of tasks. 2nd Lieutenant Francis Buckley was amused by some 'helpful' signs they encountered.

> Here on the second day, I took a small party of men, as a working party, to the shelters at the 'Sunken Road', rather nearer the line. I think we were engaged in clearing the road of mud and generally cleaning up. On the way there I saw some rather humorous notices stuck up at various points. 'This is a dangerous spot.' It was kindly meant no doubt, but on the whole no part of the Salient afforded much of a rest-cure, and it was practically all under direct observation of the enemy. We existed simply through his forbearance.[85]
>
> 2nd Lieutenant Francis Buckley, 7th Northumberland Fusiliers

Of course, some malingering soldiers would do whatever they could to avoid the working parties.

> I used to take my platoon up the line to do a lot of repair work. It was a bright morning and we'd left the Menin Road and were marching up this plank road to go further up towards the Salient. The sun was shining right in your face and all of a sudden one of the chaps fell. I went to him, had a good look at him and when he came round, I said, "Are you all right?" He said, "No, I'm not all right!" I said, "You can find your way back, can't you?" "Yes, yes!" "Right-ho, get back!" I thought that was funny, I said, "I think this fellow's swinging it!" The next morning, we got on the way again and I was walking just behind him – he didn't know I was behind him! He had his eyes on the sun, staring at the sun till it sent him dizzy! When he'd been staring a good minute or so I gave him such a push on the back! He turned round as if to say, "What's that for!" I said, "Keep your eyes on the bloody floor! Don't keep looking at that fellow up there!" He didn't do it again! You see what they do – they think of all sorts little things! It just depends on the individual.[86]
>
> Sergeant Joe Fitzpatrick, 2/6th Manchester Regiment

Most of them kept their sense of humour to see them through, even when they were assigned to the most disgusting tasks.

> A dead horse lay in the orchard, and I had to take charge of its burial. We had our unspeakable fill of burying our dead, using blankets to collect the pieces of some poor fellows, but the burial of that stinking old horse stands out in my memory as one of the most dreadful jobs we ever had to

do. Nick, gentle, fastidious Nick, was one of the burial party, and when it
was over he sat down and wrote a mock-heroic poem beginning:
"Here lies a one-time faithful gee-gee,
For a shell came and knocked him squeegee."
Thank God we could still laugh at our trials![87]
Lance Corporal William Andrews, 1/4th Black Watch

And there we have it, the theme of our book.

*   *   *

The one time they were guaranteed a good rest was on one of their rare periods of
leave. The men looked forward to this, but they also feared missing out for some
reason. This was known as 'sweating on leave'.

Leave to England had been instituted and some of the early-leave men
were now returning to the battalion from their good time in 'Blighty'.
'Frosty' Campbell was complaining to all and sundry that it would be
just like his luck to be 'smacked' before he was due for leave. Company
Sergeant Major Gallagher had just returned from leave, and he
recounted some of his experiences in London, much to the amusement
of the boys, for he was a real wag – and a little later was just going to
his dugout when a shell landed close and a fragment struck him and
killed him. Sergeant Wally Graham had come to take over Gallagher's
duties and he was railing at the sad occurrence and the strange ways of
fate when a runner told him he was wanted at company headquarters.
In a few minutes Wally came running back; he was out of breath and
his eyes were sticking out with excitement. "Out of the way e-everyb-
body! I'm for leave! (he always stuttered when excited) L-let me get
out of t-this be-f-f-fore I'm like the 'Good Gallagher'!" And seizing
the few necessaries for his trip he rushed off down Cellar Farm Avenue
and was not seen again for about a fortnight.[88]
Lieutenant Walter Belford, 11th Australian Battalion

Another Australian was equally over-excited at the prospect of leave. After all,
they really had earned it. Well, 2nd Lieutenant George Mitchell, who had recently
been commissioned, certainly thought so.

It is impossible to describe just what leave means to the soldier. For a
similar depth of happiness, one must go back to childhood days. The
leave pass with its printed and written lines is a passport to 10 days of

heaven. There is delight, even in filling the pack with all the simple needs
of 10 days. The train is a golden chariot. Songs of joy ring in one's ears.[89]
    2nd Lieutenant George Mitchell, 48th Australian Battalion

The journey back to 'Blighty' was enlivened for two weary British officers by an
encounter with some Australian counterparts in the officers' club at Boulogne
while they awaited the leave boat. An interesting clash of cultures ensued.

> We were tired, rather dirty and we were in war kit. We had our tin hats
> and gas masks slung from our shoulders, I was wearing a trench coat
> stained with blood and had in my Sam Browne belt a German Luger
> pistol in its holster. We entered a large bar room, filled with smoke and
> lots of Australian officers, most of whom were exceedingly tight. We
> thrust our way through to the bar counter, where some boozy loons
> roared at us in mock terror, "Jesus!" they howled, "Look lads! There's
> a bloody war on somewhere!" Captain Brown swore at them in English
> and Hindustani, and I gave them the benefit of certain French oaths
> which would have caused mortal offence had they comprehended
> the meaning. But as Australians seemed constitutionally incapable of
> learning any other language but their own, and only about a couple of
> thousand words of that, it didn't matter. They were bonny fighters, but
> intellectually a dead loss.[90]
>   Lieutenant Richard Dixon, 251st Battery, 53 Royal Field Artillery
>   Brigade

As they approached their homes, many realized that they were still accompanied
by a veritable menagerie of lice.

> I went home on leave in a pretty lively condition. Aunt Maggie nearly
> had a fit when the wash lady called her attention to the mobile state of my
> undergarments.[91]
>   Lieutenant Joseph Maclean, 1st Cameronians (Scottish Rifles)

The people they encountered 'back home' were friendly and superficially
appreciative, but it was soon evident that they had no real inkling of the nature of
life on the Western Front.

> I was often acclaimed a hero – in front-line trenches the word means
> nothing. More than once strangers patted me on the back and offered
> to give me a drink in a pub; but even these good-natured people did not
> want to learn how heroes live and die. Exceptionally, I was asked: "Do the

French women who wash your clothes also mend them?" and a man said, "When it's too dark to go on fighting – are you free for the evening, can you get to a cinema?"[92]

2nd Lieutenant Bernard Martin, 4th North Staffordshire Regiment

Sergeant Jack Dorgan was one of the first of his battalion to get home leave in June 1915. He was more than willing to play up to the image of the 'returning hero'!

I took off my army issue hat on the bank side and I put a bullet through it! So that when I went home back to England, wearing a hat with a bullet hole through it, I could say, "That was a near one!" And that's what I did! Members of my scout troop were all trying the hat on with the bullet hole so that they could say, "That was a near one!"[93]

Sergeant Jack Dorgan, 1/7th Northumberland Fusiliers

All too soon their leave would be over, and they would catch the leave train to get the cross-Channel ferry back to France. However, one story reveals a treasured mishap for one officer up on his arrival back in France.

The *Victoria* came in at midnight, and the first man down the gangway was Colonel Kingdon, and I was the first car. "Oh," he said, "I'm glad you're here, Organ. I was delayed last night. There was an air raid at Folkestone and the train was delayed. Go straight along to the Louvre Hotel. I won't keep you long." It was pouring with rain again. It was absolutely teeming down. The drivers in a limousine had no shelter like they've got in cars now. It was open. There was a car screen for the people in the back, and a windscreen, but the driver's sides had no doors and nothing to stop the wind and rain coming in. I pulled up at the Louvre Hotel, coat collar up right round over my neck, waterproof cape over, and cap comforter down over my ears. There was a canopy over the pavement and several steps up to the entrance of this big hotel. He went up there, and after a few minutes he came down and opened the door and I heard the door slam and off I went back the 60 miles to Blangy. When I got back there, I was frozen stiff and absolutely soaked to the skin. I got out. Opened the passenger door. No colonel! His briefcase was there, and his stick, but there was no sign of him. Well, I couldn't think what the devil had happened. I hadn't stopped on the way – I knew that. I went round to the orderly room – it was then about four o'clock in the morning – and knocked the sergeant major up. He wondered what the hell I was up to at that time in the morning. I told him; the sergeant major wasn't best pleased. He said, "You'd better report it in the morning!" But in the morning, when I went round, there was the colonel sitting behind his desk! "I'd forgotten something," he said. "I went back for my gloves after I put my briefcase and other belongings into the car! It's a good job Major Haskett-Smith had a car, or I don't know what I'd have done. He drove me home." He took it in good part, luckily.[94]

Corporal Ted Organ, Queen's Own Oxfordshire Hussars

Most men had the joys of the over-stretched French railway system to look forward to. Luckily, they were uncomplaining – not!

We had to get out and change. We were told by the railway transport officer (RTO) that our train started at 5am. It was 4.30 at the time, so we invaded an estaminet and persuaded the patron to let us have coffee. At 4.55 we returned to the station to see the train puffing out of the station. This was unheard of. For a train to start late is taken as a matter of course. For a train to start punctually elicits comment. But for a train to start before time was unheard of, a disgrace to the British Army, and many other unprintable things. So we adjourned to the office of the RTO and spoke to him on the matter in terms of honeyed sweetness. He was a blasé young man with an eyeglass through which he gazed at us inquisitively. At last, he gathered that we were complaining about his train service, and this seemed to annoy him. "Well, you know, you fellows," he exclaimed, "I weally don't wun this wotten wailway. It's pwetty pwiceless for a felloe to get wagged like this because the twain's gone. I'm not the engine dwiver!" After all we found that it wasn't the 5 o'clock train that we had seen steaming out, but the 12.15, four and three-quarter hours late. We eventually caught the 5 o'clock at 10.17![95]

Lieutenant Norman Down, 4th Gordon Highlanders

They were back to the war and all its trials and tribulations. Many would not survive to see 'Blighty' again.

Chapter 12

Over the Top

The first thing I saw in the morning were wounded Jocks coming down.
Motor ambulances to start with, then horse ambulances, then walking
wounded. I never saw so many wounded Jocks. One of the chaps said,
"Is it always like this up here?" And a Jock said, "Only on Saturdays!"[1]
  Lance Corporal Jim Davies, 12th Royal Fusiliers

T he British Army was on the offensive from 1915 to the end of 1917.
Alongside their French allies, they were fighting to clear the Germans out
of France and Belgium. The Battles of Neuve Chapelle, Aubers Ridge,
Festubert, Loos, Fromelles, the Somme, Arras and Third Ypres marked these
years with pain and crippling losses. The Germans launched their own offensives
at Second Ypres and Verdun, but otherwise took a defensive stance, which never
stopped them from making murderous counter-attacks if a single trench was
lost. The start of a great offensive could not be hidden from the other side; both
sides knew what was coming, but that did not stop them engaging in banter.
There was nothing funny about the slaughter that faced them, but they had to
laugh. What else could they do?

This concentrated effort of our great nation put forward to the end
of destroying our foe. The greatest battle in the world is on the eve of
breaking. Please God it may terminate successfully for us. Fritz I think
knows all about it. At any rate a day or two ago he put the following
notice on his wire opposite the 4th Division. "When your bombardment
starts we are going to bugger off back five miles. Kitchener is buggered.
Asquith is buggered. You're buggered. We're buggered. Let's all bugger
off home!" It is vulgar, as his humour invariably is, but the sentiments are
so eminently those of 'Tommy Atkins' that it must certainly have been a
man with a good knowledge of England and the English who wrote the
message.[2]
Captain Charles May, 22nd Manchester Regiment

Men could not help but be nervous, but they tried to swallow their fears as best they could. At least officers usually had the chance of a decent last breakfast.

> The 'just before the battle, Mother' feeling is a little uncomfortable and bewildering. There you sit in a cosy farmhouse with two or three other fellows, feeling as fit as a fiddle and eating an enormous breakfast of bacon and eggs and bread and jam; the sun pours in at the windows, the birds are twittering to each other, madame stands by the Dutch stove sucking her teeth and dispensing café au lait, the batmen are packing the valises, nothing unusual is happening, but the rumble of gunfire in the distance; and yet you have a disconcerting thought at the back of your brain that something nasty may befall during the next 24-hours, and that this may be the last breakfast some of you sitting there will eat. Yes, it certainly is a little uncomfortable, but anyway it does not last long, and the bacon and eggs are very good; nothing like a full stomach; and after all what on earth did you come out for if it was not to fight?[3]
>
> Captain John Milne, 1/4th Leicestershire Regiment

Some men could not cope and one way or another fell by the wayside, but in doing so they took a terrible risk. It is fair to say that Major Gerald Burgoyne was not sympathetic.

> I've another man for a firing party. He has just been told off for a court martial, and he should be sentenced to death. I told him he had better spend his few remaining hours in prayer and touching him on the chest, I told him, that's where the bullets would hit him. Brutal, I know, but I've no sympathy with a cur. He is always evading coming into the trenches and I hear, ever since he came out here with the battalion last August, he has scrimshanked all he could to get out of the firing line. I expect and certainly hope he will get shot. Several men have been executed for less, lately.[4]
>
> Major Gerald Burgoyne, 2nd Royal Irish Rifles

The final countdown, never more aptly named, was a matter of rising tension. Often, they could guess what was to come – they had seen it all before and recognized the grim mathematics of war.

> The usual proportion of casualties is 30 to 40 per centum, which would mean in our case 300 to 400, of which one-fourth will probably be killed outright. Some units get off lighter, but on the other hand, many catch it worse, and I know of two battalions, which entered this battle on different

occasions, and were not seen again; the whole force was extinguished. However, what is to be will be, and I think we are all fatalists long before this. It is wonderful how cheerful men are under such circumstances, always hoping for the best, determined to do well, and throughout all ranks, a feeling that it would be worthwhile getting a reasonable wound for the sake of the change and relief from fighting that it would bring.[5]

Lieutenant Colonel Herbert Hart, 1st Wellington Regiment

The officers hoped their courage would hold, that their men would follow them, and pondered on the ferocity of the German response when the whistles blew.

I shall never forget the last half hour before 'Zero', it was perfectly quiet, and the November dawn had a sharp nip of cold to herald its coming. The men lay about the parapet of the trench through which the last of the assaulting troops had passed, sipping their warming tea, cracking quiet jokes which the soldier indulges in at all times except when very tired. We officers sat in a bunch, and one thought was uppermost in all our minds – would it be a walk-over as intelligence had promised – or had this ghastly stillness a more significant meaning and would 'Zero' be ushered in by the usual heavy counter barrage and the crack, crack of the German Maxims?[6]

Major Douglas Wimberley, 232nd Machine Gun Company

The men did not usually appreciate exhortations from young subalterns they considered wet behind the ears. They wanted leadership when the moment came, but they could do without the blather.

We were a little scornful of new officers with their eagerness to advance. There was a youngster who, when our trench was being assailed by whizz-bangs walked white-faced among us and said, "Now boys, play up, and play the game!" An old NCO said, "Excuse me, Sir, this isn't a cricket match. It's a bloody war."[7]

Lance Corporal William Andrews, 1/4th Black Watch

Often the men themselves tried to lighten the mood, taking their minds off the horrors to come. Sometimes it was talking as much rubbish as the subalterns, but it was their rubbish.

From Hooge came sounds of heavy bombardment, intense rifle and machine-gun fire, and the explosion of trench mortars and bombs. The woods were lit up by Very lights and the red glare of liquid fire. Hooge looked a veritable inferno, and at any moment 'B' Company might be ordered into this maelstrom of frightfulness. As a natural result 'B' Company was pensive, wondering what it would be like with the same uncomfortable expectancy one feels in a dentist's waiting room. At this moment Joe took the situation in hand. "We're going over the top to-night, boys!" he grinned. Give your names to me all those wanting German 'elmets, German buttons and German bay'nits. I'll see you get 'em; just give your names to me and say what you want; any kind of souvenir you fancy!" and so on and so forth *ad lib*. Joe's beady eyes twinkled, his eyebrows arched, his mouth assumed all manner of ribald contortions. Joe had never been more amusing. 'B' Company rocked with mirth. The dentist's waiting room became the gallery of a music hall. The low comedian had arrived; his salary was not a pound a week, but if ever a man earned a thousand a minute Joe did then.[8]

Captain John Milne, 1/4th Leicestershire Regiment

The better officers realized that the men needed cheering up, not exhortations. Jokes, any joke, anything to take their minds off the German 5.9in shells and machine guns.

I started off again to go down the line and pass the time of day with all I came across. This meant sitting in endless shell-holes and cracking foolish jokes with the men, "Mind you wake up when the barrage starts!" "I hope your bayonet is sharp!" and so on. As 'Zero' time drew near, I saw that my revolver was loaded, a rifle also fully loaded with one in the breach and bayonet fixed slung over my shoulder, my gas mask in the alert position under my chin and my coat collar turned up and last, but by no means least, having seen that my pipe was going properly! I found the men that were coming with me all ready and anxious in a way to be over the top and over the suspense of waiting for 'Zero'. I told them that immediately the first shot of the barrage was heard they were to follow me as we must hurry to come up with the rest of the company. I do not think that any of us were at all 'windy' but the last few moments before an attack when one rather expects to be killed or wounded are somewhat tense. As usual I suppose I made damn silly jokes, generally in very questionable taste.[9]

Captain Alexander Stewart, Cameronians (Scottish Rifles)

Let the last word lie with some insouciant Cockney.

An attack was to be made by our battalion at Givenchy in 1915. The Germans must have learned of the intention – for 2-hours before it was due to begin, they sent up a strong barrage, causing many casualties. Letters and cards, which might be their last, were being sent home by our men, and a Cockney at the other end of our dugout shouted to his mate, "Harry, how d'yer spell 'delightful'?"[10]

    Private Henry Mason, 23rd London Regiment

The British barrage, on which their hopes of surviving the day generally rested, was a stupendous thing by the last years of the war. It certainly knocked Signaller Dudley Menaud-Lissenburg off his perch and into a veritable slough of despond!

It was in the early morning and a miserably wet day. I was sitting on the pole in the lavatory over a deep and narrow trench, with a sand-bagged roof supported by spars of timber overhead, situated at the end of a long communication trench running parallel to and 20 yards in rear of the line of guns. I, of course, knew the barrage was to commence that day, but with other personal matters on my mind I sat on the pole in contemplation and alone. The silence was indeed eerie! Suddenly, as if struck by an earthquake, the ground shook and the roof fell in, as hundreds of guns opened fire simultaneously. I extricated myself from the debris. Seeing blood on the shoulder of my jacket from a wound somewhere on my head, which was numbed, I panicked for a moment. I heard the lads at the guns lustily cheering and hurried to the command post, hoisting my slacks the while. Here I found Gunner Roach seated at the telephone, "What happened to you?" he enquired, as he looked at my blanched face and bleeding head. "Is it a 'Blighty'?" I asked. "No!" he replied as he examined the wound. "It's only a scratch on the lobe of your ear!" I must confess I was disappointed, but relieved.[11]

    Signaller Dudley Menaud-Lissenburg, 97th Battery, 147 Brigade, Royal Field Artillery

Then the men went over the top. As they did so, the German shells would crash down onto No Man's Land, creating a deadly wall it seemed impossible to penetrate.

Good God yes you were nervous because you expected at any moment one would be for you. Well you prayed to God, definitely! If a man tells you he hasn't then I think he tells lies. I did! I was always a little bit religious but that was the time when you really prayed hard to your 'Maker' to save you. When you got in a real bad barrage, normally you never bothered, once it had lifted you were back to your old self again. That fear didn't stay with you.[12]

    Private Ernie Rhodes, 21st Manchester Regiment

Heavy rifle and machine-gun fire was never funny, but the lucky ones reached the German front line.

> The enemy's built-up trenches were almost obliterated by the heavy fire of our guns. Trunks of trees were lying across them, anyhow, and the whole of the ground had been pulverised by shells. One badly wounded German lay writhing in agony on the ground near where we stopped. He was evidently past help. One of the signallers who had managed to get a little more than his share of rum issue, was desirous of shooting the dying German. "Bastard!" he called him, but we put a stop to that business. I saw two bullets strike the wounded German immediately afterwards and he ceased to move – so evidently someone had no scruples about it. Possibly (but not probably) someone shot him to 'put him out of his misery'. However, there were many men who shot down any of the enemy, regardless of circumstances – wounded or prisoners it made no difference – and it was noticeable that the men who did that sort of thing were loudest in condemning the German atrocities. Two wrongs evidently made a right with them.[13]
> Signaller Sydney Fuller, 8th Suffolk Regiment

Often, senior battalion officers were not far behind the men, needing to maintain some semblance of command and control in chaotic circumstances.

> Here I found a number of 'C' Company who were evidently not quite sure what their next action was, for I heard one man say, "Well, what do we do now?" I shouted out, "Now, my lads, you'll take the ruddy village," at which they laughed and clambered out of the trench with me.[14]
> Lieutenant Colonel Bernard Prior, 9th Norfolk Regiment

After September 1916, the infantry often had the support of tanks. These lumbering beasts brought a new dimension to warfare. Inside a tank was a noisy, smelly, cramped environment.

> It had a driver who worked the pedals and accelerator and so on, [and] an officer who sat beside him and worked the brakes. Then there were two men at the back – one on each side of the centre portion of the tank because on each side there was a gearing which was called a secondary gearing, so you could drive if you liked with one side of the tank in top gear and the other side in second gear – the result would be, of course, that the tracks would move unevenly and the tank would

swing in its movement and that was the chief method of turning. You had to put the clutch out and get the man at the back to put the appropriate gear in. It was a very tricky business. There were two other men on each side. A man with a six-pounder gun and the other with a machine-gun. So there were eight men in that tank altogether. There wasn't that much room for dancing![15]

Captain Mark Dillon, 'B' Battalion, Tank Corps

The infantrymen were ambivalent towards the tanks. They welcomed the support when held up by German barbed wire or strongpoints; after all, who wouldn't? But they also considered that the tanks attracted shellfire, so generally tried to keep their distance. However, there were exceptions to this general rule, as this possibly apocryphal story might indicate:

A German field gun was trying to hit one of our tanks, the fire being directed no doubt by an observation balloon. On the top of the tank was a Cockney infantryman getting a free ride and seemingly quite unconcerned at Jerry's attempts to score a direct hit on the tank. As the tank was passing our guns a shrapnel shell burst just behind it and above it. We expected to see the Cockney passenger roll off dead. All he did, however, was to put his hand to his mouth and shout to those inside the tank: "Hi, conductor! Any room inside? It's raining!"[16]

Bombardier Ambrose Boughton, 'B' Battery, Honourable Artillery Company

During an attack, tragic incidents abounded. Lieutenant Robert Graves told a poignant story of one attack and gives an indication of how the men coped.

My mouth was dry, my eyes out of focus, and my legs quaking under me. I found a water-bottle full of rum and drank about half a pint; it quieted me, and my head remained clear. Samson lay groaning about 20 yards beyond the front trench. Several attempts were made to rescue him. He had been very badly hit. Three men got killed in these attempts; two officers and two men, wounded. In the end his own orderly managed to crawl out to him. Samson waved him back, saying that he was riddled through and not worth rescuing; he sent his apologies to the company for making such a noise. We waited a couple of hours for the order to charge. The men were silent and depressed; only Sergeant Townsend was making feeble, bitter jokes about the good old British Army muddling through, and how he thanked God we still had a Navy.[17]

Lieutenant Robert Graves, 2nd Royal Welch Fusiliers

But there were amusing situations, with unlikely men thrown into the front line of battle, where they performed incredible feats – almost despite themselves. 2nd Lieutenant Reginald Russell long remembered the contribution of their latrine orderly in one desperate action!

> The 'employed man' of 'D' Company, who, by some mischance, found himself with his company on the tapes ready for the fray. Really, he should have been left with the 'details', having had much less experience of weapons of war, than of articles of sanitary utility. Never having had the use of a 'P' bomb explained to him, he found himself somewhat at a loss when, during the advance, he came across a deep dug-out, with a German officer about to mount the steps from below. The latter, noticing the bomb in Private Blank's hand, made sign of surrender and shouted in English up the steps, "Don't throw the bomb, and I will bring my men up, too!" Little did he realise that Private Blank was feeling in much more of a quandary than he, not knowing how to make the bomb explode if he wanted to![18]
>
> 2nd Lieutenant Reginald Russell, 11th Queen's Own Royal West Kent Regiment (Lewisham Battalion)

Once the killing had stopped, prisoners were thoroughly searched, often not so much for weapons – although that was an obvious consideration – but for valuables and souvenirs.

> We reached the lip of this enormous crater and lying around were many German bodies. As we went a bit further along, they began to come out from deep dugouts and throw their stick bombs. I got near enough to the entrance of the dugout to call down to them in German to surrender and they came up, hands up, quite calmly. My little corporal was standing there ushering them out and helping himself to their watches and other equipment – on the basis that somebody would get it and it might as well be him. He was a real Bermondsey boy![19]
>
> 2nd Lieutenant Arthur Hemsley, 12th East Surrey Regiment

The most coveted souvenirs were the pickelhaube helmets worn by the German infantry in the first years of the war. A chance to gain one of these was not usually to be missed.

> The dead had fallen in many strange, grotesque postures, some on their hands and knees as if they were praying. I did have a bit of a scrounge round though. I thought I might get one of those belts with '*Gott mit uns*'

on it or perhaps one of those Prussian helmets. I did come across one bloke, but when I lifted his helmet half the top of his nut was in it – it was full of brains like mincemeat. I'm not very squeamish, but I didn't fancy scraping that out.[20]

  Private Albert Conn, 8th Devonshire Regiment

Once the dugouts were cleared, these were a promising area for a diligent search.

Two or three of us went down in a fine German dugout. There were cigars, tinned food and German helmets. We all took a helmet, cigars and tobacco [but] coming out with these German helmets on we ran straight into our captain. "Yes," he said, "you all look very nice, but get some fucking digging done!"[21]

  Private Albert Andrews, 19th Manchester Regiment

If the advance was successful, then the field guns would move forwards. This could be backbreaking physical labour, and the acerbic Major Neil Fraser-Tytler happened upon a ready solution, although it was strictly against the rules of war.

We were due to cease firing and advance at 06.20, so at that hour, the backs of the gunpits having previously been pulled down, we started the **heavy** labour of man-handling the guns out of their sunk pits. Luckily at that very moment a Highlander came down the track escorting twenty-five prisoners. I called to him to go into the cookhouse and have some tea, and to hand over his rifle and the prisoners to my tender mercies. The Huns was sending over some 8-inch shell and when I ordered the prisoners to man the drag-ropes they started to argue that they ought not to be made to do it, but the arguments only lasted 30 seconds; the well-known sound of a rifle bolt going to full cock and a few well-chosen words of abuse learnt on a Pomeranian barrack square, quickly got them to work, and meanwhile our gunners were safely under cover and able to have breakfast.[22]

  Major Neil Fraser-Tytler, 'A' Battery, 150 Brigade, Royal Field Artillery

Once taken back behind the front lines, prisoners were generally well treated. However, Major David Rorie tells an amusing story of how some German officers' complaints were subtly defused:

On the evening of the 14th, a batch of some half dozen Boche officers was temporarily left in our charge until an assistant provost marshal guard was available to remove them back. We stuck them under a guard of our own in the much-battered part of our building which faced the enemy lines. Shortly afterwards I got a message asking for an interview. On entering their quarters there was much heel-clicking and saluting; and a fat, walrus-faced fellow who spoke semblable English asked, "Are you aware, sir, that we are German officers?" I murmured politely that the fact was obvious. "Are you aware, sir, that this room is not suitable accommodation for German officers?" "If you'd sent word you were coming, we'd have had it repaired!" The effect was magical! Walrus-face beamed and translated the remark to his brethren, who all saluted with pleased smiles, while their interpreter observed in the most amiable manner: "Do not further apologise!" I replied that I would not; and, looking in later, found them in very audible enjoyment of some liquid nourishment from the soup kitchen. The incident was happily closed.[23]

Major David Rorie, 1/2nd Highland Field Ambulance, Royal Army Medical Corps

But even if they were successful, the attacking troops usually faced a German counter-attack in the very near future. The British often boasted of their prowess with the 'cold steel', but the prospect of imminent close-quarters fighting tested that confidence to the limit.

You saw the Germans coming to you with fixed bayonets. The old sergeant who had been out since Mons, he said, "By God, Pat, if they get any nearer, we'll have to go and meet them with the bayonet!" I thought, "Right! I've got a round in my breech, in case I miss him with the bayonet, I can shoot him! Just pull the trigger [and] catch him that way!" But they got very near on top of us – a few feet away from us and they were coming full pelt, yelling at the top of their voices. It's a nasty feeling to think of these big Germans, all picked men, they were regular troops, done years and years conscript service.[24]

Private Pat Kennedy, 18th Manchester Regiment

After the battle had finished, what was left was a scene of true devastation: trees smashed to matchwood, buildings reduced to brick dust, debris everywhere. And amidst it, this gem.

Even in that hell of destruction, the British sense of humour was not wholly absent. In the middle of the village street lay a huge unexploded 15-inch shell, weighing about a ton. Some humourist had risked his life to linger and chalk on it, "Not to be taken away!"[25]

2nd Lieutenant Eric Bird, 144th Machine Gun Company

There was also a black humour.

> We dismounted and walked up the road to what had been the village of Fricourt. No wall seemed left more than man-high and on each side was mud and shell-holes and the woodwork thrown askew of once well-built trenches. Our guide asked the way of one of those. "Turn right by the dead major!" he was told. We went on and the road became narrower, and less distinguishable as a road. Dead men began to appear, and they seemed all to be British, and their faces looked pale green. Why, I wondered – gas, or the effect of fumes? Then we came to the dead major. He lay with his eyes open, and they were very blue, and his arm was flung out and on it showed plainly the crown and three stripes on his sleeve – he was making a most easily recognizable signpost.[26]
>
> 2nd Lieutenant Harold Mellersh, 2nd East Lancashire Regiment

When weeks or months later the French civilians were able to return to their homes, they often had little or nothing to return to.

> The French were immensely pleased at regaining part of their lost territory, though it was a pathetic sight to see some of the old people coming to look at the piles of bricks which had once been their homes. Two ladies came to Gommecourt with a key, little thinking that so far from finding a lock they would find not even a door or door-way – there was not even a brick wall more than 2 feet high.[27]
>
> Lieutenant John Hills, 5th Leicestershire Regiment

Then of course there were the wounded. Wounds ranged in severity, but the lightly wounded were generally regarded with some envy as, despite the obvious pain, they had the much craved 'Blighty Wound'.

> Near here the infantry were now digging themselves in and as we arrived one of their officers was having a slight wound dressed. The wound was situated in that region admirably suited for youthful chastisement and his breeches were down around his knees. We all laughed at the sight and he smiled back at us good humouredly.[28]
>
> Gunner Ivor Hanson, 311 Brigade, Royal Field Artillery

One delightful story indicates some of the resentment felt by front-line troops towards those who served behind the lines. This may not have been fair, but it was a natural reaction, especially in the aftermath of a battle.

> A Gordon Highlander, who, making his way back wounded from the fight, with bandaged head and arm in a sling, his kilt and hose all torn and bloody, came across a trooper of the mounted police standing in the shelter of the old church at Vermelles. As the wounded man slowly made his way past, the M.P., while he gazed at the wounds, the dirt and trickling blood of the 'kiltie', said in a condescending manner, "Some fight, Jock!" "Aye", said the Gordon, taking the cigarette from his lips, as he eyed the other up and down, from the red band on his hat to the polished boots and spurs on his feet, "and some don't."[29]
>
> Lance Corporal John Jackson, 6th Cameron Highlanders

Often men were completely unaware as to what had happened to their comrades in the press of battle.

> I regained consciousness to find myself among assorted dead bodies, including a German sergeant-major wearing a tasselled sword bayonet. His helmet with the gold eagle was in good condition except for the bullet hole in front. I don't know how long I'd been lying there and in my dazed state I tied helmet and bayonet on to me. I then crawled away from shell hole to shell hole. A British soldier, one of the walking wounded, gave me a hand in finding a first field dressing station. At the end of the war, I returned to Johannesburg and looked up an old comrade. I had grown a moustache and had filled out a bit. "What's your name?" he asked. "Bob Grimsdell, surely you know that!" "Now look", said my old comrade, "I'm sick and tired of you bums coming the old soldier trick and trying to make an easy quid, you just fuck off before I throw you out – it happens that I was next to Bob Grimsdell when he was killed at Delville!" So I just went. Our family joke, "Were you in Delville Wood?" "Yes, I was killed there!"[30]
>
> Private Bob Grimsdell, 4th South African Infantry

Before he was commissioned, Private Harold Hayward was wounded when acting as his colonel's runner. In the scheme of things, his wound was not that serious, but for a young man it was very worrying.

> A German left behind in one of their deep dugouts that hadn't been bombed had come up, seen the colonel and let fly. As soon as that had happened, he would walk on down towards our reserve lines and give himself up as a prisoner of war and no-one would have known. I was wounded in the scrotum. The bullet had come up off the ground and carried dirt with it, went through a cigarette tin and went through me.

I was carried by Lieutenant Fitz to the dugout. I never lost consciousness. Lieutenant Fitz, he did put my field dressing on me and he reassured me that nature provides two – like it provides two eyes. Well, I'm now a father![31]

Private Harold Hayward, 12th Gloucestershire Regiment

Hayward was evacuated back to England and hospitalized. However, he became irritated by the persistent questioning by one of the female visitors. His final retort was much treasured.

In this ward there was a lady from one of the 'County' families who used to come once a week. She was rather nosey – wanted to know everything. Her first visit after I was there she said, "Where was I wounded?" because of course she couldn't see any bandages and I just pointed down under the bedclothes hoping that would be sufficient. The next week she came she said, "Where were you wounded?" I knew what she was after and I said, "Guillemont!" It wasn't the particular place she wanted to know, but where the wound actually was, which being under the bed clothes she couldn't see. Finally, the next week she pointed and said, "But where are you wounded?" I was a bit fed up with this continual questioning and so I said, "Madam, if you'd been wounded where I've been wounded; you wouldn't have been wounded at all!" All the rest of the fellows in the ward guffawed somewhat loudly and she stalked out of the ward not to come back again while I was there.[32]

Private Harold Hayward, Lincoln General Hospital

Hospital visitors could be a real trial, as the bona fide Australian hero Lieutenant Albert Jacka discovered when he was badly wounded and hospitalized in England. His comrades were devastated when they later saw reports of his death in a newspaper. The explanation was simple!

What has finished him has been the kind attentions of all the old ladies in England – and not only of the old Indies, by any means; some very attractive girls found their way to his bedside. Bert, as you know, was never a ladies' man, and he had very soon had as much attention as he could put up with. One day some of us were sitting around his bed when a request to see him came from a reporter of one of the London daily newspapers. Bert turned to one of the chaps. "Go to the door and tell the beggar I'm dead!" The result was something we didn't bargain for – a big, black headline – 'Death of Jacka. Australia's First V.C. Winner Dies of Wounds.' But Bert's far from dead, don't worry.[33]

Sergeant Edgar Rule, 14th Battalion A.I.F.

The seriously wounded faced a life as a cripple, yet Captain John Staniforth's thoughts were not on their misfortune, but on a rather more pragmatic concern.

> 'One of the patients in this ward had an amputation yesterday. It occurred to me for the first time to wonder, as I sat and watched the sunset, what they do with amputated arms and legs and things after the operation. Are they given to the cat, or what? I wondered for an hour but came to no conclusion.[34]
>
> Captain John Staniforth, 4th London General Hospital, Ruskin Park

It is evident that Great War veterans had their own means of distracting themselves from the horrors that surrounded them.

Chapter 13

Advance to Victory, 1918

I am faced with this position. I have collected all bombs and small arms ammunition from casualties. Everyone has been used. I am faced with three alternatives: (a) 'To stay here with such of my men as are alive and be killed', (b) "To surrender to the enemy'. (c) To withdraw such of my men as I can. Either of these first two alternatives is distasteful to me. I propose to adopt the latter.[1]

Captain Sparks, 1/14th London Regiment (London Scottish)

In 1918, the collapse of the Russians meant that the Germans could launch a series of stunning attacks on the Western Front in the 'Spring Offensives'. This was their last chance to win the war before the arrival of the Americans, who had joined the Allies in April 1917, but would not be able to mobilize significant strength until the summer of 1918. These offensives had much in common. The German tactic of a stupendous *Feuerwalze* bombardment – aimed not only at the front lines, but also intent on devastating the British artillery gun positions and isolating the various headquarters – was not particularly innovative, but it was superbly executed. This time the British troops were thoroughly exhausted by the war, as one anonymous poet reflected in 1917.

It must be so – it's wrong to doubt
The Voluntary system's best
Your conscript, when you've dug him out
Has not the happy warrior's zest.
Because it seemed the thing to do
I joined with other volunteers
But well, I don't mind telling you I didn't reckon for three years.
Though we observe the Higher Law
And though we have our quarrel just
Were I permitted to withdraw
You wouldn't see my arse for dust.[2]

Even at this late stage of the war, humour was still an important mental protection to their sanity, as typified in one soldier's reaction to the legend of the Albert Golden Madonna statue which had been leaning forward almost at right angles to the perpendicular, leading to the belief that when the statue fell to the ground the war would end.

> The legend was that the day this Madonna fell the war would finish. I was always a bit of a comic and I says, "Why, we'll sharp rectify that!" One fellow says, "How's that?" 'Let's knock it down now – then the war will finish!"[3]
> Signaller George Cole, 'C' Bty, 253 Brigade, Royal Field Artillery

The British knew the Germans were going to attack, but not when exactly. It was a tense situation, brilliantly summarized in R.C. Sheriff's masterpiece *Journey's End*. But not all took it as seriously as they might.

> The following situation report is quoted. It was sent in morse in the usual manner to Battalion Headquarters by Captain F.W. Heath, MC, commanding 'C' Company, where it caused much amusement. Needless to say, it was not forwarded officially to Brigade.
> 'C' COMPANY SITUATION REPORT, 9/2/18
> There is nothing I can tell you,
> That you really do not know.
> Except that we are on the ridge,
> And Fritz is down below.
> When's old Fritz coming over?
> Does the general really know?
> The colonel seems to think so,
> The captain tells us "No!"
> When's someone going to tell us,
> We can "stand to" as before?
> An hour at dawn and one at dusk,
> Gawd Blimey, who wants more?[4]
> Sergeant Oliver Bailey, 1/13th London Regiment (Kensington Battalion)

When the Germans struck, those in the front lines were killed or rendered almost helpless by the power of the bombardment. They were soon surrounded and taken prisoner. The shattered remnants fell back as best they could. As some of the infantry retreated, they had practical considerations in mind: the abandoned stores and canteens that they passed *en route* were a lure many could not resist.

Here we see the British 'Tommy' at his irrepressible best. Tired and worn, he pauses for a rest. Some bright spirit lights upon a quartermaster's store filled with all manner of change of raiment. Lo! The Boche are but 2,000 yards away and coming on fast. But "Tommy" strips himself stark-naked and shouts with glee as he dons clean vest, shirt, pants, socks and what-not! One man has an armful of clean towels which he doles out to every man that passes. I gladly accept the offer of a pair of new socks, and a boon they prove, for my feet are already blistered and painful.[5]

2nd Lieutenant Frank Warren, 17 King's Royal Rifle Corps

The canteens also contained copious amounts of alcohol, which added a temptation that, across the ages, the average British soldier had rarely resisted.

The columns suddenly came upon scattered units of the famous 51st Highland Division, in groups of ten or twelve with walking wounded among them, very battle-stained, but in high humour for they had evidently helped themselves to abandoned YMCA stores. They carried in their arms a varied assortment of articles: shirts, socks, pants, bottles of wine, tins of beer, cases of whisky, boxes of cigarettes, cigars. The officers were not immune either! Some of the Scots had drunk too much and gave voice to their favourite ditties as they ambled or staggered by. From their unwashed weary faces and bedraggled kilts it was obvious to our curious gaze that continuous fighting and lack of sleep had taken their toll, hence no-one could begrudge them this demonstration of elation now that tension was relaxed as they streamed down the hill from the vicinity of Hardecourt. Andy Swanson hailed a tall lean Highlander, who carried a Lewis gun over his left shoulder and a pile of cigarette tins under his right arm, with a fancy shawl under his tin hat which added a comic touch, "Where's the auction, Mac?" The Scot relieved himself of the gun for a moment and jerked his thumb over his shoulder, "Yon storeman told us to help ourselves before they fired the canteen and we couldn't leave this loot to the bastard Germans!"[6]

Private Edward Williamson, 17th Royal Scots

When the Germans broke through, there was considerable panic in the rear areas. The German storm troopers had swiftly earned themselves a stellar reputation for their infiltration skills, which was then further enhanced by the creative power of rumour.

Huns, disguised as British officers on motorcycles, had got through into the back areas. They caused one or two serious panics by ordering villagers to clear out at once, shouting that the Hun cavalry was at hand. As may be imagined, when once a mass of motor lorries starts stampeding down a road it is not the easiest matter in the world to check them, especially when the darkness is such that it may be felt. So, at several cross-roads we posted piquets. Some staff officer asked one of my piquets what orders I had given them. The NCO replied, "The major said we were just to shoot everybody making alarm or spreading despondency, and most particularly to shoot officers!"[7]

Major Neil Fraser-Tytler, 150 Brigade, Royal Field Artillery

During the chaos there were also telling examples of the supposed national characteristics of both British soldiers and their Australian comrades.

We found a girls' high school, with beautiful beds, girls' clothes, wigs, paint and powder. A number of the men were putting on wigs, trying on the clothes, lying on the beds in their filthy, lousy clothes and enjoying every minute of it. All at once, an Australian officer, who was drunk, dropped in on us. He shouted, "Have you gone stark raving mad? Do you know that the Germans are only a quarter of a mile away, in full force, or are you just playing about, forgetting that there is a war on?" So saying, he fell, dead drunk, to the floor and was collected by his servant.[8]

Driver Rowland Luther, 'C' Battery, 92 Brigade, Royal Field Artillery

Perhaps the undying spirit and sense of the ridiculous possessed by the British soldier is exemplified by this anecdote.

Little 'Ginger' was the life and soul of our platoon until he was wounded on the Somme in 1918. As he was carried off to the dressing-station he waved his hand feebly over the side of the stretcher and whispered, "Don't tell 'Aig! He'd worry somethin' shockin'!"[9]

G.E. Morris, Royal Fusiliers

When Colonel David Rorie was captured, he underwent the usual interrogation, which gave him a wonderful story with which to regale captive audiences long after the war.

More perfunctory questioning, and we were conducted to what was possibly corps headquarters, and then to the office of the intelligence department, where a long wait ensued, fortunately beside a nice stove! Then came the real questioning, and for this we were taken separately, I suppose to see if our answers tallied. The questions were put abruptly, not to say roughly, but there was no real impoliteness. Of course, every attempt was made to extract information, but on our denial, there was no exhibition of 'frightfulness.' Some amusement was caused by my refusal to give division, brigade, brigadier's name, etc., seeing that the information was plastered over my uniform and helmet! When I refused the name of my brigadier I was told, "He is Pelham Burn and he goes on leave next week!" They knew more than I did![10]

> Colonel David Rorie, 1/2nd Highland Field Ambulance, Royal Army Medical Corps

One amusing aspect was the Tank Corps' reaction to the envisioned deployment in counter-attacks on the advancing Germans in 'penny packets'. They coined their own expressive term for this tactic.

We were moved up to near the front line in small parties. We had sections of four tanks dotted about in various concealed positions close to the line, within half a mile in some cases. The idea was that when the Germans arrived the tanks would start out and, as somebody described it, 'emerge like savage rabbits' and go into the Germans. They had absolutely no conception of using these valuable fighting machines to lead a coherent force in a counterattack. It was imposed on us, that was why we were so 'savage'. The thing was simply ridiculous.[11]

> Major Norman Dillon, 2nd Tank Battalion, Tank Corps

In one of the later German attacks there was the first ever tank–versus–tank battle near Villers-Bretonneux, when a German A7V tank advanced on three British Mark IVs (one 'male' armed with 6-pounders and two 'females' with only machine guns). Lieutenant Frank Mitchell eventually managed to put the A7V out of action, and subsequently put in a splendidly cheeky request to higher authorities for financial recognition.

I submitted a claim to the War Office for prize money for myself and crew. I pointed out that tanks, or rather landships, were first brought into existence by the Admiralty, that my landship had knocked out an enemy landship in action, and that under naval regulations a crew are entitled to prize money for sinking an enemy ship. The claim was made more by way of a joke than in earnest. A considerable silence ensued, while my letter, the first of its kind received by the military authorities, apparently travelled round from one puzzled department to another, causing much delving into regulations and shaking of heads. Then I received a very courteous reply from the financial secretary of the War Office, "It is regretted that your claim for prize money for officer and crew of the tank belonging to 'A' Company, 1st Tank Battalion, cannot be admitted, there being no funds available for the purpose of granting prize money in the Army."[12]

Lieutenant Frank Mitchell, 1st Tank Battalion

At least he tried!

*   *   *

The Americans were coming. They would make all the difference, providing a vast reservoir of manpower, inexperienced in Western Front warfare but eager – and able – to learn. There was a brashness about them that sometimes grated, and the British and Americans were certainly two nations divided by a common language.

Like Shakespeare's soldier, the Yanks were full of strange oaths. The village next to where we were resting was suddenly full of men with cowboy hats. They marched through our village in columns of three, held their rifles like Boy Scouts presenting arms with broomsticks, and spoke what sounded like a foreign language. "When we get at those cock-sucking mother-fuckers!" boasted many of them, and no-one in the 26th Battalion of the Royal Fusiliers had heard such expressions before, nor knew what they meant![13]

Lance Corporal Eric Hiscock, 26th Royal Fusiliers

The British and French helped in training, seeking to prepare the *ingénues* for the trials to come. Some officers tried their best to cement the alliance in traditional fashion.

On arrival at the mess three good 'pegs' were poured out and a suspicion of soda water added to each. The American drank with relish, and setting down his glass exclaimed, "Gee, but this sure is fine stuff!" to which one of his hosts replied, at the same time showing him the bottle, "Yes, it's Haig and Haig. Sir Douglas Haig's firm, you know!" This brought the surprising rejoinder from the American, "My, you don't say! Reckon I always allowed he was some soldier, but I did not know he ran a saloon!"[14]

Captain Charles Potter & Lieutenant Albert Fothergill, 2/6th Lancashire Fusiliers

Alcohol seems to have played a vital role in smoothing the path to a greater understanding.

> That lunch delivered the Americans into our hands, and we became the firmest friends. Scales were removed from the eyes of both Americans and British. We found that these Americans had none of the cocksureness and egotism which the modern novel portrays: officers and men were simple and unaffected and the very opposite to boastful. As the weeks went on the Americans said that they had misjudged us when at home. They wanted to know why they had not been informed our Army was such a good one, our equipment so perfect, and that our county regiments contained as good fighting material as was to be found in the Canadian and Australian Forces. Their verdict was that we had been too modest.[15]
>
> Captain Charles Potter & Lieutenant Albert Fothergill, 2/6th Lancashire Fusiliers

At the front, the Australians tried their best to teach the Americans attached to them. There was a lot to learn – and a lot of men had died learning it.

> Some Yank officers had come up. I took one in hand, and we walked to the right, where the high land overlooked the Somme Valley. He was worried. "I don't know when to duck, Aussie!" "You'll learn!" I told him. Just then came the fearsome stockwhip sound of a machine gun. The noise is terrific, but by some trick of sound, one is never under fire from that gun so heard. The Yank was on his tummy. "You don't get down for those!" I yelled above the din. He got up with a puzzled expression. We walked on for a while, outlined stark on the skyline. There came the soft hiss of bullets close round us, each making less noise than a big mosquito. I got into a shell hole and looked up to see the Yank still standing and gazing round. "Come in America," I said. "If you want to see much of the war, this is where you do get down!" He got in, "It sure has me beat how you work it out!" When the machine gunner's attention was turned elsewhere, we strolled on. With horrible suddenness a "Whizz-Bang" arrived from the left and made a fan of flame on the bank below us. We both dropped and crawled into a handy length of trench. More shells came as we crouched, the hot breath of the smoke rolling over us. "There didn't seem any doubt about that lot!" said the Yank. "No," I replied. "Your instincts were sound that time!"[16]
>
> 2nd Lieutenant George Mitchell, 48th Australian Battalion

The Americans learnt fast!

With the Americans onside, the counter-attacks began in July 1918. They began a series of battles which forced the Germans back, with every one of the Allied nations playing a crucial part. But casualties were severe in any kind of open warfare.

> In July 1918, at a casualty clearing station occupying temporary quarters in the old College of St. Vincent at ruined Senlis we dealt with 7,000 wounded in eight days. One night when we were more busy than usual an ambulance car brought up a load of gas-blinded men. A little man whose voice proclaimed the city of his birth – arm broken and face blistered with mustard gas, though he alone of the party could see – jumped out, looked around, and then whispered in my ear, "All serene, Guv'nor, leave 'em to me." He turned towards the car and shouted inside, "Dalston Junction, change here for Hackney, Bow, and Poplar!" Then gently helping each man to alight, he placed them in a line with right hand on the shoulder of the man in front, took his position forward and led them all in, calling softly as he advanced, "Slow march, left, left, I had a good job and I left it!"[17]
>
> Private Henry Lowde, 63rd Casualty Clearing Station, Royal Army Medical Corps

The tide of war was turning, but there was still the same dark humour, never better expressed than by an epitaph penned by some anonymous Australian on a recently dug German grave:

> Some of the graves dotting a battlefield had inscriptions, often macabre as in the case of one I saw – that of a German killed during an Australian advance. To the man's rifle had been pinned a sheet of cardboard on which was scrawled in chalk:
> 'Here you lie, brother Boche!
> Your Pals won't bury you!
> Hindenburg won't bury you!
> Your Kaiser won't bury you – they can't!
> But the poor bloody Aussie will bury you – because YOU STINK!'[18]
>
> 2nd Lieutenant John Fleming, 'U' Bty, 16 Brigade, Royal Horse Artillery

As they passed over the disputed battlefields, there seemed to be a proliferation of amusing notices.

There were several German dugouts with notice boards directing "Zum Unterstand" ("To the dugout"). The wits among the transport at once chalked up underneath, "And Zum Don't!"[19]

Lieutenant Colonel William Lowe, 18th Durham Light Infantry

Herbert Hart, now promoted to command a brigade, found himself in a most unusual headquarters as they advanced. He could not resist the obvious joke.

Finally, I took up my headquarters in the vault below a roadside shrine, wherein a telephone was installed, and the bricked-in coffins on one side of the vault served as a table for my maps and orders. It was a very strenuous day indeed. Often in the war, I had thought a grave would maybe prove a final resting place in France, but I never had anticipated directing a battle from a grave![20]

Brigadier General Herbert Hart, Headquarters, 3 (Rifle) New Zealand Brigade

As the pace of the advance quickened, it was obvious they were winning, but there were many different reactions to the approach at last of victory and peace.

A frightful gloom began to settle upon us all. I do not think the men could have carried on much longer if they had not hoped that the end was near. The imagination seemed to be unable to look further forward than 3-months. It must be over then. I wrote in my diary:

'PEACE OPINIONS AT THE FRONT.

Front Line: 'Peace at any price, for Christ's sake!'

Battalion Headquarters: 'Peace soon? Too good to be true. If only!'

Brigade Headquarters: 'Ah well, we've had enough of this!'

Division Headquarters: 'Peace? Oh, not yet. We must have another smash at 'em first!'

Corps Headquarters: 'No peace, now or ever. Fight on like hell, damn you.'

The Base: 'Peace likely? I 'ope to Gawd it ain't true. This is good enough for me. It'll suit me for life.!'[21]

Lance Corporal William Andrews, 1/4th Black Watch

As they advanced, the troops found themselves the liberators of villages and towns up and down the front, but not all British officers were enamoured with being forced into close physical proximity with the 'great unwashed'.

The civilian inhabitants, too, had come out of their cellars and proceeded to treat us as their deliverers with "Gallic" fervour. It was rather an embarrassing situation when at your approach old women who had sallied forth to find water for their morning ablutions dropped their buckets, threw their arms round your neck and kissed you on both cheeks; you felt touched by the honour, but wished at the same time that soap and water could have taken precedence to those greetings in the public street.[22]

Captain Charles Potter & Lieutenant Albert Fothergill, 2/6th Lancashire Fusiliers

Peace was coming, but when? The fighting continued, although on the British front it diminished shortly after the Battle of the Sambre on 4 November. Common sense and logistical necessity combined to slow the pace of the advance as peace loomed.

A certain company commander, picking up his box respirator, found that he had thrown it off into a patch of filth; copious oaths followed, and he vowed that he would murder the next Boche he saw. Some half hour later, a cyclist patrol met us, escorting one undersized little prisoner, splay footed and bespectacled. The company was delighted, and with one accord hailed their commander with cries of, "Now's your chance, Sir!"[23]

Lieutenant John Hills, 5th Leicestershire Regiment

Then, at last, the day came: 11 November 1918. the focus for many of all their hopes and dreams for the future, but it was often a dreadful anti-climax.

Rumour circulated that an armistice was to be signed at 11am. A mounted officer proceeding up the line had broken the news to one of our men, but we still had our doubts. At about 11am we were ordered to 'Fall in!' on the roadside at the farm entrance. We were given the 'Stand at ease!' and 'Stand easy!' Then Lieutenant Cook said to us casually, "Well boys, I'm pleased to inform you that the bloody war is over!"[24]

Gunner Ivor Hanson, 311 Brigade, Royal Field Artillery

Behind the front line there was more opportunity to celebrate, and Private Frederick Noakes neatly sums up the ecstatic mood:

Suddenly, through the pandemonium which always preceded 'Lights Out' could be heard the sound of distant cheering, apparently from the far side of the camp. At first it was greeted with sarcastic laughter and a few ironical counter-cheers, but the sound increased, and presently the throbbing of a drum mingled with the shouting. At that, the noise in the hut was suddenly silenced. Men gazed at each other with eager, questioning eyes. "Can it be?" was the unspoken query. "It is!" and with a simultaneous movement, everybody huddled on their clothes and poured out on to the parade ground. On all sides, the other huts were disgorging their occupants and in a few minutes the huge open space was black with excited men. The rumour and the cheering spread like a conflagration, "Germany has surrendered!" and the whole eight or ten thousand of us yelled ourselves hoarse. With one accord, the whole throng burst into unanimous song:

"Take me back to dear old Blighty,
Put me on the train for London town;
Drop me over there, any-blooming-where
Birmingham, Leeds or Manchester
Well, I don't care!"

Backwards and forwards we swayed, arms linked, shouting, cheering and singing. The uproar was indescribable, and it never occurred to us to doubt the truth of the rumour. I remember thinking, "This is the happiest moment of my life. I must fix it in my memory for ever!"[25]

Private Frederick Noakes, Cayeux Camp

The war was finally over.

Epitaph

The Spirit of the place is felt today by all who stand before the Menin Gate and gaze on the Latin inscription to the British dead, '*Pro Rege, Pro Patria.*' The same spirit was felt by every British soldier who passed through the Menin Gate and read the unseen writing on the ramparts, 'See Wipers and die!'[1]

Captain John Milne, 1/4th Leicestershire Regiment

The Great War was never a 'war to end war'; that was just a catchy slogan. But it was a belief that helped men to keep on going *in extremis*. They thought that this dreadful agony was a 'one off' and that, somehow, they were fighting for a better future; that their children might never have to suffer what they were undergoing. They were fond hopes that would soon be disabused in the post-war years.

We were told that this was 'the war to end war' and some of us at least believed it. It may sound extraordinarily naïve, but I think one had to believe it. All the mud, blood and bestiality only made sense on the assumption that it was the last time civilised man would ever have to suffer it. I could not believe that anyone who had been through it could ever allow it to happen again. I thought that the ordinary man on both sides would rise up as one and kick any politician in the teeth who even mentioned the possibility of war.[2]

Lieutenant John Nettleton, 2 Rifle Brigade

Some thought the whole thing was a worldwide outburst of insanity.

The German prayer book found in the pillbox at Poelcapelle – on the cover, '*Mit Jefuf in der Feld*', and inside a coloured picture of Christ looking with pity on a dead German soldier. The same picture as in our own field prayer book, 'With Jesus in the Field'. The only appreciable difference being in the uniform of the dead soldier – German in one,

khaki in the other – and the feeling experienced on seeing that picture compared with one of our own, that the whole war was a horrible mistake.[3]
    Signaller Sydney Fuller, 8th Suffolk Regiment

After it was over, men tried to encapsulate their feelings in memoirs, dull treatises, songs and poems. The literature of the war is incredible. Almost every unit produced a history recounting 'their' war. Some are little more than a war diary, but others bring battalion characters back to life and are full of anecdotes. War memoirs proliferated: there are literally thousands, recording events from every point of view. Then of course there are the poets, bringing cultured sensibilities to bear on life and death in the trenches. Yet, sometimes, simplicity seems to pack more punch, as in this one entitled 'History of the War':

A Trench,
A Stench,
Some scraps of French,
Some horrible German vapours;
A Shell,
A Yell,
No more to tell,
Bar a paragraph in the papers![4]
    Private Frank Pope, 10th Battalion, King's Royal Rifle Corps

But to return to our overarching theme – the character of the British soldier at war. That is what this has all been about. Others have – and hopefully still will – write the stories of soldiers of Germany, France, Russia, America and all the other nations, too many to list. But this work has been devoted to the British 'Tommy'. At times he is a comic cliché, but he is often possessed of incredible courage and stamina.

His one privilege is to grouse. He was ease-loving and pleasure-seeking; now he submits to the most rigorous discipline. His time is divided between soul-saddening drill and detestable trenches. His amusements are 'slating the Army' and 'strafing the enemy'. He anathematises the Army wholeheartedly, root and branch, from top to bottom, lock, stock and barrel. He criticises its organisation, methods, and all its works. He is irreverent about 'Red Hats'. He is starved, sweated, insulted, 'fed up', and far from home. He says the 'Army is an Ass', and if he had his time over again – well, he would join it again.[5]
    Private Edward Loxdale, 15th London Regiment (Civil Service Rifles)

They would 'join it again' because, whatever people may think today, there is little doubt that for the most part the British soldiers knew why they had gone to war and genuinely believed that the Germans had to be stopped. There is much evidence to indicate that they were right, although no country was entirely innocent in those days of imperial ambitions and rapacious capitalism.

As a final word, it may be considered that the awful conditions and horrors of the Western Front gave the soldier little choice but to laugh or cry. Over the course of these pages, we hope you have joined them in their laughter; perhaps now, upon quiet reflection of the reality of what you have read, we can pause and maybe also shed a tear in their memory.

Acknowledgements

Firstly, we would like to thank Taff Gillingham for taking the time to read the book and provide a heartfelt preface. Also thanks to all our friends who have helped us in the production of the book. In particular Mat McLachlan who had the idea for the podcast which is what started the whole thing off; Richard Van Emden has been a constant inspiration, plus the dynamic duo of Phil Wood and John Paylor who were kind enough to check the original manuscript. We would also like to thank our long suffering wives Polly and Janet for all the help and support. It has been a pleasure working with Tara Moran, Harriet Fielding, Olivia (Liv) Camozzi-Jones and all the team at P&S. Here's to the next one! Peter Hart & Gary Bain

Endnotes

Preface

1. IWM SOUND, H. Bretton, AC 11029, Reel 4.
2. L. Sotheby, *Lionel Sotheby's Great War* (Athens, OH: Ohio University Press, 1997), pp.15–16.
3. R. Van Emden, *The Soldier's War: The Great War through Veterans' Eyes* (London: Bloomsbury, 2008), p.43.

Chapter 1: First Clash of Arms, 1914

1. J.C. Squire, Poem: 'God Heard the Embattled Nations'.
2. IWM DOCS: R.H. Kelly, typescript letters, 2/8/1914.
3. E. Roe (ed. P. Downham), *Diary of an Old Contemptible, From Mons to Baghdad, 1914–1919* (Barnsley: Pen & Sword, 2004), pp.3–4.
4. R. Graves, *Goodbye to All That* (London: Penguin Books, 1960), p.77.
5. R. Graves, *Goodbye to All That* (London: Penguin Books, 1960), pp.79–80.
6. A.A.E. Gyde, *Contemptible* (London: Heinemann, 1916), pp.5–6.
7. Peter Vansittart, *Voices from the Great War* (London: Pimlico, 2003), p.x.
8. E. Spears, *Liaison 1914* (London: Eyre & Spottiswood, 1930), p.72.
9. IWM SOUND: E.E. Dorman-Smith (Later known as E.E. Dorman O'Gowan), AC 4184, Reel 1.
10. R. Van Emden, *The Soldier's War: The Great War through Veterans' Eyes* (London: Bloomsbury, 2008), p.43.
11. T. Snow (ed. D. Snow & M. Pottle), *The Confusion of Command* (London: Frontline Books, 2011), p.17.
12. IWM DOCS: S.C.M. Archibald, microfilm account, p.90.
13. IWM DOCS: D.M. Laurie, typescript diary, 27/8/1914.
14. IWM SOUND: J. Armstrong, AC 10920, Reel 2.
15. R. Van Emden, *The Soldier's War: The Great War through Veterans' Eyes* (London: Bloomsbury, 2008), p.99.
16. C.B. Purdom, *Everyman at War* (London: J.M. Dent, 1930), pp.17–18.
17. IWM SOUND ARCHIVE: T. Painting, AC 00212, Reel 6.
18. C.I. Stockwell, quoted by C.H. Dudley Ward, *Regimental Records of the Royal Welch Fusiliers* (London: Forster Groom & Co Ltd, 1928), p.112.

19. IWM SOUND: H.G.R. Williams, AC 24878, Reel 1. Recorded by Keith Chambers.

Chapter 2: Back Home

1. W.A. Andrews, *Haunting Years: The Commentaries of a War Territorial* (London: Hutchinson & Co, 1930), p.13.
2. Laurie Milner, *Leeds Pals: A History of the 15th (Service) Battalion, West Yorkshire Regiment, 1914–1918* (Barnsley: Leo Cooper, 1993), pp.22, 25.
3. R. Van Emden, *The Soldier's War: The Great War through Veterans' Eyes* (London: Bloomsbury, 2008), p.34.
4. IWM SOUND: J.L. Lovegrove, AC 08231, Reel 1.
5. J.F. Tucker, *Johnny Get Your Gun: A Personal Narrative of the Somme, Ypres and Arras* (London: William Kimber & Co, 1978), p.21.
6. F.A. Voight, *Combed Out* (London: Jonathan Cape, 1929), pp.12–13.
7. T.M. Banks and R.A. Chell, *With the 10th Essex in France* (London: Burt & Sons, 1921), p.6.
8. N.D. Cliff, *To Hell and Back with the Guards* (Braunton: Merlin Books Ltd, 1988), p.17.
9. J.H.M. Staniforth, *At War With the 16th Irish Division, 1914–1918: The Staniforth Letters* (Barnsley: Pen & Sword Military, 2012), pp.8–9.
10. F.E. Noakes, *The Distant Drum: A Memoir of a Guardsman in the Great War* (London: Frontline Books, 2010), pp.15–16.
11. F.E. Noakes, *The Distant Drum: A Memoir of a Guardsman in the Great War* (London: Frontline Books, 2010), pp.15–16.
12. J.H.M. Staniforth, *At War With the 16th Irish Division, 1914–1918: The Staniforth Letters* (Barnsley: Pen & Sword Military, 2012), pp.35–36.
13. H.E.L. Mellersh, *Schoolboy into War* (London: William Kimber, 1978), p.51.
14. F.E. Noakes, *The Distant Drum: A Memoir of a Guardsman in the Great War* (London: Frontline Books, 2010), p.27.
15. L. Bird, *Machine Gunner on the Somme* (Brighton: Reveille Press, 2012), p.1.
16. IWM SOUND: F. Dixon, AC 00737, Reel 2.
17. T. Chalmers, *An Epic of Glasgow: History of the 15th Battalion Light Infantry* (Glasgow: John McCallum & Co, 1934), pp.8–9.
18. T. Chalmers, *An Epic of Glasgow: History of the 15th Battalion Light Infantry* (Glasgow: John McCallum & Co, 1934), pp.8–9.

Chapter 3: Off to War

1. IWM DOCS: R.A. Backhurst, Manuscript Account, p.7
2. IWM SOUND: T. Haddock, AC 10753, Reel 2.

3. E.J. Needham, *The First Three Months: The Impressions of an Amateur Subaltern* (Aldershot, UK: Gale and Polden, 1933), pp.15–16.

4. J. Chojecki & M. LoCicero, *We are All Flourishing: The Letters and Diary of Captain Walter J.J. Coats MC, 1914–1919* (Solihull: Helion & Co, 2016), pp.39–40.

5. C.H. Potter & A.S.C. Fothergill, *The History of the 2/6th Lancashire Fusiliers* (Rochdale: General Printing Works, 1927), pp.29–30.

6. J. Milne, *In the Footsteps of the 1/4th Leicestershire Regiment, August 1914 to November 1918* (Leicester: Edgar Backus, 1935), p.3.

7. R. Van Emden & Steve Humphries, *Veterans* (Barnsley: Leo Cooper, 1998), pp.24–25.

8. F.E. Noakes, *The Distant Drum: A Memoir of a Guardsman in the Great War* (London: Frontline Books, 2010), p.38.

9. N.C. Down, *Temporary Heroes* (Barnsley: Pen & Sword Military, 2014), p.14.

10. B. Livermore, *Long 'Un: A Damn Bad Soldier* (Batley: Harry Hayes, 1974), p.22.

11. J. Baynes & H. Maclean, *A Tale of Two Captains* (Edinburgh: The Pentland Press, 1990), p.77.

12. B. Peacock, *Tinker's Mufti: Memoirs of a Part-Time Soldier* (London: Seeley Service & Co, 1974), p.49.

13. P. Digby, *Pyramids and Poppies, The 1st SA Infantry Brigade in Libya, France and Flanders 1915–1919* (Solihull: Helion & Company Ltd, 2016), pp.166–67.

14. L. Sotheby, *Lionel Sotheby's Great War* (Athens, OH: Ohio University Press, 1997), p.14.

15. W.C. Belford, *'Legs-Eleven' Being the story of the 11th Battalion AIF in the Great War* (Uckfield: The Naval & Military Press Ltd, 2011), pp.259–60.

16. R.O. Russell, *The History of the 11th (Lewisham) Battalion, The Queen's Own Royal West Kent Regiment* (London: Lewisham Newspaper Co Ltd, 1934), p.33.

17. H. Stinton, *Harry's War: A British Tommy's Experiences in the Trenches in World War One* (London: Conway Books, 2008), p.32.

Chapter 4: Conditions in the Trenches

1. IWM DOCS: M.W. Murray, transcript diary, p.100.

2. D. Bell, *A Soldier's Diary of the Great War* (London: Faber & Gwyer, 1929), pp.115–16.

3. F.E. Noakes, *The Distant Drum: A Memoir of a Guardsman in the Great War* (London: Frontline Books, 2010), p.157.

4. R.H. Roy, *The Journal of Private Fraser 1914–1918 Canadian Expeditionary Force* (Ontario: CEF Books, 1998), pp.32–33.

5. G.D. Mitchell, *Backs to the Wall: A Larrikin on the Western Front* (Sydney: Allen & Unwin, 2007), pp.35–36.

6. N.C. Down, *Temporary Heroes* (Barnsley: Pen & Sword Military, 2014), p.113.

7. H.J. Wenyon & H.S. Brown, *The History of the Eighth Battalion, The Queen's Own Royal West Kent Regiment, 1914–1919* (London: Hazell, Watson & Viney, 1921), pp.108–09.

8. W.C. Belford, *'Legs-Eleven' Being the story of the 11th Battalion AIF in the Great War* (Uckfield: The Naval & Military Press Ltd, 2011), pp.36–33. We have taken the liberty of filling in what Belford modestly left as asterisks in his book.

9. B. Hammond, *Cambrai 1917: The Myth of the First Great Tank Battle* (London: Weidenfield & Nicholson, 2008), pp.25–26.

10. R. Holmes, *Tommy: the British Soldier on the Western Front 1914–1918* (London: Harper Perennial, 2005), p.249.

11. J. Chojecki & M. LoCicero, *We are All Flourishing: The Letters and Diary of Captain Walter J.J. Coats MC, 1914–1919* (Solihull: Helion & Co, 2016), p.226.

12. E.L. Bird, *Machine Gunner on the Somme* (Brighton: Reveille Press, 2012), p.27.

13. H. Stinton, *Harry's War: A British Tommy's Experiences in the Trenches in World War One* (London: Conway Books, 2008), p.73.

14. R. Van Emden, *The Soldier's War: the Great War through Veterans' Eyes* (London: Bloomsbury, 2008), pp.227–28.

15. W.C. Belford, *'Legs-Eleven' Being the story of the 11th Battalion AIF in the Great War* (Uckfield: The Naval & Military Press Ltd, 2011), p.360.

16. F.E. Noakes, *The Distant Drum: A Memoir of a Guardsman in the Great War* (London: Frontline Books, 2010), pp.148–49.

17. Frank Warren, *Honour Satisfied, A Dorset Rifleman at War 1916–1918* (Swindon: The Crowood Press, 1990), p.60.

18. J.H.M. Staniforth, *At War With the 16th Irish Division, 1914–1918: The Staniforth Letters* (Barnsley: Pen & Sword Military, 2012), p.78.

19. G. Harrison, *To Fight Alongside Friends: The First World War Diaries of Charlie May* (London: William Collins, 2014), p.116.

20. E.N. Gladden, *Ypres 1917: A Personal Account* (London: William Kimber & Co Ltd, 1967), p.94.

21. A.M. McGilchrist, *The Liverpool Scottish, 1900–1919* (Liverpool: Henry Young & Sons Ltd, 1930), p.141.

22. IWM SOUND: T. Phillips, SR 9489, Reel 4.

23. IWM SOUND: G. Harbottle, AC 9474, Reel 5.

24. T.M. Banks and R.A. Chell, *With the 10th Essex in France* (London: Burt & Sons, 1921), p.131.

25. N. Atter, *With Valour and Distinction: The Actions of the 2nd Battalion Leicestershire Regiment, 1914–1918* (Warwick: Helion & Co Ltd, 2019), p.26.

26. Reginald H. Roy (ed.), *The Journal of Private Fraser 1914–1918, Canadian Expeditionary Force* (Ontario: CEF Books, 1998), pp.52–53.

27. A.J.H. Stewart, *A Very Unimportant Officer* (London: Hodder & Stoughton, 2008), p.125.

28. IWM SOUND: T. Phillips, SR 9489, Reel 4.

29. S. Graham, *A Private in the Guards* (London: Macmillan & Co Ltd, 1919), p.248.

30. IWM DOCS: H.R. Butt, Typescript diary, 12/11/1916.

31. IWM DOCS: L. Gameson, Typescript, 4/10/1916.

32. E.S.C. Vaughan, *Some Desperate Glory: The Diary of a Young Officer, 1917* (London: Frederick Warne Publishers Ltd, 1981), pp. 9–96.

33. N.D. Cliff, *To Hell and Back with the Guards* (Braunton: Merlin Books Ltd, 1988), p.56.

34. W.C. Belford, *'Legs-Eleven' Being the story of the 11th Battalion AIF in the Great War* (Uckfield: The Naval & Military Press Ltd, 2011), p.272.

35. IWM SOUND: Ivor Watkins, AC 12232, Reel 5.

36. IWM SOUND: Jack Dorgan, AC 9253, Reel 14.

37. IWM SOUND: E.C. Bigwood, AC 10115, Reel 1.

38. IWM SOUND: Donald Price, AC 10168, Reel 4.

39. S. Hurst, *The Public Schools Battalion in the Great War, 'Goodbye Piccadilly'* (Barnsley: Pen & Sword Military, 2007), p.101.

40. G.D. Mitchell, *Backs to the Wall: A Larrikin on the Western Front* (Sydney: Allen & Unwin, 2007), p.48.

41. IWM DOCS: L. Ganeson, Typescript, p.60.

42. W.C. Belford, *'Legs-Eleven' Being the story of the 11th Battalion AIF in the Great War,* (Uckfield: The Naval & Military Press Ltd, 2011), p.337.

43. E.J. Rule, *Jacka's Mob: a narrative of the Great War* (Melbourne: Military Melbourne, 1999), p.34.

44. S. Hurst, *The Public Schools Battalion in the Great War, 'Goodbye Piccadilly'* (Barnsley: Pen & Sword Military, 2007), p.101.

45. IWM SOUND: S. Stewart, AC 10169, Reel 5.

46. F.E. Noakes, *The Distant Drum: A Memoir of a Guardsman in the Great War* (London: Frontline Books, 2010), pp.177–78.

47. E. Shepherd, *A Sergeant-Major's War from Hill 60 to the Somme* (Wiltshire: The Crowood Press, 1987), p.20.

48. IWM SOUND: F.E. Sumpter, SR 09520, Reel 3.

49. IWM SOUND: M. Rymer Jones, AC 10699, Reel 8.

50. IWM SOUND: Jack Dorgan, AC 9253, Reel 14.

51. Harold R. Williams, *An Anzac on the Western Front, The personal reflections of an Australian Infantryman from 1916–1918* (Barnsley: Pen & Sword Ltd, 2012), p.70.

52. F.C. Hitchcock, *Stand To: A Diary of the Trenches 1915–1918* (Norwich: Gliddon Books, 1988), p.122.

53. IWM SOUND: H.G.R. Williams, AC 24878, Reel 1. Recorded by Keith Chambers.

54. J. Milne, *In the Footsteps of the 1/4th Leicestershire Regiment, August 1914 to November 1918* (Leicester: Edgar Backus, 1935), p.43.

55. F.E. Noakes, *The Distant Drum: A Memoir of a Guardsman in the Great War* (London: Frontline Books, 2010), p.72.

56. IWM SOUND: E.C. Bigwood, AC 10115, Reel 1.

57. Harold R. Williams, *An Anzac on the Western Front, The personal reflections of an Australian Infantryman from 1916–1918* (Barnsley: Pen & Sword Ltd, 2012), p.58.

58. IWM SOUND: P. Jackson, AC 10417, Reel 2.

59. Anon, *The Best 500 Cockney War Stories* (Stroud: Amberley Publishing, 2012), p.23.

60. IWM DOCS: H.D. Paviere, Typescript account, pp.40–41.

61. G.D. Mitchell, *Backs to the Wall: A Larrikin on the Western Front* (Sydney: Allen & Unwin, 2007), pp.38–39.

62. A.G. Empey, *Over the Top* (New York: The Knickerbocker Press, 1917), pp.22–23.

63. F.E. Noakes, *The Distant Drum: A Memoir of a Guardsman in the Great War* (London: Frontline Books, 2010), p.69.

64. R. Graves, *Goodbye to All That* (London: Penguin Books, 1960), p.107.

65. IWM DOCS: L. Ganeson, Typescript diary and notes, 10/1916.

66. IWM SOUND: I. Watkins, SR 12232, Reel 5.

67. IWM SOUND: W.G. Shipway, AC 10118, Reel 3.

68. E.N. Gladden, *Ypres 1917: A Personal Account* (London: William Kimber & Co Ltd, 1967), p.100.

69. IWM SOUND: J.P. Fidler, AC 24879, Reel 1. Recorded by Keith Chambers.

70. J. Tyndale-Biscoe, *Gunner Subaltern 1914–1918* (London: Leo Cooper, 1971), p.83.

71. J.F. Tucker, *Johnny Get Your Gun: A Personal Narrative of the Somme, Ypres and Arras* (London: William Kimber & Co, 1978), pp.137–38.

72. C.E. Wurtzburg, *The History of the 2/6th Battalion, The King's Liverpool Regiment, 1914–1919* (Aldershot: Gale & Polden Ltd, 1920), pp.47–48.

73. G. Ashurst, *My Bit: A Lancashire Fusilier at War, 1914–18* (Wiltshire: The Crowood Press, 1987), p.93.

74. A.M. McGilchrist, *The Liverpool Scottish, 1900–1919* (Liverpool: Henry Young & Sons Ltd, 1930), p.68.

75. D. Rorie, *A Medico's Luck in the War* (Aberdeen: Milne & Hutchison, 1929), pp.16–17.

76. A.M. McGilchrist, *The Liverpool Scottish, 1900–1919* (Liverpool: Henry Young & Sons Ltd, 1930), p.68.

77. G. Ashurst, *My Bit: A Lancashire Fusilier at War, 1914–18* (Wiltshire: The Crowood Press, 1987), p.93.

78. A.M. McGilchrist, *The Liverpool Scottish, 1900–1919* (Liverpool: Henry Young & Sons Ltd, 1930), p.141.

79. B. Hammond, *Cambrai 1917: The Myth of the First Great Tank Battle* (London: Weidenfield & Nicholson, 2008), p.281.

80. R.O. Russell, *The History of the 11th (Lewisham) Battalion, The Queen's Own Royal West Kent Regiment* (London: Lewisham Newspaper Co Ltd, 1934), p.54.

81. R. Van Emden, *The Soldier's War: the Great War through Veterans' Eyes* (London: Bloomsbury, 2008), pp.99–100.

82. G. Harrison, *To Fight Alongside Friends: The First World War Diaries of Charlie May* (London: William Collins, 2014), pp.118–19.

83. G. Harrison, *To Fight Alongside Friends: The First World War Diaries of Charlie May* (London: William Collins, 2014), p.119.

84. IWM DOCS: A.V. Conn, Typescript account.

85. IWM SOUND: G. Ashurst, AC 9875, Reel 7.

86. R.O. Russell, *The History of the 11th (Lewisham) Battalion, The Queen's Own Royal West Kent Regiment* (London: Lewisham Newspaper Co Ltd, 1934), p.86.

87. IWM SOUND: D. Price, AC 10168, Reel 6.

88. IWM SOUND: H. Wells, AC 22740, Reel 3.

89. IWM SOUND: L. McCormack, AC 22739, Reel 3.

90. E.L. Bird, *Machine Gunner on the Somme* (Brighton: Reveille Press, 2012), p.31.

91. J. Chojecki & M. LoCicero, *We are All Flourishing: The Letters and Diary of Captain Walter J.J. Coats MC, 1914–1919* (Solihull: Helion & Co, 2016), pp.125–26.

92. L. Sotheby, *Lionel Sotheby's Great War* (Athens, OH: Ohio University Press, 1997), p.53.

93. C.H. Potter & A.S.C. Fothergill, *The History of the 2/6th Lancashire Fusiliers* (Rochdale: General Printing Works, 1927), p.61.

94. J. Milne, *In the Footsteps of the 1/4th Leicestershire Regiment, August 1914 to November 1918* (Leicester: Edgar Backus, 1935), p.41.

95. Reginald H. Roy (ed.), *The Journal of Private Fraser 1914–1918 Canadian Expeditionary Force* (Ontario: CEF Books, 1998), p.94.

96. N. Boyack, *Behind the Lines: The Lives of New Zealand Soldiers in the First World War* (Wellington: Allen & Unwin, 1989), pp.108–09.

97. R. Graves, *Goodbye to All That* (London: Penguin Books, 1960), pp.113–14.

Chapter 5: Fighting in the Trenches

1. L. Sotheby, *Lionel Sotheby's Great War* (Athens, OH: Ohio University Press, 1997), p.71.
2. IWM SOUND: Jack Dorgan, AC 9253, Reel 15.
3. S. Hurst, *The Public Schools Battalion in the Great War, 'Goodbye Piccadilly'* (Barnsley: Pen & Sword Military, 2007), p.151.
4. IWM SOUND: A.J. Smith, AC 9433, Reel 10.
5. B. Livermore, *Long 'Un: A Damn Bad Soldier* (Batley: Harry Hayes, 1974), p.60.
6. IWM SOUND: M.L. Walkington, AC 09132, Reel 2.
7. G. Burgoyne, *The Burgoyne Diaries* (London: Thomas Harmsworth Publishing, 1985), p.80.
8. Anon, *The Best 500 Cockney War Stories* (Stroud: Amberley Publishing, 2012), pp.13–14.
9. C.A. Cuthbert Keeson, *The History and Records of Queen Victoria's Rifles, 1792–1922* (London: Constable & Company Ltd, 1923), pp.136–37.
10. IWM SOUND: H. Hayward, AC 9422, Reel 6.
11. B. Bairnsfather, *Bullets & Billets* (London: Grant Richard Ltd, 1916), pp.55–56.
12. F Shepherd, *A Sergeant-Major's War from Hill 60 to the Somme* (Wiltshire: The Crowood Press, 1987), p.49.
13. A.G. Empey, *Over the Top* (New York: The Knickerbocker Press, 1917), pp.34–35.
14. J.H.M. Staniforth, *At War With the 16th Irish Division, 1914–1918: The Staniforth Letters* (Barnsley: Pen & Sword Military, 1912), p.130.
15. W.C. Belford, *'Legs-Eleven' Being the story of the 11th Battalion AIF in the Great War* (Uckfield: The Naval & Military Press Ltd, 2011), p.241.
16. IWM SOUND: I. Watkins, AC 12232, Reel 6.
17. IWM SOUND: Stewart Sibbald, AC 10169, Reel 6.
18. A.V. Wheeler-Holohan & G.M.C. Wyatt, *The Rangers Historical Records* (London: Harrison & Sons Ltd, 1921), pp.31–32.
19. W.C. Belford, *'Legs-Eleven' Being the story of the 11th Battalion AIF in the Great War* (Uckfield: The Naval & Military Press Ltd, 2011), p.339.
20. IWM SOUND: H.J. Rogers, AC 19072, Reel 2.
21. R. Graves, *Goodbye to All That* (London: Penguin Books, 1960), p.103.
22. E. Gleichen, *The Doings of the Fifteenth Infantry Brigade, August 1914 to March 1915* (Edinburgh & London: William Blackwood & Sons, 1917), p.273.
23. J. Hills, The *Fifth Leicestershire* (Loughborough: The Echo Press, 1919), p.161.
24. W.A. Andrews, *Haunting Years: The Commentaries of a War Territorial* (London: Hutchinson & Co, 1930), p.139.

25. J.H.M. Staniforth, *At War With the 16th Irish Division, 1914–1918: The Staniforth Letters* (Barnsley: Pen & Sword Military, 1912), pp.89–90.
26. J. Tyndale-Biscoe, *Gunner Subaltern 1914–1918* (London: Leo Cooper Ltd, 1971), p.44.
27. W.C. Belford, *'Legs-Eleven' Being the story of the 11th Battalion AIF in the Great War* (Uckfield: The Naval & Military Press Ltd, 2011), p.240.
28. N.C. Down, *Temporary Heroes* (Barnsley: Pen & Sword Military, 2014), p.76.
29. W.C. Belford, *'Legs-Eleven' Being the story of the 11th Battalion AIF in the Great War* (Uckfield: The Naval & Military Press Ltd, 2011), p.238.
30. N.C. Down, *Temporary Heroes* (Barnsley: Pen & Sword Military, 2014), pp.83–84.
31. J. Hills, *The Fifth Leicestershire* (Loughborough: The Echo Press, 1919), p.56.
32. Anon, *The Best 500 Cockney War Stories* (Stroud: Amberley Publishing, 2012), p.87.
33. J.G.W. Hyndson, *From Mons to the First Battle of Ypres* (London: Wyman & Sons Ltd, 1933), pp.118–19.
34. A. Wolff, *Subalterns of the Foot, Three World War 1 Diaries of Officers of the Cheshire Regiment* (Worcester: Square One Publications, 1992), p.9.
35. N.C. Down, *Temporary Heroes* (Barnsley: Pen & Sword Military, 2014), pp.90–91.
36. C.E. Wurtzburg, *The History of the 2/6th Battalion, The King's Liverpool Regiment, 1914–1919* (Aldershot: Gale & Polden Ltd, 1920), pp.62–63.
37. IWM SOUND: L. Gordon Davies, AC 09343, Reel 6.
38. L. Sotheby, *Lionel Sotheby's Great War* (Athens, OH: Ohio University Press, 1997), p.81.
39. G.D. Mitchell, *Backs to the Wall: A Larrikin on the Western Front* (Sydney: Allen & Unwin, 2007), p.42.
40. R.O. Russell, *The History of the 11th (Lewisham) Battalion, The Queen's Own Royal West Kent Regiment* (London: Lewisham Newspaper Co Ltd, 1934), p.47.
41. E.N.F. Ellison (ed. D.R. Lewis), *Remembrances of Hell: The First World War Diary of Norman F. Ellison* (Shrewsbury: Airlife, 1997), p.40.
42. A. Simpson & T. Donovan, *Voices from the Trenches: Life and Death on the Western Front* (Stroud: Tempus, 2006), p.180.
43. IWM SOUND: J.R. Mallalieu, AC 09417, Reel 8.
44. S. Hurst, *The Public Schools Battalion in the Great War, 'Goodbye Piccadilly'* (Barnsley: Pen & Sword Military, 2007), p.109.
45. G. Chapman, *A Passionate Prodigality* (London: Ivor Nicholson & Watson Ltd, 1933), p.86.
46. J. Jackson, *Private 12768 Memoir of a Tommy* (Stroud: Tempus Publishing Limited, 2004), pp.54–55.

47. T.M. Banks and R.A. Chell, *With the 10th Essex in France* (London: Burt & Sons, 1921), p.81.
48. J.F. Tucker, *Johnny Get Your Gun: A Personal Narrative of the Somme, Ypres and Arras* (London: William Kimber & Co, 1978), p.56.
49. P. Pederson, *The Anzacs: Gallipoli to the Western Front* (Victoria: Penguin Group Australia, 2007), p.157.
50. C. Hope, *Frank Speaking from Suvla to Schweidnitz* (Bromley: H&K Ltd, 2021), p.133.
51. G. Chapman, *A Passionate Prodigality* (London: Ivor Nicholson & Watson Ltd, 1933), pp.71–72.
52. J. Hills, *The Fifth Leicestershire* (Loughborough: The Echo Press, 1919), p.111.
53. N.C. Down, *Temporary Heroes* (Barnsley: Pen & Sword Military, 2014), pp.184–85.
54. E.J. Rule, *Jacka's Mob: a narrative of the Great War* (Melbourne: Military Melbourne, 1999), p.119.
55. IWM DOCS: D.N. Menaud-Lissenburg, Typescript memoir, p.175.
56. J. Goss, *A Border Battalion: The 7/8th King's Own Scottish Borderers* (Edinburgh: T.N. Foulis, 1920), p.124.
57. C.H. Potter & A.S.C. Fothergill, *The History of the 2/6th Lancashire Fusiliers* (Rochdale: General Printing Works, 1927), pp.47–48.
58. IWM SOUND: L.J. Barley, AC 00321, Reel 4.
59. G. Harrison, *To Fight Alongside Friends: The First World War Diaries of Charlie May* (London: William Collins, 2014), pp.85–86.
60. G. Harrison, *To Fight Alongside Friends: The First World War Diaries of Charlie May* (London: William Collins, 2014), p.63.
61. L. Sellers, *The Hood Battalion, Royal Naval Division: Antwerp, Gallipoli, France 1914–1918* (Barnsley: Leo Cooper, 1995), p.166.
62. IWM SOUND: F. Dixon, AC 00737, Reel 5.
63. B. Peacock, *Tinker's Mufti: Memoirs of a Part-Time Soldier* (London: Seeley Service & Co, 1974), p.61.
64. A.M. McGilchrist, *The Liverpool Scottish, 1900–1919* (Liverpool: Henry Young & Sons Ltd, 1930), pp.59–60.
65. J. Hills, *The Fifth Leicestershire* (Loughborough: The Echo Press, 1919), pp.168–69.
66. IWM SOUND: H. Hall, AC 16466, Reel 1.
67. A.M. McGilchrist, *The Liverpool Scottish, 1900–1919* (Liverpool: Henry Young & Sons Ltd, 1930), p.102.
68. D.V. Kelly, *39 Months with the Tigers, 1915–1918* (Eastbourne: Ernest Benn Ltd, 1930), pp.39–40.
69. J. Baynes & H. Maclean, *A Tale of Two Captains* (Edinburgh: The Pentland Press, 1990), p.114.

Chapter 6: The Men All Loved Me!

1. H.E.L. Mellersh, *Schoolboy Into War* (London: William Kimber, 1978), p.93.
2. C.H. Weston, *Three Years with the New Zealanders* (London: Skeffington & Son, 1918), pp.88–89.
3. G. Burgoyne, *The Burgoyne Diaries* (London: Thomas Harmsworth Publishing, 1985), pp.24–25, 35.
4. N.C. Down, *Temporary Heroes* (Barnsley: Pen & Sword Military, 2014), pp.23–24.
5. C.H. Potter & A.S.C. Fothergill, *The History of the 2/6th Lancashire Fusiliers* (Rochdale: General Printing Works, 1927), p.5.
6. IWM SOUND: R. Johnson, AC 9172, Reel 1.
7. D. Rorie, *A Medico's Luck in the War* (Aberdeen: Milne & Hutchison, 1929), p.134.
8. J. Hills, *The Fifth Leicestershire* (Loughborough: The Echo Press, 1919), p.187.
9. E.L. Bird, *Machine Gunner on the Somme* (Brighton: Reveille Press, 2012), p.60. Swearwords interpreted from context.
10. IWM SOUND: S.H. Firth, AC 10146, Reel 4.
11. F. Warren, *Honour Satisfied, A Dorset Rifleman at War 1916–1918* (Swindon: The Crowood Press, 1990), p.43.
12. G. Chapman, *A Passionate Prodigality* (London: Ivor Nicholson & Watson Ltd, 1933), p.304.
13. N.C. Down, *Temporary Heroes* (Barnsley: Pen & Sword Military, 2014), p.162.
14. R.O. Russell, *The History of the 11th (Lewisham) Battalion, The Queen's Own Royal West Kent Regiment* (London: Lewisham Newspaper Co Ltd, 1934), pp.122–23.
15. N.D. Cliff, *To Hell and Back with the Guards* (Braunton: Merlin Books Ltd, 1988), p.71.
16. IWM SOUND: J.R. Mallalieu, AC 09417, Reel 7.
17. R.O. Russell, *The History of the 11th (Lewisham) Battalion, The Queen's Own Royal West Kent Regiment* (London: Lewisham Newspaper Co Ltd, 1934), p.125.
18. N.C. Down, *Temporary Heroes* (Barnsley: Pen & Sword Military, 2014), p.48.
19. B. Hammond, *Cambrai 1917: The Myth of the First Great Tank Battle* (London: Weidenfield & Nicholson, 2008), p.275.
20. G. Harrison, *To Fight Alongside Friends: The First World War Diaries of Charlie May* (London: William Collins, 2014), pp.46, 75–76.
21. IWM SOUND: N.M. Dillon, SR 09552, Reel 5.
22. N.C. Down, *Temporary Heroes* (Barnsley: Pen & Sword Military, 2014), pp.216–17.
23. E.S.C. Vaughan, *Some Desperate Glory: The Diary of a Young Officer, 1917* (London: Frederick Warne Publishers Ltd, 1981), pp.147–48.

24. E.S.C. Vaughan, *Some Desperate Glory: The Diary of a Young Officer, 1917* (London: Frederick Warne Publishers Ltd, 1981), pp.148–49.

25. C.H. Potter & A.S.C. Fothergill, *The History of the 2/6th Lancashire Fusiliers* (Rochdale: General Printing Works, 1927), pp.44–45.

26. N.C. Down, *Temporary Heroes* (Barnsley: Pen & Sword Military, 2014), pp.93–94.

27. R. Holmes, *Tommy the British Soldier on the Western Front 1914–1918* (London: Harper Perennial, 2005), p.323.

28. IWM SOUND: W.E. Grover, AC 10441, Reel 7.

Chapter 7: Friends and Enemies

1. IWM SOUND: F.E. Sumpter, SR 09520, Reel 3.

2. G. Chapman, *A Passionate Prodigality* (London: Ivor Nicholson & Watson Ltd, 1933), pp.171–72.

3. IWM DOCS: C.C. Miller, Transcript account, 'A Letter from India to my daughters in England', p.29.

4. IWM DOCS: T.S. Louch, Typescript account, pp.32–33.

5. E.S. Underhill, *A Year on the Western Front* (London: London Stamp Exchange, 1988), p.14.

6. B. Gillard, *Good Old Somersets, An 'Old Contemptible' Battalion in 1914* (Leicester: Matador, 2004), p.60.

7. IWM SOUND ARCHIVE: Y.R.N. Probert, AC 1083, Reel 3.

8. G.D. Mitchell, *Backs to the Wall: A Larrikin on the Western Front* (Sydney: Allen & Unwin, 2007), p.41.

9. IWM SOUND ARCHIVE: J. Davies, AC 9750, Reel 13.

10. P. Pederson, *The Anzacs: Gallipoli to the Western Front* (Victoria: Penguin Group Australia, 2007), p.259.

11. Tim Cook, *Eyewitnesses at the Somme, A Muddy & Bloody Campaign 1916–1918* (Barnsley: Pen & Sword Military, 2017), p.91.

12. Harold R. Williams, *An Anzac on the Western Front, The personal reflections of an Australian Infantryman from 1916–1918* (Barnsley: Pen & Sword Ltd, 2012), pp.139–40.

13. IWM DOCS: F.P. Cook, Transcript account, p.59.

14. G. Ashurst, *My Bit: A Lancashire Fusilier at War, 1914–18* (Wiltshire: The Crowood Press, 1987), p.93.

15. S. Hurst, *The Public Schools Battalion in the Great War, 'Goodbye Piccadilly'* (Barnsley: Pen & Sword Military, 2007), p.83.

16. J. Chojecki & M. LoCicero, *We are All Flourishing: The Letters and Diary of Captain Walter J.J. Coats MC, 1914–1919* (Solihull: Helion & Co, 2016), p.132.

17. G. Chapman, *A Passionate Prodigality* (London: Ivor Nicholson & Watson Ltd, 1933), p.72.
18. I.L. Read, *Of Those We Have Loved* (Bishop Auckland: The Pentland Press, 1994), pp.60–61.
19. N.C. Down, *Temporary Heroes* (Barnsley: Pen & Sword Military, 2014), p.101.
20. E.J. Rule, *Jacka's Mob: a narrative of the Great War* (Melbourne: Military Melbourne, 1999), p.23.
21. N.C. Down, *Temporary Heroes* (Barnsley: Pen & Sword Military, 2014), p.84.
22. N.C. Down, *Temporary Heroes* (Barnsley: Pen & Sword Military, 2014), p.86.
23. W.D. Lowe, *War History of the 18th (S) Battalion Durham Light Infantry* (London: Oxford University Press, 1920), p.9.
24. J.H.M. Staniforth, *At War With the 16th Irish Division, 1914–1918: The Staniforth Letters* (Barnsley: Pen & Sword Military, 2012), p.66.

Chapter 8: Gunners

1. N. Fraser-Tytler, *Field Guns in France* (London: Hutchinson & Co, 1922), p.223.
2. IWM DOCS: D.N. Menaud-Lissenburg, Typescript memoir, pp.168–69.
3. IWM DOCS: A.J. Heraty, Typescript memoir, p.54.
4. IWM SOUND: M.R. Jones, AC 10699, Reel 2.
5. J.I. Hanson & A. Wakefield, *Plough & Scatter: the Diary-Journal of a First World War Gunner* (Yeovil: Haynes Publishing, 2009), p.188.
6. N. Fraser-Tytler, *Field Guns in France* (London: Hutchinson & Co, 1922), pp.210–11.
7. N. Fraser-Tytler, *Field Guns in France* (London: Hutchinson & Co, 1922), p.38.
8. Anon, *The Best 500 Cockney War Stories* (Stroud: Amberley Publishing, 2012), p.19.
9. N. Fraser-Tytler, *Field Guns in France* (London: Hutchinson & Co, 1922), p.94.
10. IWM SOUND: C. Denys, AC 9876, Reel 6.
11. N. Fraser-Tytler, *Field Guns in France* (London: Hutchinson & Co, 1922), pp.76–77.
12. J. Tyndale-Biscoe, *Gunner Subaltern 1914–1918* (London: Leo Cooper, 1971), pp.79–80.
13. J. Tyndale-Biscoe, *Gunner Subaltern 1914–1918* (London: Leo Cooper, 1971), pp.80–81.
14. J. H.M. Staniforth, *At War With the 16th Irish Division, 1914–1918: The Staniforth Letters* (Barnsley: Pen & Sword Military, 1912), p.66.
15. W.C. Belford, *'Legs-Eleven' Being the story of the 11th Battalion AIF in the Great War* (Uckfield: The Naval & Military Press Ltd, 2011), pp.364–65.

16. W.C. Belford, *'Legs-Eleven' Being the story of the 11th Battalion AIF in the Great War* (Uckfield: The Naval & Military Press Ltd, 2011), pp.364–65.

17. W.C. Belford, *'Legs-Eleven' Being the story of the 11th Battalion AIF in the Great War* (Uckfield: The Naval & Military Press Ltd, 2011), p.387.

18. W.D. Croft, *Three Years with the 9th (Scottish) Division* (London: John Murray, 1919), pp.84–85.

Chapter 9: You Can't Eat the Wireless!

1. IWM SOUND: R.C. Cooney, AC 00494, Reel 5.

2. J. Tyndale-Biscoe, *Gunner Subaltern 1914–1918* (London: Leo Cooper Ltd, 1971), p.39.

3. IWM SOUND: J.W. Mortimer, AC 24859, Reel 1. Recorded by Keith Chambers.

4. H.J. Wenyon & H.S. Brown, *The History of the Eighth Battalion, The Queen's Own Royal West Kent Regiment, 1914–1919* (London: Hazell, Watson & Viney, 1921), pp.123–24.

5. J. Hills, *The Fifth Leicestershire* (Loughborough: The Echo Press, 1919), p.150.

6. G.V. Dennis, *A Kitchener Man's Bit* (York: MERH Books, 1994), pp.59–60.

7. G.V. Dennis, *A Kitchener Man's Bit* (York: MERH Books, 1994), pp.59–60.

8. W.D. Lowe, *War History of the 18th (S) Battalion Durham Light Infantry* (London: Oxford University Press, 1920), p.32.

9. IWM SOUND: A. Hemsley, AC 09927, Reel 7.

10. IWM SOUND: A. Hemsley, AC 09927, Reel 7.

11. IWM SOUND: A. Hemsley, AC 09927, Reel 7.

12. A.M. McGilchrist, *The Liverpool Scottish, 1900–1919* (Liverpool: Henry Young & Sons Ltd, 1930), pp.55–56.

13. IWM SOUND: A. Hemsley, AC 09927, Reel 7.

14. IWM SOUND: A. Hemsley, AC 09927, Reel 7.

15. IWM DOCS: B. Chaney, Typescript account, pp.131–32.

Chapter 10: Donkey's Bollocks!

1. Lieutenant McClymont parody of Siegfried Sassoon poem, 'The General'.

2. A.J.H. Stewart, *A Very Unimportant Officer* (London: Hodder & Stoughton, 2008), pp.150–51.

3. N.C. Down, *Temporary Heroes* (Barnsley: Pen & Sword Military, 2014), p.48.

4. N.C. Down, *Temporary Heroes* (Barnsley: Pen & Sword Military, 2014), pp.117–18.

5. D.V. Kelly, *39 Months with the Tigers, 1915–1918* (Eastbourne: Ernest Benn Ltd, 1930), p.53.

6. J. Charteris, *At G.H.Q.* (London: Cassell & Co, 1931), p.164.

7. J. Charteris, *At G.H.Q.* (London: Cassell & Co, 1931), p.134.

8. A.M. McGilchrist, *The Liverpool Scottish, 1900–1919* (Liverpool: Henry Young & Sons Ltd, 1930), p.58.

9. T.M. Banks and R.A. Chell, *With the 10th Essex in France* (London: Burt & Sons, 1921), p.165.

10. R.O. Russell, *The History of the 11th (Lewisham) Battalion, The Queen's Own Royal West Kent Regiment* (London: Lewisham Newspaper Co Ltd, 1934), p.106.

11. T. Chalmers, *A Saga of Scotland: History of the 16th Battalion Light Infantry* (Glasgow: John McCallum & Co, 1930), p.45.

12. IWM SOUND: A. Jefferies, AC 19760, Reel 2.

13. B. Peacock, *Tinker's Mufti: Memoirs of a Part-Time Soldier* (London: Seeley Service & Co, 1974), p.67.

14. N.C. Down, *Temporary Heroes* (Barnsley: Pen & Sword Military, 2014), pp.39–40.

15. R. Macleod, 'An artillery officer in the First World War' (Typescript diary: no known publisher or date), 13/7/1917.

16. W.C. Belford, *'Legs-Eleven' Being the story of the 11th Battalion AIF in the Great War* (Uckfield: The Naval & Military Press Ltd, 2011), p.352.

17. IWM SOUND: F. Dixon, AC 00737, Reel 16.

18. C.H. Potter & A.S.C. Fothergill, *The History of the 2/6th Lancashire Fusiliers* (Rochdale: General Printing Works, 1927), pp.36–37.

19. G. Chapman, *A Passionate Prodigality* (London: Ivor Nicholson & Watson Ltd, 1933), pp.79–80.

20. C.H. Potter & A.S.C. Fothergill, *The History of the 2/6th Lancashire Fusiliers* (Rochdale: General Printing Works, 1927), p.87.

21. W.F.A. Wadham & J. Crossley, *The Fourth Battalion: The King's Own (Royal Lancaster Regiment) and the Great War* (London: Cowther and Goodman, 1935), p.6.

22. IWM SOUND: M.E.S. Laws, AC 00390, Reel 5.

23. IWM SOUND: A. Jefferies, AC 19760, Reel 2.

24. D. Jerrold, *Georgian Adventure* (London: Right Book Club, 1937), pp.176–77.

25. A.P. Herbert poem.

Chapter 11: Out of the Line

1. A. Simpson & T. Donovan, *Voices from the Trenches: Life and Death on the Western Front* (Stroud: Tempus, 2006), p.12.

2. J. Chojecki & M. LoCicero, *We are All Flourishing: The Letters and Diary of Captain Walter J.J. Coats MC, 1914–1919* (Solihull: Helion & Co, 2016), pp.140–41.

3. I.L. Read, *Of Those We Have Loved* (Bishop Auckland: The Pentland Press, 1994), p.22.

4. N.C. Down, *Temporary Heroes* (Barnsley: Pen & Sword Military, 2014), pp.34–35.

5. Anon, *The Best 500 Cockney War Stories* (Stroud: Amberley Publishing, 2012), p.25.

6. N.D. Cliff, *To Hell and Back with the Guards* (Braunton: Merlin Books Ltd, 1988), p.43.

7. IWM SOUND: F. Dixon, AC 00737, Reel 16.

8. G. Chapman, *A Passionate Prodigality* (London: Ivor Nicholson & Watson Ltd, 1933), p.254.

9. O.F. Bailey & H.M. Hollier, *The Kensingtons: 13th London Regiment* (London: Regimental Old Comrades Association 1935, 2014), p.132.

10. J. Tyndale-Biscoe, *Gunner Subaltern 1914–1918* (London: Leo Cooper Ltd, 1971), p.56.

11. J.F. Tucker, *Johnny Get Your Gun: A Personal Narrative of the Somme, Ypres and Arras* (London: William Kimber & Co, 1978), p.145.

12.

13. G. Harrison, *To Fight Alongside Friends: The First World War Diaries of Charlie May* (London: William Collins, 2014), p.14.

14. W.C. Belford, *'Legs-Eleven' Being the story of the 11th Battalion AIF in the Great War* (Uckfield: The Naval & Military Press Ltd, 2011), p. 221.

15. L. Sotheby, *Lionel Sotheby's Great War* (Athens, OH: Ohio University Press, 1997), p.40.

16. H. Stinton, *Harry's War: A British Tommy's Experiences in the Trenches in World War One* (London: Conway Books, 2008), pp.140–41.

17. IWM SOUND: A. Hemsley, AC 09927, Reel 7.

18. L. Sotheby, *Lionel Sotheby's Great War* (Athens, OH: Ohio University Press, 1997), p.51.

19. H. Hart (ed. J. Crawford), *The Devil's Own War: The Diary of Herbert Hart* (Auckland: Exisle Publishing, 2009), p.111.

20. J.C. Dunn, *The War the Infantry Knew* (London: Janes Publishing Company, 1987), p.166.

21. C.H. Potter & A.S.C Fothergill, *The History of the 2/6th Lancashire Fusiliers* (Rochdale: General Printing Works, 1927), p.35.

22. E.N.F. Ellison (ed. D.R. Lewis), *Remembrances of Hell: The First World War Diary of Norman F. Ellison* (Shrewsbury: Airlife, 1997), pp.27–28.

23. G. Chapman, *A Passionate Prodigality* (London: Ivor Nicholson & Watson Ltd, 1933), p.212.

24. N.C. Down, *Temporary Heroes* (Barnsley: Pen & Sword Military, 2014), p.13.

25. G. Harrison, *To Fight Alongside Friends: The First World War Diaries of Charlie May* (London: William Collins, 2014), p.19.
26. M. Pottle & J.G.G. Ledingham (eds), *We Hope to Get Word Tomorrow: The Garvin Family Letters, 1914–1916* (London: Frontline Books, 2009), p.82.
27. W.C. Belford, *'Legs-Eleven' Being the story of the 11th Battalion AIF in the Great War* (Uckfield: The Naval & Military Press Ltd, 2011), p.263.
28. W.C. Belford, *'Legs-Eleven' Being the story of the 11th Battalion AIF in the Great War* (Uckfield: The Naval & Military Press Ltd, 2011), p.255.
29. B. Cherry, *They Didn't Want to Die Virgins: Sex and Morale in the British Army on the Western Front 1914–18* (Solihull: Helion & Company Limited, 2016), p.146.
30. R.B. Talbot-Kelly, *A Subaltern's Odyssey: A Memoir of the Great War, 1915–1917* (London: William Kimber & Co, 1980), p.104.
31. IWM SOUND: J.L. Lovegrove, AC 08231, Reel 4.
32. N.C. Down, *Temporary Heroes* (Barnsley: Pen & Sword Military, 2014), pp.18–19.
33. E.N. Gladden, *Ypres 1917: A Personal Account* (London: William Kimber & Co Ltd, 1967), p.28.
34. D. Rorie, *A Medico's Luck in the War* (Aberdeen: Milne & Hutchison, 1929), p.51.
35. O.F. Bailey & H.M. Hollier, *The Kensingtons: 13th London Regiment* (London: Regimental Old Comrades Association 1935, 2014), p.62.
36. S. Graham, *A Private in the Guards* (London: Macmillan & Co Ltd, 1919), p.205.
37. Harold R. Williams, *An Anzac on the Western Front: The personal reflections of an Australian Infantryman from 1916–1918* (Barnsley: Pen & Sword Ltd, 2012), p.31.
38. J. Milne, *In the Footsteps of the 1/4th Leicestershire Regiment, August 1914 to November 1918* (Leicester: Edgar Backus, 1935), p.29.
39. L. Sotheby, *Lionel Sotheby's Great War* (Athens, OH: Ohio University Press, 1997), p.36.
40. E.N. Gladden, *Ypres 1917: A Personal Account* (London: William Kimber & Co Ltd, 1967), pp.85–86.
41. IWM SOUND: E.R. Booth, AC 09263, Reel 2.
42. H. Stinton, *Harry's War: A British Tommy's Experiences in the Trenches in World War One* (London: Conway Books, 2008), p.144.
43. H. Stinton, *Harry's War: A British Tommy's Experiences in the Trenches in World War One* (London: Conway Books, 2008), p.60.
44. C.H. Lander, *Lander's War, 1914–1919* (Eastbourne: Menin House, 2010), p.40.
45. E.L. Bird, *Machine Gunner on the Somme* (Brighton: Reveille Press, 2012), pp.89–90.

46. R.O. Russell, *The History of the 11th (Lewisham) Battalion, The Queen's Own Royal West Kent Regiment* (London: Lewisham Newspaper Co Ltd, 1934), p.25.

47. IWM SOUND: H.J. Hayward, AC 09422, Reel 14.

48. B. Cherry, *They Didn't Want To Die Virgins: Sex and Morale in the British Army on the Western Front 1914–18* (Solihull: Helion & Company Limited, 2016), pp.83–84.

49. IWM DOCS: C.H. Dudley Ward, Manuscript diary, pp.472–73.

50. W.C. Belford, *'Legs-Eleven' Being the story of the 11th Battalion AIF in the Great War* (Uckfield: The Naval & Military Press Ltd, 2011), p.304.

51. B. Cherry, *They Didn't Want To Die Virgins: Sex and Morale in the British Army on the Western Front 1914–18* (Solihull: Helion & Company Limited, 2016), p.77.

52. IWM SOUND: H. Wells, AC 22740, Reel 3.

53. R. Graves, *Goodbye to All That* (London: Penguin Books, 1960), p.125.

54. I.L. Read, *Of Those We Have Loved* (Bishop Auckland: The Pentland Press, 1994), pp.227–28.

55. IWM SOUND: G. Ashurst, SR 09875, Reel 8.

56. G. Ashurst, *My Bit: A Lancashire Fusilier at War, 1914–18* (Wiltshire: The Crowood Press, 1987), pp.48–49.

57. B. Cherry, *They Didn't Want To Die Virgins: Sex and Morale in the British Army on the Western Front 1914–18* (Solihull: Helion & Company Limited, 2016), p.71.

58. G. Ashurst, *My Bit: A Lancashire Fusilier at War, 1914–18* (Wiltshire: The Crowood Press, 1987), p.50.

59. IWM DOCS: D. Starrett, Typescript account, p.61.

60. N.C. Down, *Temporary Heroes* (Barnsley: Pen & Sword Military, 2014), p.72.

61. E.N. Gladden, *Ypres 1917: A Personal Account* (London: William Kimber & Co Ltd, 1967), pp.160–61.

62. E. Hiscock, *The Bells of Hell go Ting-a-Ling-a-Ling* (London: Arlington Books, 1976), pp.40–42.

63. C.H. Potter & A.S.C. Fothergill, *The History of the 2/6th Lancashire Fusiliers* (Rochdale: General Printing Works, 1927), p.37.

64. IWM SOUND: T. Keele, AC 09428, Reel 9.

65. T. Chalmers, *An Epic of Glasgow: History of the 15th Battalion Light Infantry* (Glasgow: John McCallum & Co, 1934), pp.51–52.

66. N.C. Down, *Temporary Heroes* (Barnsley: Pen & Sword Military, 2014), p.30.

67. R. Holmes, *Tommy: the British Soldier on the Western Front 1914–1918* (London: Harper Perennial, 2005), p.517.

68. IWM SOUND: L. Gordon Davies, AC 09343, Reel 6.

69. J. Milne, *In the Footsteps of the1/4th Leicestershire Regiment, August 1914 to November 1918* (Leicester: Edgar Backus, 1935), p.35.

70. W. C. Belford, *'Legs-Eleven' Being the story of the 11th Battalion AIF in the Great War* (Uckfield: The Naval & Military Press Ltd, 2011), p.459.

71. R.O. Russell, *The History of the 11th (Lewisham) Battalion, The Queen's Own Royal West Kent Regiment* (London: Lewisham Newspaper Co Ltd, 1934), p.108.

72. R. Graves, *Goodbye to All That* (London: Penguin Books, 1960), p.112.

73. J. Hills, *The Fifth Leicestershire* (Loughborough: The Echo Press, 1919), p.164.

74. C.H. Weston, *Three Years with the New Zealanders* (London: Skeffington & Son, 1918), p.77.

75. H. Stinton, *Harry's War: A British Tommy's Experiences in the Trenches in World War One* (London: Conway Books, 2008), p.202.

76. R. Van Emden, *The Soldier's War: the Great War through Veterans' Eyes* (London: Bloomsbury, 2008), p.268.

77. IWM SOUND: Norman Edwards, AC 14932, Reel 2.

78. J. Milne, *In the Footsteps of the 1/4th Leicestershire Regiment, August 1914 to November 1918* (Leicester: Edgar Backus, 1935), p.118.

79. J. Hills, *The Fifth Leicestershire* (Loughborough: The Echo Press, 1919), p.128.

80. L. Sotheby, *Lionel Sotheby's Great War* (Athens, OH: Ohio University Press, 1997), p.59.

81. B. Hammond, *Cambrai 1917: The Myth of the First Great Tank Battle* (London: Weidenfield & Nicholson, 2008), p.87.

82. N.C. Down, *Temporary Heroes* (Barnsley: Pen & Sword Military, 2014), pp.48–49.

83. R. Van Emden, *The Soldier's War: the Great War through Veterans' Eyes* (London: Bloomsbury, 2008), p.102.

84. Various, *The History of the Prince of Wales Own Civil Service Rifles* (London: Wyman and Sons, 1921), pp.69–70.

85. Francis Buckley, *Recollections of the Great War: Three years on campaign in France and Flanders with the Northumberland Fusiliers* (Barnsley: Pen & Sword Military, 2015), pp.28–29.

86. IWM SOUND: J. Fitzpatrick, AC 10767, Reel 11.

87. W.A. Andrews, *Haunting Years: The Commentaries of a War Territorial* (London: Hutchinson & Co, 1930), p.142.

88. W.C. Belford, *'Legs-Eleven' Being the story of the 11th Battalion AIF in the Great War* (Uckfield: The Naval & Military Press Ltd, 2011), pp.246–47.

89. G.D. Mitchell, *Backs to the Wall: A Larrikin on the Western Front* (Sydney: Allen & Unwin, 2007), p.200.

90. IWM DOCS: R.G. Dixon, Typescript account, 'The Wheels of Darkness', p.99.

91. J. Baynes & H. Maclean, *A Tale of Two Captains* (Edinburgh: The Pentland Press, 1990), p.131.

92. B. Martin, *Poor Bloody Infantry: A Subaltern on the Western Front, 1916–17* (London: John Murray, 1987), p.137.

93. IWM SOUND: J. Dorgan, AC 9253, Reel 15.

94. Lyn MacDonald, *To the Last Man: Spring 1918* (London: Viking, Penguin Group, 1998), pp.30–31.

95. N.C. Down, *Temporary Heroes* (Barnsley: Pen & Sword Military, 2014), p.71.

Chapter 12: Over the Top

1. IWM SOUND: J. Davies, AC 9750, Reel 4.

2. IWM DOCS: C.C. May, Typescript diary, 16/6/1916.

3. J. Milne, *In the Footsteps of the 1/4th Leicestershire Regiment, August 1914 to November 1918* (Leicester: Edgar Backus, 1935), p.14.

4. G. Burgoyne, *The Burgoyne Diaries* (London: Thomas Harmsworth Publishing, 1985), p.132.

5. H. Hart (ed. J. Crawford), *The Devil's Own War: The Diary of Herbert Hart* (Auckland: Exisle Publishing, 2009), p.137.

6. B. Hammond, *Cambrai 1917: The Myth of the First Great Tank Battle* (London: Weidenfield & Nicholson, 2008), pp.109–10.

7. W.A. Andrews, *Haunting Years: The Commentaries of a War Territorial* (London: Hutchinson & Co, 1930), p.143.

8. J. Milne, *In the Footsteps of the 1/4th Leicestershire Regiment, August 1914 to November 1918* (Leicester: Edgar Backus, 1935), pp.45–46.

9. A.J.H. Stewart, *A Very Unimportant Officer* (London: Hodder & Stoughton, 2008), pp.202–04.

10. Anon, *The Best 500 Cockney War Stories* (Stroud: Amberley Publishing, 2012), p.70.

11. IWM DOCS: D.N. Menaud-Lissenburg, Typescript memoir, p.178.

12. IWM SOUND: E. Rhodes, AC 10914, Reel 5.

13. IWM DOCS: S.T. Fuller, diary, 30/7/1917.

14. B. Hammond, *Cambrai 1917: The Myth of the First Great Tank Battle* (London: Weidenfield & Nicholson, 2008), p.136.

15. B. Hammond, *Cambrai 1917: The Myth of the First Great Tank Battle* (London: Weidenfield & Nicholson, 2008), pp.44–45.

16. Anon, *The Best 500 Cockney War Stories* (Stroud: Amberley Publishing, 2012), pp.13–14.

17. R. Graves, *Goodbye to All That* (London: Penguin Books, 1960), p.164.

18. R.O. Russell, *The History of the 11th (Lewisham) Battalion, The Queen's Own Royal West Kent Regiment* (London: Lewisham Newspaper Co Ltd, 1934), p.71.

19. IWM SOUND: A. Hemsley, AC 09927, Reel 7.
20. IWM DOCS: A.V. Conn, Typescript account.
21. A.W. Andrews (ed. S. Richardson), *Orders are Orders: A Manchester Pal on the Somme* (Manchester: Neil Richardson, 1987), pp.50–51.
22. N. Fraser-Tytler, *Field Guns in France* (London: Hutchinson & Co, 1922), pp.195–96.
23. D. Rorie, *A Medico's Luck in the War* (Aberdeen: Milne & Hutchison, 1929), p.111.
24. IWM SOUND: P.J. Kennedy, AC 13679, Reel 1.
25. E.L. Bird, *Machine Gunner on the Somme* (Brighton: Reveille Press, 2012), p.48.
26. H.E.L. Mellersh, *Schoolboy Into War* (London: William Kimber, 1978), p.88.
27. J. Hills, *The Fifth Leicestershire* (Loughborough: The Echo Press, 1919), pp.174–75.
28. J.I. Hanson & A. Wakefield, *Plough & Scatter: the Diary-Journal of a First World War Gunner* (Yeovil: Haynes Publishing, 2009), p.212.
29. J. Jackson, *Private 12768: Memoir of a Tommy* (Stroud: Tempus Publishing Limited, 2004), pp.50–51.
30. P. Digby, *Pyramids and Poppies, The 1st SA Infantry Brigade in Libya, France and Flanders 1915–1919* (Solihull: Helion & Company Ltd, 2016), pp.160–61.
31. IWM SOUND: H. Hayward, AC 9422, Reel 11.
32. IWM SOUND: H. Hayward, AC 9422, Reel 12.
33. E.J. Rule, *Jacka's Mob: a narrative of the Great War* (Melbourne: Military Melbourne, 1999), p.48.
34. J.H.M. Staniforth, *At War With the 16th Irish Division, 1914–1918: The Staniforth Letters* (Barnsley: Pen & Sword Military, 1912), p.120.

Chapter 13: Advance to Victory, 1918

1. J.H. Lindsay, *The London Scottish in the Great War* (London: Regimental Headquarters, 1925), p.114.
2. S. Hurst, *The Public Schools Battalion in the Great War, 'Goodbye Piccadilly'* (Barnsley: Pen & Sword Military, 2007), p.229.
3. IWM SOUND: G. Cole, AC 9535, Reel 4.
4. O.F. Bailey & H.M. Hollier, *The Kensingtons: 13th London Regiment* (London: Regimental Old Comrades Association 1935, 2014), p.132.
5. IWM DOCS: F. Warren, Transcript diary, 23/3/1918.
6. IWM DOCS: P.E. Williamson, Typescript account, pp.36–37.
7. N. Fraser-Tytler, *Field Guns in France* (London: Hutchinson & Co, 1922), p.232.
8. IWM DOCS: R.M. Luthor, Typescript account, p.44.

9. Anon, *The Best 500 Cockney War Stories* (Stroud: Amberley Publishing, 2012), p.42.

10. D. Rorie, *A Medico's Luck in the War* (Aberdeen: Milne & Hutchison, 1929), p.177.

11. IWM SOUND: N.M. Dillon, AC 9752, Reel 12.

12. F. Mitchell, *Tank Warfare: The Story of the Tanks in the Great War* (London: Thomas Nelson & Sons Ltd, 1933), p.198.

13. E. Hiscock, *The Bells of Hell go Ting-a-Ling-a-Ling* (London: Arlington Books, 1976), p.86.

14. C.H. Potter & A.S.C. Fothergill, *The History of the 2/6th Lancashire Fusiliers* (Rochdale: General Printing Works, 1927), p.162.

15. C.H. Potter & A.S.C. Fothergill, *The History of the 2/6th Lancashire Fusiliers* (Rochdale: General Printing Works, 1927), p.161.

16. G.D. Mitchell, *Backs to the Wall: A Larrikin on the Western Front* (Sydney: Allen & Unwin, 2007), p.277.

17. Anon, *The Best 500 Cockney War Stories* (Stroud: Amberley Publishing, 2012), p.43.

18. IWM DOCS: J.F. Fleming-Bernard, Typescript Account, p.62.

19. W.D. Lowe, *War History of the 18th (S) Battalion Durham Light Infantry* (London: Oxford University Press, 1920), p.139.

20. H. Hart (ed. J. Crawford), *The Devil's Own War: The Diary of Herbert Hart* (Auckland: Exisle Publishing, 2009), p.253.

21. W.A. Andrews, *Haunting Years: The Commentaries of a War Territorial* (London: Hutchinson & Co, 1930), p.205.

22. C.H. Potter & A.S.C. Fothergill, *The History of the 2/6th Lancashire Fusiliers* (Rochdale: General Printing Works, 1927), p.187.

23. J. Hills, *The Fifth Leicestershire* (Loughborough: The Echo Press, 1919), p.370.

24. J.I. Hanson & A. Wakefield, *Plough & Scatter: the Diary-Journal of a First World War Gunner* (Yeovil: Haynes Publishing, 2009), p.300.

25. F.E. Noakes, *The Distant Drum: A Memoir of a Guardsman in the Great War* (London: Frontline Books, 2010), p.191.

Epitaph

1. J. Milne, *In the Footsteps of the 1/4th Leicestershire Regiment, August 1914 to November 1918* (Leicester: Edgar Backus, 1935), p.31.

2. IWM DOCS: J. Nettleton, Typescript account, p.197.

3. IWM DOCS: S.T. Fuller, diary, postscript.

4. R. Van Emden, *The Soldier's War: the Great War through Veterans' Eyes* (London: Bloomsbury, 2008), p.290.

5. J. Knight, *The Civil Service Rifles in the Great War* (Barnsley: Pen & Sword Military), 2004), p.62.